VOLUME

DAVE MONROE is an instructor at the Applied Ethics Institute of St. Petersburg College, Florida, and adjunct instructor of philosophy at the University of Tampa. He is the co-editor of *Food & Philosophy*, with Fritz Allhoff (Wiley-Blackwell, 2007).

SERIES EDITOR

FRITZ ALLHOFF is an Assistant Professor in the Philosophy Department at Western Michigan University, as well as a Senior Research Fellow at the Australian National University's Centre for Applied Philosophy and Public Ethics. In addition to editing the *Philosophy for Everyone* series, Allhoff is the volume editor or co-editor for several titles, including *Wine & Philosophy* (Wiley-Blackwell, 2007), *Whiskey & Philosophy* (with Marcus P. Adams, Wiley, 2009), and *Food & Philosophy* (with Dave Monroe, Wiley-Blackwell, 2007).

PHILOSOPHY FOR EVERYONE

Series editor: Fritz Allhoff

Not so much a subject matter, philosophy is a way of thinking. Thinking not just about the Big Questions, but about little ones too. This series invites everyone to ponder things they care about, big or small, significant, serious ... or just curious.

Running & Philosophy:
A Marathon for the Mind
Edited by Michael W. Austin

Wine & Philosophy:
A Symposium on Thinking and Drinking
Edited by Fritz Allhoff

Food & Philosophy:
Eat, Think and Be Merry
Edited by Fritz Allhoff and Dave Monroe

Beer & Philosophy:
The Unexamined Beer Isn't Worth Drinking
Edited by Steven D. Hales

Whiskey & Philosophy:
A Small Batch of Spirited Ideas
Edited by Fritz Allhoff and Marcus P. Adams

College Sex – Philosophy for Everyone: Philosophers With Benefits
Edited by Michael Bruce
and Robert M. Stewart

Cycling – Philosophy for Everyone:
A Philosophical Tour de Force
Edited by Jesús Ilundáin-Agurruza
and Michael W. Austin

Climbing – Philosophy for Everyone:
Because It's There
Edited by Stephen E. Schmid

Hunting – Philosophy for Everyone:
In Search of the Wild Life
Edited by Nathan Kowalsky

Christmas – Philosophy for Everyone:
Better Than a Lump of Coal
Edited by Scott C. Lowe

Cannabis – Philosophy for Everyone:
What Were We Just Talking About?
Edited by Dale Jacquette

Porn – Philosophy for Everyone:
How to Think With Kink
Edited by Dave Monroe

Serial Killers – Philosophy for Everyone: Being and Killing
Edited by S. Waller

Dating – Philosophy for Everyone:
Flirting With Big Ideas
Edited by Kristie Miller and Marlene Clark

Gardening – Philosophy for Everyone:
Cultivating Wisdom
Edited by Dan O'Brien

Motherhood – Philosophy for Everyone: The Birth of Wisdom
Edited by Sheila Lintott

Fatherhood – Philosophy for Everyone: The Dao of Daddy
Edited by Lon S. Nease
and Michael W. Austin

Forthcoming books in the series:

Fashion – Philosophy for Everyone
Edited by Jessica Wolfendale
and Jeanette Kennett

Coffee – Philosophy for Everyone
Edited by Scott Parker
and Michael W. Austin

Blues – Philosophy for Everyone
Edited by Abrol Fairweather
and Jesse Steinberg

Edited by Dave Monroe

PORN
PHILOSOPHY FOR EVERYONE
How to Think with Kink

Foreword by Gram Ponante

A John Wiley & Sons, Ltd., Publication

Blackwell Publishing was acquired by John Wiley & Sons in February 2007.
Blackwell's publishing program has been merged with Wiley's global Scientific,
Technical, and Medical business to form Wiley-Blackwell.

Registered Office
John Wiley & Sons Ltd, The Atrium, Southern Gate, Chichester, West Sussex, PO19
8SQ, United Kingdom

Editorial Offices
350 Main Street, Malden, MA 02148-5020, USA
9600 Garsington Road, Oxford, OX4 2DQ, UK
The Atrium, Southern Gate, Chichester, West Sussex, PO19 8SQ, UK

For details of our global editorial offices, for customer services, and for information
about how to apply for permission to reuse the copyright material in this book
please see our website at www.wiley.com/wiley-blackwell.

The right of Dave Monroe to be identified as the author of the editorial material in
this work has been asserted in accordance with the UK Copyright, Designs and
Patents Act 1988.

Library of Congress Cataloging-in-Publication Data
Porn – Philosophy for Everyone: how to think with kink / edited by Dave Monroe;
foreword by Gram Ponante.
    p.   cm —(Philosophy for everyone)
    Includes bibliographical references.
    ISBN 978-1-4051-9962-9 (pbk.: alk. paper)   1. Pornography.   2. Philosophy.
I. Monroe, Dave.   II. Title: Porn – Philosophy for Everyone.
    HQ471.P585 2010
    176'.7—dc22

                                                    2010004891

A catalogue record for this book is available from the British Library.

Set in 10/12.5pt Plantin by SPi Publisher Services, Pondicherry, India
Printed in Singapore

1   2010

For Rhonda,
my loudest cheerleader
and constant inspiration

CONTENTS

FOREWORD

Filling in the Cave

In Plato's Myth of the Cave, the philosopher attributes to his mentor, Socrates, the spinning of a pleasing allegory about a group of prisoners sitting manacled in a subterranean cave, forced to look at the shadows projected on a wall by a group of actors, let us say, parading on an elevated walkway between the prisoners' backs and a roaring fire.

Socrates asks, "Isn't it reasonable to assume that the prisoners believe the shadows to be real, the echoes to be learned discourse, and the ability to predict what shadow comes next as a skill worthy of the highest reward of the prisoners' society?" In other words, look at what we can get up to in the absence of the "real."

This is a searing (depending on the proximity of the fire to the prisoners) indictment of blind, spoon-fed cultures then and now, to be sure. But, while we willingly accept the idea of a proto-Skinnerian world in which a group of prisoners has *for no discernible reason* been chained in an upright position since childhood and forced to gaze at flickering projections, as told by a man who thought it best to put his words in the mouth of someone else having a discussion with yet a third party (Plato's older brother, Glaucon), we might be allowed to speculate on some of the questions that might have popped up in that ancient Athenian peanut gallery, such as, "Were they at least naked shadows?"

In my several years covering the business, lifestyles, and ethics (that last one contains the fewest billable hours) of the porn industry, I often doubt the reality of a job whose hazards include slipping on milk that has just been shot out of an oiled 19-year-old's ass. I keep turning around to look for the fire.

But if we are tempted to think of porn (derived from the Greek word for prostitute) as those images on the wall, and ourselves as the prisoners forced to watch and believe it, then we would have to accept that the parties that lit the fire, erected the walkway, and hired the actors were smarter than us, or at least had some plan for our lives.

My friends, I have met the people who make the *Dirtpipe Milkshakes* series, and I can assure you that they will not be contesting your spelling bee title. Nor do they care where you go once you push the offending DVD or computer away from you. No, I think *porn* is the wall, and the images change depending on how we choose to look at them.

You might have noticed that porn has the quality of becoming less satisfying the more complicated it gets. Throw in a plot (or even – *shudder* – a B story) and the pornographer increases his chances of breaking something that previously hummed along like some shaved steampunk perpetual motion machine; for millennia we have been aware that one simply *can't go wrong* with people having sex, and that modern pornography's success has not been in presenting variations of the sexual act but in providing the media for its presentation to be more accessible.

We can argue about what is the "right" kind of porn and how something with that elusive description should appeal to women, couples, minorities, sensitive Caucasian men, the aged, and beings yet to appear, but no one says that watching other people (or oneself) fuck is not intriguing in a marrow-level, continuance-of-the-species kind of way.

It is when elements are added to stimulate the newer neighbors of our monkey brains that porn becomes less "real." It is then we notice the boom dipping into the frame, then we realize the performers just got the script that morning, that in any case they never expected to be performing *Medea* when they got bra-busting saline injections, and then we scoff at a dolly shot when a simple close-up will do.

Early texts of Plato's *Republic*, in which the Myth of the Cave appeared, used the word *gaze* to describe how its audience regarded the pictures on the wall. The reason we gaze at pornography, rather than be engaged by it, is because the very basic and elemental strivings and exertions depicted therein are ours to interpret. We gaze because porn becomes what we want it to be; it is a cave to be filled in.

That is why we spare porn the rigorous character breakdowns we would require of *Dude, Where's My Car?* This is why we forgive porn for labeling as MILF the 23-year-old who has never borne children, as Asian a Swede, as a naughty schoolgirl someone who is not and never was. But the uniform is all they – and you, the viewer – need to begin the crazy joyride of projection. So porn is the wall and the viewer is both the prisoner and the fire; the actors are whoever you want them to be, because I can tell you they are not in "real life" what you have made them.

Porn as a phenomenon seems to have generated a perfect ratio of content to comment. For as many issues of *Barely Legal*, *Screw My Wife, Please*, and *Dirty Debutantes* generated annually, there are scholarly treatises about Why We Like Porn; or Is It OK That We Like Porn? or; Are We Bad People for Encouraging Other People To Like Porn?

I would like to throw my hat in the ring and say that porn is not real, but you are, and that porn serves the same purpose that monster trucks, professional wrestling, TMZ, and eating candy do: they are all fixed points at which existing thoughts can coalesce. It helps, then, that those entertainments are fairly thought-agnostic on their own.

Maybe Plato projected his own allegory of the cave onto Socrates because he thought the name "Socrates" might make the theory sexier – less Platonic. In the adult business we understand this, hence Linda Hopkins became Tera Patrick and Jenna Massoli became Jenna Jameson. What is porn if not the thoughtful practice of projecting something onto the most attractive surface?

ACKNOWLEDGMENTS

First, I would like to thank all of the contributors; they are the true authors of this anthology. Many of these people I have only communicated with by phone or email, but they already seem like friends. I deeply appreciate the quality of their writing and their good spirits in working with me on crafting this volume. Sometimes it may have seemed that I was the source of unending questions, feedback, suggestions, and perhaps, irritation. Nevertheless, the authors were, without exception, diligent, patient, and a pleasure to work with; I am grateful for their excellent essays. It is noteworthy to recognize their background diversity, too; they come from various academic professions, law, and even inside the porn industry itself, which had the effect of extending my own knowledge. I am grateful for that, as well!

Second, I would like to thank those who have directly or indirectly helped me throughout the production of this book, including my mother, Mary Turfe, and my brothers, Chris and Andrew Monroe; my cousin Ian Verhine; Nathan Bunker-Otto, my dear friend, and Jason at Vegas Showgirls in Saint Petersburg; Tom Brommage, Eric Berling, and Joe Ellin, for stepping in to help with other academic obligations; my students and colleagues at Saint Petersburg College and University of Tampa; and, especially, my wife Rhonda. I cannot imagine what life would be like without her loving support and willingness to promote my various projects, including a book about porn! Precious few wives would be willing to indulge their husbands' spending long hours talking to porn stars, watching porn, and devoting weekends editing papers and writing about the jizz biz. I am fortunate to be so lucky.

Third, I would like to thank my publisher. Wiley-Blackwell has been behind this project from its inception, and shown remarkable enthusiasm for a project about an admittedly controversial topic. In particular, I recognize the efforts of Fritz Allhoff, Jeff Dean, and Tiffany Mok. Fritz, the series editor of the *Philosophy for Everyone* line, has shown unflagging confidence in this volume, the series, and in me. I especially appreciate his ardent desire to produce excellent books, and I thank him for his constant guidance, suggestions, and feedback in helping me attain that end. Jeff, the acquisitions editor for philosophy at Wiley-Blackwell, has also been a great source of help, enthusiasm, and ideas. Tiffany helped guide me through the business side of putting together an anthology, something about which I was woefully ignorant, and I could not have done it without her. Any editor should be grateful for such wise guidance!

Finally, I thank you, the reader: enjoy the volume! The next time you engage with porn, think about it!

Dave Monroe
Saint Petersburg, FL

DIRTY MINDEDNESS

An Introduction to *Porn – Philosophy for Everyone*

In the pages of this anthology, the reader will find a tantalizing spread of essays about pornography. Like "gonzo" videos, the essays within are broadly arranged by topic; this allows you to "fast forward" or "rewind" to the issues that turn you on. I am confident, however, that you will find each section stimulating, as every essay is uniquely delightful and intellectually arousing.

Some may wonder whether the world needs more writing about pornography; after all, there is no dearth of academic literature on the subject. Porn has been a topic in feminist, legal, and general ethical discussions since at least the 1970s. So what is the motive for producing this anthology? The answer is simple. We have, as a culture, become more dirty minded. Yet discussions of the porn industry and its attendant issues seem largely to be limited to academic or legal contexts, locker rooms or bedchambers. In other words, the ubiquity of the subject appears to outrun the scope of the discourse. This anthology seeks to broaden the conversation about pornography, both by expanding the range of questions about porn that academics might address and by opening the conversation to those who are most familiar with it – the creators and users of porn.

The contemporary porn industry and the hordes of porn consumers have never been larger. The explosion of porn on the Internet has expanded the industry in previously undreamt ways. Nude busty women, lesbian sex, and money shots are a mere Google search away; access to porn no longer involves skulking into the shady parts of town to visit the adult theatre or video store. What's more, porn's relationship to pop culture has changed since the "Golden Age" of the 1970s. Porn has lampooned or perverted Hollywood story lines since then (one thinks of memorable titles like *Edward Penishands*), but it is evident that the dynamic has shifted. Hollywood films, television, popular magazines, and literature are now frequently giving homage to the porn industry. There is scarcely a reality show on TV that does not feature some current or former Playboy model. Movies like *Zach and Miri Make a Porno* celebrate, rather than denigrate, porn. "Crossovers" are surprisingly common, as well. Once, having acted in porn was equivalent to branding oneself with a scarlet letter. Actresses like Traci Lords worked tirelessly to transition into doing mainstream films and TV. Now, however, there seem to be no such stigmas. The crossover runs the other direction, as well; Kelly McCarty, Miss USA 1991 and soap opera star, signed a contract with Vivid Video in 2008.

Furthermore, celebrity sex tapes are increasingly available to the libidinous celebrity obsessed public. Non-industry performers are getting in on the act, too. Popular, and controversial, videos like the *Girls Gone Wild* series feature not adult actresses, but rambunctious college-aged girls willing to flash for cash. Similarly, "amateur" porn is an emerging trend on the internet – couples film their coitus and broadcast it for others to see. The rest of us, in startling numbers, are tuning in to watch.

With porn's new dimensions come new issues to discuss. What are the ramifications of this pornographic proliferation? What moral dimensions are there to the explosion of technology and the availability of porn? How does porn potentially affect our relationships with others? Are there special ethical concerns that present themselves when amateurs act like porn professionals? How does the virtual bombardment of pornographic images affect our psychology? Does porn offer any social benefits? Do old legal concepts about porn hold up under a new cultural paradigm of dirty mindedness? What are some contemporary issues in gay porn? These and other novel issues are discussed within.

That is not to say, however, that this volume fails to address the classic issues constellated around porn. Concerns about the nature of free speech and whether porn falls under that concept, the putative artistic value of porn, gender issues, discussions of possible harms related to porn, are all covered. Thus, the reader interested in standing academic debates about porn will not be left feeling as if they have taken a cold shower.

Porn – Philosophy for Everyone is also a "crossover" book. Inside, you will find essays written not just by academic philosophers, but lawyers, psychologists, and other scholars. Our contributors come from around the world; we have Canadian, British, and Australian writers as well as American. The jewels in our crossover crown, though, are essays written or contributed to by porn industry insiders like Dylan Ryder, the Fabulous Mz. Berlin, and Roger T. Pipe. Their provocative first-hand insights about the porn business are not to be missed!

So, we who have created this anthology invite you to go behind the green door, get a little dirty minded, and think with kink! We have no doubt that you will be seduced by the tantalizing topics thrown under hot light by our authors, and be intellectually aroused. Enjoy!

In the second part of this introduction, I offer you a tour of this volume, and briefly discuss some of the issues addressed therein. I hope that you are satisfied with the spread, but of course would not object if at the end you yearn for more!

We start with a foreword by Gram Ponante, who is "America's Beloved Porn Journalist." I am delighted that Gram wrote the foreword, as I did not want just anyone to kick off the volume. Gram is well connected in the industry, and thus has an insider's view of the porn business. Moreover, he is known for his critical observations and sometimes trenchant commentary regarding what he sees. He takes a philosophical approach to his work, in other words, and thus is naturally sympathetic to this anthology. As such, he is the perfect person to write the foreword.

After the foreword, we move into our first unit, a kind of foreplay to prime us for the rest of the book. I have subtitled the section Sundry Sexy Thoughts because, unlike the forthcoming units, there is no shared underlying philosophical context. Nevertheless, the essays within are alluring on their own. We start with an essay by Dylan Ryder, a contemporary porn dynamo, and yours truly. Our offering takes up the prudential question of whether a porn performer's individual life is necessarily worse off by virtue of being in the porn industry. We argue that it is not, and that there is no essential connection between the Jizz Biz and the quality of one's life. In making our case, we draw distinctions between various ways of valuing human lives, and argue that the common-sense view that porn stars have worse lives than "normal" folks conflates, or confuses, moral value with welfare; i.e., quality of life. Next is an essay by Andrew Aberdein, a lighthearted chapter exploring the historical connection between pornographic and philosophical literature. There is a history of porno-philosophical writing and imagery, he shows us, mostly aiming to contrast rational versus irrational forms of persuasion. He offers us a shocking, and hilarious, example of femdom representations of Aristotle and Phyllis. His essay ends with an argument attempting to show that the porno-philosophical connection raises problems for contemporary arguments against pornography.

The next unit, The Pornographic Mind, consists of essays focusing on psychological considerations relating to pornography, especially those regarding the audience. This seems a natural starting point; porn appeals to *something* within our psychology, or else it would lack the massive popularity it enjoys. What happens to our mind when we are porn spectators? Are our beliefs about the mental states of porn performers veridical? Is there a kind of rebelliousness against social norms going on in our minds when we view certain kinds of porn? These fascinating questions frame the issues in this section. The unit starts with a delightfully irreverent and entertaining essay by Anne K. Gordon and Shane W. Kraus, evolutionary psychologists. They performed empirical studies about the scope of belief in porn audiences about the genuineness of female orgasms in porn films. Their study reveals that men are more likely than women to believe that girls in porn actually get off, and conclude that, among its other putative negative effects, porn makes men bad lovers! Next is an essay by Theodore Bach, who explains the scope of porn consumption on the model of psychological simulation. Briefly, we use our own mind to model that of another individual, like an engineer would use a model airplane to simulate its activity. According to Bach, it is likely that the porn viewer engages in this kind of mental modeling; one thinks and feels as if he or she is actually experiencing the depicted sex acts. The upshots of this fact, he argues, are some potentially negative social implications. The final essay in this unit is written by Casey McKittrick. He addresses some of the psychological issues present in the gay "barebacking" video subgenre. "Barebacking" is an erotic celebration of condomless anal sex, and represents a substantial minority seeking to reclaim a loss of intimacy resulting from the AIDS epidemic in the gay community. The exchange of semen in gay sex is labeled as paradigmatically "risky" behavior, which results in a taboo in gay porn against condomless sex scenes. McKittrick explores Freudian psychological bases for the motive to produce, participate, and view bareback videos, while remaining neutral with respect to attendant moral implications. I am excited to include his essay, as precious little philosophical literature addresses male homosexual pornography.

The next section, Between the Sheets, deals with ethical issues relating to porn. While some consideration is given to the classical arguments about the exploitation, objectification, and harms that seem attached to the adult entertainment business, the focus of this section is on unusual topics, such as whether masturbating to porn constitutes cheating in a monogamous relationship. That being said, the first essay, by Tait Szabo, is a defense of the porn viewer's freedom to watch porn without moral guilt. He argues for his thesis on the basis of John Stuart Mill's Harm Principle, which roughly states that unless our actions result in genuine harm to others, we are free to pursue and enjoy whatever we wish. Szabo attempts to show that porn does not result in the sorts of harms anti-porn arguments generally posit; thus, we have no basis to condemn it, and are free to guiltlessly enjoy it. Next is an essay by Fiona Woollard. Her arguments focus on the question of whether self-gratification via porn constitutes a breach of monogamy norms. Is the moral outrage or feeling of betrayal that commonly accompanies catching your partner masturbating to Jenna reasonable? Woollard considers two possible grounds for that outrage; she categorically rejects that solo use of porn is a kind of infidelity, while conceding that some porn is damaging to relationships because it reinforces harmful attitudes that undermine loving partnerships. However, she notes, this is not true of all pornography. Darci Doll, in the unit's final essay, offers us a cautionary tale drawn from celebrity sex tapes. Doll argues that there are benefits of taping one' sex life, particularly in the case of celebrities who use it as a vehicle to fame, but that associated pitfalls ought to give us pause before consenting to make "private" porn. Doll is careful to distinguish morally legitimate ways of producing and distributing private sex tapes, and warns that the benefits of releasing sex tapes frequently accrue to the wrong people, if anyone.

As we hope the law follows morality, our next section centers on legal questions and philosophy of law and pornography. The authors of these essays take issue with some classic questions, such as the nature and definition of "obscenity" and the limits of free speech. If "obscenity" is not protected by our right to free speech, just what counts as "obscene"? Is there some objective way of defining it, or does the term merely denote a subjective kind of judgment or response? The first essay in the Talking Dirty section takes up this issue. Jacob M. Held argues that the concept of obscenity is insufficiently defined to ground legislation limiting our freedom of expression. This obscurity results in the inability to take inter-pretation out of the hands of individual judges, who are forced to rule on cases with no clear standard of the obscene. As a result, we citizens cannot have fair warning of what obscenity laws prescribe, and thus such laws fail to realize the form of law that being subject to rule of law requires. Following Held, Mimi Marinucci argues that we ought not to cave in to censorship laws, not because there is nothing wrong or harmful with porn as it stands, but because allowing more expansive censorship laws threatens other avenues of expression. Censorship serves the interests of the dominant culture (male, in this case) and so should be avoided. Rather than worrying about censoring porn, she suggests, we ought to support the production of more socially responsible kinds of pornography, including feminist porn. Lastly, J. K. Miles advances the claim that defending porn on the grounds of free speech or free expression is a failed cause. He argues that certain relevant differences between political or religious speech and porn suffice to distinguish the cases enough that porn is disqualified from protection by constitutional rights to free speech. One difference is that public displays of porn, unlike public speeches about politics or sermons, would *coerce* the audience into behaving in a way they may not want to – that is, watching porn. Speeches and sermons do not force you into an act against your will, whereas public displays of porn would. Therefore, porn would attempt to persuade without rational consent. This fact, Miles argues, takes porn out of the sphere of protected speech. However, he suggests that the freedom to use porn could be defended on other grounds.

The Art of Dirty unit concerns the question whether porn has artistic merit. Porn and art share media: print, film, photography, painting, and so forth. Can porn be elevated to the status of fine art? Are artworks ever *also* pornographic, or is art necessarily non-pornographic? Christopher Bartel, Lawrence Howe, and David Rose address these questions, and others, in the scope of this section. Bartel argues that the distinction between what is pornographic and what is artistic is not a function of the work in question, but is given by a distinction in ways of valuing that thing. We can take an artistic interest in a piece, e.g., appreciating its formal qualities, or a pornographic interest in it, e.g., getting turned on by the content of the work. These attitudes, he argues, are mutually exclusive; one cannot take an artistic interest in a painting, say, while one takes a pornographic interest in it. Bartel also wonders whether it is possible to gain an artistic attitude for an artwork *via* having a pornographic interest in it, and concludes that this is impossible on the basis of the exclusivity of our interests. Howe, on the other hand, works to sharpen distinctions between fine art, erotica, and pornography, and considers whether the categories overlap. Howe argues that what shows or supports the distinction is the aesthetic attitude, i.e., contemplative distance, or disinterestedness in the object of one's appreciation. Pornography does not allow us to enter the aesthetic attitude, partly due to its apparent lack of other aesthetic qualities; e.g., proportion, unity in diversity, and so on. Porn differs from erotica, on the other hand, in that erotica promotes a sympathetic relation between the viewer and represented objects, which is missing in porn. The distinction between erotica and fine art is harder to draw, he concedes, but he ultimately concludes that erotica is closer to fine art than to porn. David Rose, in the unit's last essay, considers reasons generally given to treat pornographic works as different from other aesthetic objects. Rose argues that standard moral reasons, e.g., that porn is exploitative, coercive, harmful to women, and so on, are insufficient to ground legislation against porn because they neither identify a characteristic wrongness unique to porn nor ensure consensus. However, Rose argues that there is such a ground for legislation because proper artistic objects play a special role in the promotion of societal values, relationships, and a culture's self-identity, whereas porn degrades them.

The next unit is about the interpenetration of technology and porn. Clearly, improvements in technology have opened new horizons for the porn industry; its product is easier than ever to obtain and use, is cheaper to produce and distribute via Internet sites, and digital interactivity expands rapidly. Roger T. Pipe, a porn critic, offers an insider's perspective on the affects of this technological explosion. He takes us through the history of the contemporary adult film industry, from the raincoater days of XXX theatres to the current Internet era, and wonders whether or not these "advances" have been for the better. Matthew Brophy recognizes new moral problems emerging with innovative porn technologies, and prognosticates further issues as more advanced virtual realities arise. If porn becomes qualitatively indistinguishable from normal sex, and we can determine the precise characteristics of our ideal lovers with a click of a button, Brophy argues this will undermine traditional virtues requisite for human flourishing, and promote moral vice.

Our final unit, Kink, takes up special issues in "alternative" or "fringe" porn. With McKittrick's essay being the sole exception, our earlier essays have dealt with "mainstream" porn. Defining mainstream porn is difficult, but I think the standard form is the sort of porn that is found on most websites and adult videos; i.e., heterosexual porn, usually with some oral sex and a few positions thrown in for spice, culminating in "the money shot." Alternative or fringe porn deviates from that model.

The first essay in this section, by Chad Parkhill, investigates the seeming oddity of heterosexual men enjoying girl-girl pornography; since male sexuality is excluded in lesbian porn, why do men find it so attractive? Appealing to Lacanian psychoanalysis, Parkhill distinguishes between kinds of pleasure men can have in watching lesbian porn, *plaisir* and *jouissance*, arguing that the latter involves an "ego shattering" pleasure that precludes male "intrusion." For that reason, he concludes that *jouissance* is the morally preferable kind of pleasure for men to feel when watching girl-girl porn. In the next essay, Ummni Khan argues against the rough legal treatment of sadomasochistic porn. Khan argues that in the case of SM porn, legal systems have systematically ignored the role of consent in mitigating "violence" in SM contexts, and as a result have propagated violence against the SM community. The violence comes in three forms: physical, phenomenological, and epistemic. Physical violence consists in disproportionate legal punishments and imprisonment in violation of the principle of proportionality of punishment. Phenomenological violence consists in enforcing a stipulated "true" sexuality that is likely not consonant with an individual's experiences, and epistemic violence restricts the freedom of individuals on the basis of judgments that are false or obscure, or lacking in sufficient justification. Thus, governments *systematically wrong* those who are into SM porn. The final essay in this section, and indeed, the anthology itself, is an interview with the Fabulous Mz. Berlin. Berlin is a popular dominatrix who acts in, directs, and produces BDSM films. Additionally, she works as an actress in "vanilla" XXX. In the interview, Berlin answers questions about the porn industry in general, as well as her experiences as a dominatrix. She discusses the nature of informed consent, the role that concept plays in determining acceptable contexts for filming dirty movies, the nature of torture, fluid gender roles, and various other exciting topics. Her thoughts are fittingly the last – ruminations from an educated woman both on the inside and at the boundaries of the porn industry.

In closing, I hope that you enjoy this volume as much as I enjoyed working on it. I also hope that it helps you think philosophically about porn. Enjoy!

PART I

LIGHTS, CAMERA, ACTION!
SUNDRY SEXY THOUGHTS

CHAPTER I

THE JIZZ BIZ AND QUALITY OF LIFE

 Dylan Ryder, co-author of this essay, is a contemporary porn star. Her job involves having sex with various men and women, and having that sex recorded for the voyeuristic enjoyment of others. It goes without saying that this job is unlike most of ours; we spend time in offices day-dreaming at water coolers, slaving away on factory floors, cooking and serving food, teaching classes, or at sundry other occupations. She gets paid to have sex on camera, to bare what most of us would not dare – our naked bodies and sexual activities. Dylan's job is not a "normal" occupation, at least in the sense that it is unusual. But what do you think of when you think about *the life* a porn star leads? Some of you may romanticize about the sexual pleasure they seem to enjoy, or perhaps think that the "rock star" life-style many porn stars, like Jenna Jameson, lead is attractive and fun. Being a porn star holds a taboo allure, one might think, a way of life that is more "exciting," and better than, the life one currently lives. Dylan and Dave suspect that those beliefs are held by a small minority. More likely, the majority opinion is that the life of a porn star is *worse* than average.

It seems that the pre-reflective, common-sense opinion about a porn star's quality of life holds that because (as the arguments usually go) porn stars are objectified, coerced, degraded, or exploited, their lives must be *worse off* than the lives of "normal people." Don't movies like

Boogie Nights show us that "something must be wrong or missing" in someone's life that drives one into the porn business, and that once in things only get worse? Most people believe that porn professionals are drug addicts, have been sexually abused in their present or past, or are coerced or forced into the business by someone else, usually an abusive pimp. After all, what sort of decent, self-respecting person would have sex on camera – for money?

Our essay explores the prudential question of whether a porn actor's life is necessarily better or worse off by virtue of his or her profession. The issue, we take it, is about one's individual welfare, or the *quality* of one's individual life. That is, one might say, how "well" or "ill" one's life is going. We will call this "prudential" value: the value of one's own life to oneself. So, in short, the claim for which we will argue is that being involved in porn does not necessarily interfere with one's having a prudentially "good life."

Our arguments will attempt to demonstrate that popular opinion is mistaken; even if it is true that the *porn business* is an immoral institution, which we do not believe it is, it does not follow that the individual porn actor's life is worse off. In defense of our claim, we will discuss what we take to be the "common-sense" popular opinion sketched above, elaborate what we take to be mistaken assumptions behind it, and argue against them. We will also distinguish between various ways of valuing a human life, and suggest that part of the impetus for the common-sense view rests on confusing a distinction between the "moral" quality of life and prudential quality of life, aka "wellbeing" or "welfare."[1] We will argue in favor of this distinction in an effort to show that there is no necessary connection between moral or immoral things happening to a person and the quality of that person's life. Furthermore, we will consider potential objections to our conclusion, including the classic "Happy Slave" thought experiment that seems to give reason to reject our claims. In the end, we do not think these objections succeed. Being a porn star does not necessarily impede the prudential value of one's life.

Eeew! Sucks to be a Porn Star!

Before we get into a discussion of our rejection of popular opinion, we ought to outline, in a little more detail, just what that is. Again, we take the main thesis to be the belief that something must be wrong in a porn star's life if they are making porn, and that the wrongness perpetuated by the porn industry must affect the individual welfare of that porn star. For instance, a defender of the popular opinion may point out that it is not "normal" to have sex for money and record it for others' enjoyment; porn actors display an abnormal level of exhibitionism, and that must reveal some kind of psychological defect, more compelling addiction, or coercion. There are voids in that person's life, in other words, that she or he mistakenly turns to porn to fill. Furthermore, one may say, it is not normal to place so little "value" on sexual activity, and that may indicate a history or current track record of sexual abuse. On the basis of this thinking, getting into the porn business seems to show that there is *already* some diminution of welfare that drives one into the business. Thereafter, it may appear, things get worse.

Popular opinion also sees the porn industry as propagating poor quality of life. Those who produce porn films are guilty of coercing performers into doing things they may not be comfortable with, degrading them, exploiting their damaged circumstances (e.g., taking advantage of the fact that a porn star may have a drug habit to support), and objectifying them as a matter of course; that is, treating them as "things" rather than persons. Given that they are victims of, or complicit in, so much "wrongdoing," we must conclude that the lives of porn stars are worse off than most of ours.

We believe that the popularity and plausibility of this opinion rests on several assumptions. First, there is the assumption that departing from "normal" sexual behavior represents a kind of character defect. Second, there is an assumption that sex acts have a special significance that the porn actor does not recognize or ignores due to some interfering factor. Third, and most significant, is the assumption that there is a necessary connection between morality and welfare. One could attribute these assumptions to certain religious-based views about the significance of sexual activity and definitions stipulating "normal" sexual behavior. Undoubtedly, many who hold the popular opinion accept these assumptions on the basis of their religious backgrounds. However, that may not be true, especially with respect to the belief that moral quality of life is essential to one's welfare.[2] Aristotle defends this view, telling us that virtue is a necessary condition for *eudaemonia*, or "faring well." That is, if we are not virtuous, we have no hope of a satisfying, good life. Of course, we reject this view and its assumptions, so we will turn now to our arguments against them.

Get Out Of My Bed!

It is manifestly false that porn stars are scummy people universally lacking in character, have drug problems, were sexually abused, have bad family lives, have mental defects, or any of the panoply of assumed flaws. Dylan, for example, has spent a great deal of time doing non-profit work for charities that "normal" people tend to praise; in fact, she was a substance abuse counselor for prison inmates preparing for their release. She has lived a regular life in which she competed in sports, was free from sexual assault, and so forth. She currently attends college, and has a great relationship with her parents and siblings. There are some, like Dylan, who simply like the business, embrace their sexuality, and relish putting it on display for the enjoyment of others. No doubt there are some who have the aforementioned issues, but the assumption that porn performers must be somehow defective to get into the business is false.

Does departing from "normal" sexual behavior represent some kind of character defect? This assumption is problematic. There are certainly clear cases in which one departs too radically from sexual norms, such as molesting children. The moral issue is clear – it involves victimizing and exploiting people who are powerless to defend themselves and cannot give informed consent.[3] But what about cases that involve fully developed adults making informed choices to act on certain non-standard sexual preferences? Such individuals exercise their autonomy in a way that does not involve actively harming others. Does this represent a kind of "character defect"? It may, if we understand "character" in this context as conforming to some Pauline standard of sexual morality, or believe that a specific kind of sex life contributes to human flourishing, e.g., monogamy. If that were actually true, then perhaps there is some substance to this assumption and our sexuality assumes a special significance.

Whether or not this is true, however, is a matter of debate. It is not our purpose here to settle this matter entirely, so we will only pause to throw doubt on the assumption that "normal" sexual mores are justified or that they have any special connection to the prudential value of our lives. In the absence of some purpose-driven worldview, it is difficult to elaborate why sex ought to have the significance generally attached to it. If one does not go in for that sort of thing, then there's little reason, outside of mere social convention, to believe that there is a well-defined "sexual normality." What if sexual norms are just a matter of social convention?

𝄞

Insisting that porn stars should follow social norms *because* they are social norms is not justified. After all, there are better and worse social norms and practices, and we ought to give some defense of why a particular set of norms and practices is acceptable. That is part of the point at issue here, so to say that porn stars are "abnormal" because they do not practice monogamy, are exhibitionists, and get paid for "doing it" is no help. The fact that most people do not act like porn stars in bed does not, by itself, mean that what the porn stars are doing is wrong. That is not to say that we cannot place limits on acceptable sexual behavior, as we have suggested above. Informed consent and lack of harm seem to place those limits nicely. But those limits do not depend on "what most people do."

Even if there is some moral significance to "normal" sex, and some morally right way to do it, that does not establish a necessary connection to our wellbeing. It may be true that being in "normal" sexual relationships makes available to us prudential goods that we might otherwise not realize. However, a connection between those further goods, such as constant companionship, and our welfare would require demonstration, and the connection is likely to be contingent or accidental at best. Showing a relationship may be possible, but those prudential goods would have to be proven *better* than the goods provided by "abnormal" practices, and that is a tall order. However, there is reason to be dubious of the claim that sex plays a special role in wellbeing to begin with. There are some, e.g., priests and clerics of various religions, who *abstain* from any sort of sexual activity, and it would be presumptuous of us to assume that they are necessarily worse off for it.

What about the Aristotelian claim that virtue is a necessary condition for human flourishing? Will being morally good climax in my own wellbeing, or at least make wellbeing possible? Putting it bluntly, no. Many philosophers have noted that one can conceive of a perfectly *immoral* person enjoying personal welfare in spite of his wickedness; doing so does not result in contradiction, which means such a case is logically possible. Thus, being virtuous is not necessary for our personal welfare. What of other moral theories? Is *acting* morally a condition of the good life? Again, it does not seem so. Utilitarianism's value maximizing principle leaves open the possibility, despite the fact that the valued end is both morally and prudentially valuable, that doing the "right thing" would force us to sacrifice our own welfare for that of others. Kant's deontology severs clean the connection between welfare and ethics; we are obligated to follow morality's principles *regardless* of how it affects the quality of our lives. Taking a cue from the utilitarians and Kant, then, we should understand morality as setting limits on our quality of life, or at least the ways in which we are allowed to pursue it. However, being moral is not a *condition* for our wellbeing, and it is perfectly conceivable that a villain could enjoy as much prudential quality of life as the rest of us. Thus, even if those working in the porn industry are *doing* something immoral, or have tarnished characters, it does not follow that they are "worse off" from the perspective of their own welfare. Neither does it follow that having immoral things happen to us necessarily inhibits our welfare. To see why the latter is true, we need to sharpen the distinction between moral and prudential value.

Ways of Valuing Lives

There are as many ways of valuing lives as there are kinds of values. A life may be morally valuable, aesthetically valuable, intellectually valuable, historically valuable, and so on. For any such value, we can say with a straight face that one leads a "good" or "bad" life; that is, good or bad relative to whatever value we mean when we make the judgment. Sometimes these evaluations overlap. Mother Teresa, for instance, lived a morally and historically significant (that is, good) life. While these values are distinct, the fact that they often overlap and the fact that we use the same evaluative terms for each (good, bad, and so forth) creates ambiguity. This ambiguity is responsible, we think, for the concern that the porn industry propagates poor quality of life. It is based on confusing, once again, the moral quality of one's life with one's welfare.

What exactly distinguishes moral quality of life from prudential wellbeing? When we are talking about the welfare, or wellbeing, of an individual we mean roughly how well or ill that person's life is going. There must be someone whose life is going well, and furthermore, that person must be able to recognize that it is so. Prudential value is the value of your life from *your* perspective; there is an essentially subjective element to welfare. What constitutes welfare varies from person to person, so Dylan's beliefs about what makes her life worthwhile could radically differ from Dave's. For example, Dylan may think her life is better off because of her ability to swim, exercise, or have sex for a living, while Dave finds satisfaction in teaching. If Dave tells us that teaching contributes to his life being "good," or worthwhile, he is not saying at the same time that we all ought to teach and attain that good. Given the subjective nature of welfare, it also seems that the person best positioned to *make* welfare judgments is the individual whose life is in question. Dylan is the best judge of how Dylan's life is going, in other words.

Morality, if it is worth its salt, is not "optional" in the way our welfare seem to be. Morality and its dictates seem to be universal and not purely contingent on our subjective mental states; that is, if there are moral rules Dave ought to follow or character traits that Dylan ought to develop, then so ought everyone else. Judgments about the moral standing of one's life, then, need not involve reference to anything subjective. Judging the wickedness of Hitler or Dahmer does not depend at all on whether *they* thought what they were doing was wrong, in other words. It is perfectly possible that one could fail to recognize a diminished or increased moral quality of life. But this, we suggest, is *not* true with one's own welfare, precisely because what constitutes one's welfare *depends upon* one's own subjective viewpoint.[4] The two ways of judging the "quality of one's life" are distinct, and thus it is possible that one could have a low moral life-value and high welfare, or vice versa.

If we are right, then we have advanced our claim that even if the porn business is immoral and subjects its employees to moral harms, it does not follow that the particular porn performer's wellbeing is necessarily diminished.

"Not so fast, my friend," Lee Corso might exclaim at this point. "There is an objection to your view that you have not considered." That is true. So, in the next section, we will consider some important objections to our argument and attempt to show that they fall short of the mark.

Climax: Happy Slaves, Oppression, and Quality of Life

Suppose we were to consider the lot of a slave. What would we think when we considered her life? Most of us, when asked if that slave had a high quality of life, would think that she endures the *worst* kind of life. The slave is oppressed, compelled to work against her will, and enjoys very little opportunity for advancement or prospects for what we might normally associate with factors contributing to wellbeing. Nevertheless, if asked, our slave might report that her life is just fine. In fact, she may claim that she enjoys a high degree of wellbeing. Our intuitions seem to be at variance with her subjective judgment about how her life is going; while she may report satisfaction with her life, we recognize immediately that something is amiss. Intuitively, we see that oppression and slavery *reduce* quality of life.

What the aptly named Happy Slave example supposedly shows is that in order to make sense of these judgments, we must draw a distinction between subjective quality of life (or wellbeing) and objective quality of life. The subjective sort simply depends on the perspectives, preferences, desires, or whatever, of a person (consonant with our position outlined above), but the objective judgment that the slave's life *is* worse off, despite her subjective mind states, requires some external, objective understanding of wellbeing. Thus, wellbeing does not simply *amount to* whatever we like or find worthwhile – something else matters, too. If this is true, then one may be mistaken about whether one actually enjoys a meaningful level of wellbeing.

We can replace the "happy slave" with the "happy porn star" and we get essentially the question that is the target of our essay. Why isn't the porn star simply *wrong* about her quality of life? It may *seem to her* as if her life is a good one, but *in fact* it is not. To establish our claim that being a porn star does not necessarily diminish one's wellbeing, then, requires our dealing with the Happy Slave problem.

Fortunately, others working in the context of medical ethics have blazed a trail for us to follow. Ron Amundson, in defense of the plausibility of subjective accounts of wellbeing, argues against the intuitions "shown" by the Happy Slave problem by pointing out some epistemological problems. We seem to have an upper hand in understanding the slave's plight because we are third-person observers, that is, outsiders, who recognize the objectification, coercion, and so forth. And we think "if only the slave knew what was good for her, she would recognize how horrible her life really is." That may be true, Amundson concedes, but that special standpoint does not generalize beyond *obvious* cases like slavery. There are many cases in which third-personal knowledge of a person's situation does not yield grounds for accurate judgments about another person's welfare. Amundson points out that precisely the opposite is true with respect to physical disability. A curious fact about quality of life reports from disabled people is that they tend to be about the same, or sometimes even better, than those of "normal" people. That is, their subjective quality of life does not differ on the basis of physical limitations, despite the fact that our "intuitions" tell us that such a life is worse than normal. Who is really in the right position to make the judgment that disability decreases quality of life: a disabled person or an outsider? The answer seems clear – the person who has

DYLAN RYDER AND DAVE MONROE

endured the disability knows better the quality of her life than those of us who have not "walked a mile in her shoes." Furthermore, Amundson argues, unless we have a robust understanding of what "objective" quality of life consists in, we have no way of telling whether our judgments about the wellbeing of the disabled are legitimate, or the result of social stigmas.[5]

One could apply the same response, changing what needs to be changed, to the case of the porn star. Is it more like the plight of the slave, or the plight of the disabled? What are the "objective" factors that determine our wellbeing? Do our judgments about the quality of porn star lives simply reflect a social stigma? We are inclined to think the latter is true. Are there objective factors that determine our quality of life? Perhaps there are, but we suspect that *any* putative objective factor offered as an answer will be susceptible to the "anomaly" seen above in the case of physical disability. Our lives may lack some, or many, of the putative objective "facts" about wellbeing, yet nevertheless our subjective reports of prudential value could be "normal" or better. We make psychological adjustments to the objective conditions of our lives, and those adjustments preserve the possibility of our maintaining a high degree of wellbeing.

We are not convinced that the Happy Slave shows what it wants to show in the first place. Are we forced to conclude that there must be some objective factor to wellbeing on the basis of the fact that we make the third-person judgment that the slave is worse off? No. We believe that this example has force precisely because it confuses or conflates the distinction made above concerning moral and prudential value. It is clear that something is *wrong* in the slave case – something immoral occurs when people are forced into servitude against their will, oppressed, and so forth. The patent immorality of the situation confuses us into accepting that the slave's life must be worse off; she is the non-consensual victim of a wicked institution, cruel treatment, and restrictions on her autonomy. Her life is *morally* worse off, that much is clear. Nevertheless, as we argued above, this does not determine anything with respect to her wellbeing. She may, without contradiction, genuinely judge that her quality of life is high, despite the fact that she suffers ill use at the hands of others. Again, changing what needs to be changed, the same applies to the case of a porn performer.

One might point out that we have good reason to doubt the *sincerity* of a porn star's subjective report about her wellbeing. How do we know that when a porn performer, like Dylan, tells us her life is great and that she enjoys porn she really *means* it? Is it not likely that her claims are coerced, either directly and indirectly, and if so, why should we believe what she says? The same may be true of the slave, women in oppressive cultures, and regular dudes who work for Budweiser. It is a common occurrence. Few of us are willing to risk getting in trouble by not "towing the party line," as it were. The porn star risks her livelihood by being honest. Telling the truth about how much porn star lives suck would be a quick route to the industry blacklist.

We concede that this is possible, in practice. Some porn employees may simply be towing the party line when they tell us how much they love their jobs, working in the industry, having hot nasty sex for money, and so on. But suppose we fixed the conditions under which they made assertions about their wellbeing. Suppose we could assure that no one in the industry would ever discover what they said, and do so in a way that promised no repercussions or loss of livelihood? Why then would we doubt what they told us? In principle, the interference or coercion would be obviated, so we would have no reason to doubt their sincerity. Besides, this is an empirical question we could resolve with the right kind of blind survey, and is somewhat beside the point of whether a porn star *could* enjoy a high quality of life despite her industry.

The last objection we will consider might go as follows: "Suppose you are right that being exploited, coerced, and so on does not necessarily diminish one's wellbeing. Doesn't this seem to excuse the bad behavior of oppressive individuals and institutions? For example, one may argue that 'since so-and-so (insert victim or victim group here) is not necessarily "worse off" for my oppression, there is little reason for me to stop doing what I am doing.' After all, no one is necessarily 'hurt' by the oppressive activity – one can live a fulfilling life in spite of it all."

In response, we concede that in practice some may rationalize their bad behavior in this way. However, it does not follow that one legitimately justifies their oppressive conduct by appealing to the fact that the oppression does not necessarily diminish the wellbeing of the oppressed. We have distinguished moral value from wellbeing, so where there are genuinely oppressive or exploitative institutions or individuals, we can condemn them on independent moral grounds. An adequate moral theory should enable us to make these judgments irrespective of whether or not the victims of moral villainy are "worse off" prudentially. Incidentally, we are not convinced that the porn biz is an institution of oppression, like slavery, guilty and in need of condemnation. We will leave those arguments to others writing in this anthology, though.

Afterglow

If our arguments are correct, we have shown that popular opinion about the wellbeing of porn stars is misguided. It is not true that all porn performers are character deficient or flawed, and even if some are it may make no difference to whether they find their lives satisfying. Neither is it necessarily true that working in porn contributes to a lack of wellbeing; some porn stars may find great satisfaction in their work, even if the porn business treats them badly. What constitutes their wellbeing is something that only they, individually, can determine, and it is not for us to pity them or think "we know better" on the basis of misguided social stigmas.

NOTES

1 Note that we are not interested in developing a robust account of welfare. We will base the distinction between morality and quality of life on features we believe to be essential to any adequate theory of welfare; e.g., the fact that welfare judgments require a first-personal component, or the perspective of the person whose life it is.
2 For a defense of this kind of view, see Vincent Punzo, "Morality and Human Sexuality" in *Reflective Naturalism* (Upper Saddle River: Prentice-Hall, 1969).
3 We assume that minors are not cognitively developed or informed enough to rationally decide to engage in sex with those older than them.
4 Again, we are not interested in deciding the source of those standards, such as desire-satisfaction, personal pleasure, and so forth. Our goal is not to elaborate a fully defended account of welfare, but we are convinced that whatever it is, it is essentially subjective.
5 Ron Amundson, "Disability, Ideology, and Quality of Life: A Bias in Biomedical Ethics," in D. Wasserman et al. (eds.) *Quality of Life and the Human Difference: Genetic Testing, Healthcare and Disability* (New York: Cambridge University Press, 2005), pp. 110–13.

CHAPTER 2

STRANGE BEDFELLOWS

The Interpenetration of Philosophy and Pornography

Have You Anything *Philosophical?*

Patrons of pre-revolutionary French bookshops who requested "livres philosophiques" did not receive what their modern counterparts would expect. As the book dealer Hubert Cazin explained to the officers holding him in the Bastille, the term was "a conventional expression in the book trade to characterize everything that is forbidden."[1] Research by historian Robert Darnton in the extensive archives of the eighteenth-century Swiss publisher Société typographique de Neuchâtel has shown that this use of "philosophical books" was widespread. The term encompassed categories of book we now keep separate: the irreligious, the seditious, the libelous, but above all the pornographic.

What should we make of this curious practice? An initial suspicion would be that Cazin and his colleagues were just trying to put the authorities off the scent. Satisfying the French appetite for clandestine literature was a risky endeavor, but lucrative for the determined and ingenious. One stratagem was to "marry" the unbound sheets of such material with sheets from blameless works, interleaving them to escape detection by customs officers.[2] Perhaps the euphemism "philosophical books" worked the same way – hiding the explicit and salacious in a tedious-sounding category censors would be quick to overlook. However, reality is considerably stranger. Firstly, many of the ideas which the French censor found too controversial were in some respect philosophical, such as challenges to the authority of the monarchy or the Catholic Church. But that does not explain the classification of overt pornography as philosophical. Secondly, although some of the works fit happily into modern categories, whether as respectable Enlightenment classics or disreputable libertine smut, many others are hopelessly hybridized: improbable marriages of philosophy and pornography.

Closer inspection of some individual works and their authors may make the situation clearer. Denis Diderot (1713–84) was one of the giants of the French Enlightenment. Best known as the principal editor and contributor of the *Encyclopédie*, a 35-volume treasury of scientifically and politically progressive thought, and as the author of works disseminating innovative philosophical ideas, he was also responsible for *Les Bijoux indiscrets* (1748).[3] This novel concerns one "Sultan Mangogul" (a thinly veiled caricature of Louis XV), who acquires a magic ring with which he may command women's genitals to speak. The central conceit, that the women's lower lips speak truths their upper lips disavow, is not original to Diderot, and may be traced back to the thirteenth-century fable "Le Chevalier Qui Fist Parler les Cons."[4] Despite its apparent misogyny, this idea has been appropriated by feminist philosophers such as Luce Irigaray as a positive metaphor for the subtleties of female communication.[5] Diderot's excursions into the erotic were not restricted to his youth. At the opposite end of his career he published *Supplément au voyage de Bougainville* (1772). This fictional work expands the description of Tahiti by the explorer Louis-Antoine, Comte de Bougainville (1729–1811) into a utopian vision of free love, and a powerful statement of the Enlightenment myth of the "noble savage": that life in a state of nature would be free and blissful.

The philosophical writings of Jean-Baptiste de Boyer, Marquis d'Argens (1704–71) were almost as numerous as those of Diderot, but are now little read. His principal claim to literary immortality may be *Thérèse philosophe* (1748), a sexually explicit work he never publicly acknowledged. The title translates as "Thérèse, Philosopher" and may allude to an early Enlightenment manifesto, *Le Philosophe* (1743),[6] attributed to César Chesneau Dumarsais (1676–1756) and later reworked by both Diderot and Voltaire. Dumarsais presents an ideal of the (male) philosopher: committed to reason, which he follows wherever it leads, impatient with religious superstition and conventional morality, conscious of how subject he is to external causes, but determined to understand their influence upon him. Argens's novel concludes with a similar statement of Enlightenment values:

> [W]e do not think as we like. The soul has no will, and is only influenced by the senses; that is to say by matter. Reason enlightens us, but cannot determine our actions. Self-love (the pleasure we hope for or the pain we try to avoid) is the motivating force for all our decisions. . . . There is no religion for God is sufficient unto Himself.[7]

However, Thérèse acquires these insights from primarily sexual experience. Withdrawn from her convent by a mother concerned that celibacy is fatally weakening her constitution, she first seeks refuge with a celebrated divine, Father Dirrag, an anagrammatic allusion to Jean-Baptiste Girard (1680–1733), a Jesuit whose alleged seduction of a female pupil was a recent scandal. Dirrag is revealed to Thérèse as a hypocrite – she eavesdrops as he persuades a naive (or concupiscent) pupil, through materialist arguments masquerading as Christianity, to accept as spiritual exercises a series of increasingly sexual acts, culminating with an orgasm the pupil mistakes for a transport of religious ecstasy. Thérèse is rescued by a family friend, Mme C., who it transpires is cheerfully cohabiting with another priest, the Abbé T. Again, the still virginal but increasingly voyeuristic Thérèse observes them at close quarters, as they alternate between sexual and philosophical intercourse. Eventually, after an interlude conversing with a retired prostitute (a venerable theme, as we shall see), Thérèse finds contentment as the mistress of an intellectual count who bets his library against her virginity that she will be unable to spend two weeks reading the former without volunteering to surrender the latter. Thus, the textual and the sexual intermingle in the novel's form and content.

By far the best known, indeed infamous, of French Enlightenment pornographers is Donatien-Alphonse-François, Marquis de Sade (1740–1814). He is less well known as a philosopher. None of his publications are primarily philosophical in the twenty-first-century sense, although commentators have professed to extract significant philosophical content. This should not surprise – his works are similar in structure to *Thérèse philosophe*: explicit sex interrupted by philosophical argument, or vice versa, depending on your priorities. For example, in his dialogue *La Philosophie dans le boudoir* (1795) the initially virginal Eugénie receives (enthusiastically) a hands-on sexual education from three older debauchees, one of whom breaks off mid-orgy to read aloud a recently purchased

𝄞 ANDREW ABERDEIN

pamphlet, "Frenchmen! One more effort, if you truly wish to be republicans!" This argues for the abolition of capital punishment, on the novel grounds that the crimes for which it was traditionally exacted, calumny, theft, immorality, and murder, are not crimes at all, since entirely natural. This argument is typical of Sade – he categorically rejects the cheerful optimism about human nature we saw in Diderot's vision of Tahiti, while apparently endorsing the Enlightenment argument that laws of nature should trump the laws of man. Sade's view of life in a state of nature is at least as bleak as Thomas Hobbes's "nasty, brutish and short," and the nastiness is explored in remorseless detail and at prodigious length. Even *Philosophie*, the shortest and most light-hearted of his pornographic works, culminates with Eugénie raping and, by implication, murdering her own mother. The tricky question Sade's interpreters have never resolved is whether he should be read as a satirist, showing by the blackest of comedy how the Enlightenment project can lead to an abominable conclusion, or whether he sincerely embraces those abominations.

These three examples demonstrate not only that some "philosophical books" were written by actual philosophers, but also the intimacy of the synthesis of philosophy with pornography widespread in the literary undergrowth of the French Enlightenment.

A Deeper Exploration

One way of understanding the surprising connection between pornography and philosophy is to explore their shared history. The history of pornography, however, raises questions of definition which go beyond the scope of this chapter. Firstly, I shall make no attempt to distinguish pornography from erotica; secondly, I propose to understand them both as texts and images intended to produce sexual arousal. This is a conscious oversimplification, even for twenty-first-century pornography. It may be criticized as excluding some material, or including too much, or as resting on a fundamentally wrong-headed approach. Matters become far worse when we go back in time. It has been argued that the word "pornography" is a nineteenth-century neologism.[8] Of course, we could say with US Supreme Court Justice Potter Stewart that we know pornography when we see it.[9] Surely historical "pornography" had a similar effect on its consumers as the modern sort, whatever they called it? This appeal to common sense is plausible, but can lead us astray the further back we go. Victorian archeologists excavating Pompeii confidently designated any building with sexually explicit wall paintings as a brothel, eventually identifying 35 of them, 80 times as many per capita as Rome itself.[10] Modern classicists interpret the material differently, concluding that the Romans had, by modern standards, an astonishingly broad-minded approach to interior décor. Shorn of context, the Pompeiian wall paintings strike us as pornographic, but perhaps the Romans saw them differently. Projecting our own standards into the past can lead to profound misunderstanding.

Nevertheless, these worries can be answered directly for at least one work: *L'Ecole des filles* (1655), whose pretensions to philosophy are explicit in its subtitle, *La Philosophie des dames*. Its authorship has never been satisfactorily established, although its publishers, Jean L'Ange and Michel Millot, were respectively fined and hanged in effigy as putative authors.[11] The reader response to this book is unusually well documented. The English diarist Samuel Pepys (1633–1703) records encountering it at a bookshop on 13 January 1668. His initial expectations of a suitable present for his wife are overturned by a quick browse, but on 8 February he returns to buy a copy for himself. The following night he reads it:

> I did read through *L'Escholle des Filles*; a lewd book, but what doth me no wrong to read for information sake (but it did hazer [cause] my prick para [to] stand all the while, and una vez to decharger [to discharge once]); and after I had done it, I burned it, that it might not be among my books to my shame; and so at night to supper and then to bed.[12]

The ejaculatory effect, ineffectually concealed by Pepys's macaronic jargon, and indeed the subsequent incineration, are recognizable in more modern porn consumers. The book which so moved Pepys is a dialogue between two women, in which the experienced Susanne instructs the prospective bride Fanchon in sexual technique. Its claims to philosophical interest may seem slim, but it has been read as both satirizing and utilizing the new scientific method of René Descartes – after a "discourse on method," a "process of discovery . . . unfolds: isolation in a heated room, elimination of customary prejudices and external authorities, introspection and lucidly ordered exposition of the fundamentals derived from it."[13]

The device of a young woman receiving sexual education from a more experienced woman is widespread; we saw it in *Thérèse philosophe* and *La Philosophie dans le boudoir*. The older woman is often, although not invariably, a current or former prostitute, hence such works are sometimes described as whore or courtesan dialogues. Numerous other contemporary examples could be cited; the common inspiration seems to be the *Ragionamenti*, or *Dialogues*, of Pietro Aretino (1492–1556) which first appeared in 1536, with a sequel in 1556. Aretino, a Renaissance humanist, made an even more influential contribution to erotic literature, the *Sonetti sopra I 'XVI Modi'* (1524), or "sonnets on the sixteen ways of doing it." These verses were inspired by a series of prints anatomically detailed enough to land their engraver in a papal prison. Aretino successfully lobbied the pope for his release – and then composed the accompanying sonnets.[14] The first of the *Ragionamenti* is a debate between two women, Nanna and Antonia, as to which of the three careers available to women – wife, nun, or whore – Nanna should choose for her daughter Pippa. They decide on the last, since "the nun betrays her holy vows and the married woman murders the holy bond of matrimony, but the whore violates neither her monastery nor her husband."[15] In the sequel Pippa receives an education in her future career.

The *Ragionamenti* are in part a satire on the more earnest dialogues of Aretino's contemporary Renaissance humanists. They in turn were inspired by the resurgence of interest in Plato, whose principal works were translated into Latin in the fifteenth century, having being unknown in Western Europe for centuries.[16] Of particular influence was Plato's *Symposium*, a dialogue debating the nature of love. The preferred theory involves an ascent from mere physical lust to more rarefied forms of love, culminating in an abstract intellectual ideal. The Renaissance reading of this passage is the source for the concept of "platonic love" – although our use of that idea overlooks its roots in physical intimacy. An even closer connection between sex and philosophy may be found elsewhere in Plato's work. In his *Republic* Plato has Socrates characterize philosophy as at "the mercy of others who aren't good enough for her, and who defile her and gain her the kind of tarnished reputation you say her detractors ascribe to her – for going about with people who are either worthless or obnoxious."[17] This sexual metaphor for philosophy may mark the inception of its relationship with pornography.

Plato is the best-known author of Socratic dialogues, in which philosophical ideas are developed in conversation between Socrates and supportive or hostile interlocutors. Socratic dialogues were written both by former pupils such as Plato and Xenophon, and by later writers with no direct acquaintance with Socrates. Since Socrates left behind no writings of his own, such works are our only access to his thought, but it is clear that the Socratic dialogue developed a life of its own as a leading genre of ancient philosophy. Correspondingly, the courtesan dialogue was a leading genre of ancient pornography. The best-known surviving example is that of Lucian, the second-century AD humorist, whose work is likely to have influenced Aretino.[18]

Crossovers – dialogues between philosophers and courtesans – are surprisingly common.[19] This juxtaposition seems to have served a variety of purposes for ancient authors. It could be satirical: Epicurus and his school were often linked to courtesans in this way, since he admitted women and taught that pleasure was the highest good. (The innuendo was misleading, since the Epicurean ideal was closer to the avoidance of pain than unbridled hedonism.) But one of the most frequent purposes of these comparisons is to reflect on persuasion, something both professions have in common, whether by deduction or seduction. This could serve to unite or separate philosophers and courtesans, as demonstrated by two younger contemporaries of Lucian. Alciphron finds a lowest common denominator: "the means by which they persuade are different; but one end – gain – is the goal for both"; whereas Aelian has Socrates distinguish himself from a courtesan in terms of his comparative lack of success: "you lead all of your followers on the downward path while I force them to move toward virtue. The ascent is steep and unfamiliar for most people."[20] I shall return to these two modes of persuasion in the final section.

The Lay of Aristotle

Although Plato's works were scarcely known in the Middle Ages, Aristotle was so strongly associated with philosophy that he could be referred to just as "The Philosopher." Yet many medieval and early modern depictions of Aristotle show him naked, on all fours, and being whipped by a woman riding on his back, as in figure 2.1.[21] An analysis of this unexpected predilection for female domination may clarify the relationship between physicality and philosophy. The narrative behind these images describes Aristotle's humbling by the mistress of his pupil, Alexander the Great. The earliest known version is Henri d'Andeli's thirteenth-century *Lay of Aristotle*, which was frequently retold. Whether or not Andeli invented the story, no modern commentator supposes it to have any connection to the historical Aristotle.[22] In the story Alexander, campaigning

ᴧ ANDREW ABERDEIN

FIGURE 2.1   *Aristotle and Phyllis* by Hans Baldung, 1513.

in India, is distracted from his duties by an affair with a local girl. (Andeli does not name the girl. Later sources generally call her Phyllis, or occasionally Campaspe, seemingly by confusion with a different legendary mistress of Alexander.) Aristotle advises him to break it off, counseling that "Your heart has so far strayed as to forget / the rule of moderation: hero's goal."[23] Phyllis finds out, and devises a plan to get her revenge. As she tells Alexander:

> Against me then, as you shall see tomorrow,
> your master's subtle skill in dialectic,
> his intellect, his vaunted golden mean
> will not prevail. Rise early and you'll see
> how Nature takes the measure of your master.[24]

The "golden mean" is the same "rule of moderation" which Aristotle pressed on Alexander. In Aristotle's ethics virtue is a middle way which practical reason should navigate between opposed extremities of vice. Phyllis identifies herself with a Nature powerful enough to sweep aside such subtle ethical calculus. The following morning she disports herself outside Aristotle's study so seductively that he attempts to ravish her. She affects to consent, but on one condition:

> I find a great desire has overcome me
> to make of you my steed and ride you now
> across the greensward underneath the trees.
> And you must be (no villain rider I!)
> saddled to carry me in elegance.[25]

The plan is enacted, to the amusement of Alexander in his concealed viewpoint. After absorbing the absurd spectacle, he reveals the trick to Aristotle. But it is the philosopher who has the last word:

> In one short hour, Love omnipotent
> has toppled all my wisdom's wide empire.
> Now learn from this: if I, both old and wise,
> have yet been driven to commit a deed
> mad even to dream of, shocking to perform,
> you, lusty youth, will surely not go free.[26]

The story, and especially its comic denouement, was a frequent subject for medieval and Renaissance art. Figure 2.1, the second of two versions by Hans Baldung, a pupil of Albrecht Dürer, is characteristic. There is no saddle, but like most artists, Baldung has added a bridle and riding crop to this scene of pioneering pony-play.

This story can be read two ways. For Andeli and his contemporaries, Aristotle is right: Nature must be subordinated to reason (and by extension, woman to man). The narrative illustrates the perilous consequences of ignoring this injunction. But, on the view defended by Diderot or Argens, Phyllis is right: Nature cannot be subordinated to reason. If even Aristotle cannot abide by his own injunctions, what chance would Alexander or the rest of us have? The difference between these two perspectives may determine how the hybridization of pornography with philosophy is received. On Aristotle's account, it is a bizarre anomaly; on Phyllis's, an intelligible continuity. Conversely, philosophical arguments for the censorship of pornography would be incongruous to Phyllis, but welcomed by Aristotle.

ANDREW ABERDEIN

Tying Up Loose Ends

We have seen that Phyllis's perspective has had a hand in many different theses. The most philosophically central of these is the analysis of persuasion. I will conclude with a novel application of this analysis, which may help defend Phyllis's diversity against "Aristotelian" censorship. But first I should address the outstanding problem of classification. The categories which we apply to the world, and especially the categories which we apply to human activity, may appear to be natural and unalterable, but they have histories, and may be transformed in a few generations. We have already seen that "pornography" is one such category. "Philosophy" is another. The term is not a new one – it can be traced back two and a half millennia. But its use has altered throughout that period. For example, much of what we now call science was called philosophy by its discoverers. The use of "philosophy" in the eighteenth-century French book trade was extraordinary, but it was part of a complex history of changing meaning.

The nineteenth century saw increasing academic specialization and professionalization. Philosophy and science drew apart, but the universities came to monopolize them both. New venues for publication opened up, and the general market became less important. Moreover, university professors became concerned with respectability in ways that had not troubled the amateurs of past generations. In the later nineteenth century the study of sexuality came within the scope of academic science. Although some of this work repeated that of the previous century, it did so on very different terms, professing to substitute the dispassionate objectivity of a narrow elite for particularity and mass audience appeal. Concepts of free speech also evolved in the nineteenth century. New liberal democracies expected a freedom of political speech, both on the hustings and in print, alien to absolutist monarchies such as pre-revolutionary France. But such freedom did not extend to all varieties of banned speech. Hence pornography emerged as a separate category of material that could be safely banned by societies otherwise congratulating themselves on their freedoms. These processes may explain the rarity of philosophical pornography in the last two centuries.

Yet there have been occasional revivals. New York philosophy professor John Lange is much better known as John Norman, author of the Gor series, a sequence of more than two dozen fantasy novels increasingly concerned with depicting and justifying the sexual subordination of women to men. As he states in a typical passage, "In the Gorean view, female slavery is a societal institution which enables the female, as most Earth societies would not, to exhibit, in a reinforcing environment, her biological nature. It provides a rich soil in which the flower of her beauty and nature, and its submission to a man, may thrive."[27] The Gor books were bestsellers in the 1970s, but dwindled in popularity in the 1980s, and struggled to find a publisher in the 1990s – something Lange attributes to feminist conspiracy.[28] However, in recent years his work has found a new audience, and inspired a vast, mostly Internet-based sexual subculture.[29] (Not a boast many philosophers can make!) Curiously, significant proportions of both audiences appear to be female.[30] In his one philosophical monograph, Lange stated "it cannot be denied that there is a certain schizophrenic charm in embracing an immoral theory at a suitably abstract level while in practice devoting oneself earnestly to worthy endeavors, redoubling as though in compensation one's efforts to bring about a more just state of affairs in the world."[31] It is tempting to read this autobiographically, as suggesting that the attitude to gender relations in his novels is satirical. But other statements would suggest that he is sincere – indeed, it would be consistent for him to view his novels as the "worthy endeavors" and gender equality as the "immoral theory."

In recent decades, philosophical engagement with pornography has mostly comprised arguments for its censorship. Paradoxically, Lange's novels may undercut one of the most sophisticated of these, that pornography tacitly subordinates women.[32] Lange intermingles his pornography with explicit philosophical advocacy of such subordination. This poses a dilemma. Prospective censors must choose between banning the whole thing or just the pornography. If they endorse the former, they concede that their project is not just aimed at disposable entertainment, but strikes directly at freedom of thought (if freedom includes the freedom to be wrong). But what grounds could they have for sparing the philosophy? It endorses conclusions just as obnoxious as the pornography. The only practical basis for tolerating philosophical arguments for conclusions forbidden to pornography would seem to be that the philosophy is less harmful, that is, less persuasive than the pornography. Lange's philosophy may well be less persuasive than his pornography, but if his arguments are so weak, then the feminist counterarguments must be exceptionally strong. Hence censorship would be unnecessary, unless even these exceptionally strong arguments are weaker than pornography, that is, unless philosophy is *in general* less persuasive than pornography. But if this depressing observation is true, how could anyone be persuaded by the philosophical arguments for censorship, since they are to be weighed against pornography which, even the censors must admit, indeed insist, is more persuasive? Of course, this does not mean that what they say is not true, only that if it is then it will not be persuasive. Which suggests that if their argument is persuasive, then their conclusion must be false.

NOTES

1 Robert Darnton, *The Forbidden Best-Sellers of Pre-Revolutionary France* (London: Fontana, 1996), p. 7.
2 Ibid., p. 17.
3 Translations of both of the Diderot novels discussed may be found in Michel Feher (ed.) *The Libertine Reader: Eroticism and Enlightenment in Eighteenth-Century France* (New York: Zone Books, 1997).
4 Robert Hellmann and Richard O'Gorman (eds.) *Fabliaux: Ribald Tales from the Old French* (New York: Thomas Y. Crowell, 1965), pp. 105 ff.
5 Mary D. Sheriff, "Labia," in Colin Blakemore and Sheila Jennett (eds.) *The Oxford Companion to the Body* (Oxford: Oxford University Press, 2001).
6 Published in 1743, but circulated earlier in manuscript.
7 Jean-Baptiste de Boyer, Marquis d'Argens, *Thérèse philosophe*, trans. Robert Darnton. In Darnton, *Forbidden Best-Sellers*, p. 299.
8 Notably by Walter Kendrick, *The Secret Museum: Pornography in Modern Culture* (Berkeley: University of California Press, 1987).
9 Quoted in Isabel Tang, *Pornography: The Secret History of Civilization* (London: Macmillan, 1999), p. 23.
10 Ibid., p. 35.
11 Joan DeJean, "The Politics of Pornography: L'Ecole des Filles," in Lynn Hunt (ed.) *The Invention of Pornography: Obscenity and the Origins of Modernity, 1500–1800* (New York: Zone Books, 1996), p. 112.
12 Quoted in James Grantham Turner, *Schooling Sex: Libertine Literature and Erotic Education in Italy, France, and England 1534–1685* (Oxford: Oxford University Press, 2003), p. 2.
13 Ibid., p. 128.
14 Paula Findlen, "Humanism, Politics and Pornography in Renaissance Italy," in Hunt, *Invention of Pornography*, pp. 95 f.
15 Pietro Aretino, *Dialogues*, trans. Raymond Rosenthal (New York: Marsilio, 1994), p. 158.
16 C. M. Woodhouse, "How Plato Won the West," in M. Holroyd (ed.) *Essays by Divers Hands*, vol. 42 (London: Royal Society of Literature, 1982), p. 122.
17 Plato, *Republic*, trans. Robin Waterfield (Oxford: Oxford University Press, 1993), 495c.
18 Findlen, "Humanism, Politics and Pornography in Renaissance Italy," p. 78.

19 Laura McClure, *Courtesans at Table: Gender and Greek Literary Culture in Athenaeus* (London: Routledge, 2003), p. 102.

20 Both quoted in McClure, *Courtesans at Table*, p. 102.

21 For a valuable survey of these images, see Ayers Bagley, *Study and Love: Aristotle's Fall* (Minneapolis: Society of Professors of Education, 1986).

22 Simon Blackburn, *Lust* (New York: Oxford University Press, 2004), p. 10.

23 Henri d'Andeli, "The Lay of Aristotle," trans. Stephen G. Nichols, Jr. In Angel Flores (ed.) *Masterpieces of World Literature: The Medieval Age* (New York: Dell, 1963), p. 334.

24 Ibid., p. 336.

25 Ibid., p. 339.

26 Ibid., p. 340.

27 John Norman, *Hunters of Gor* (1974), quoted in Peter Fitting, "Violence and Utopia: John Norman and Pat Califia," *Utopian Studies* 11, 1 (2000): 93.

28 Fitting, "Violence and Utopia," p. 102.

29 Shaowen Bardzell and William Odom, "Experience of Embodied Space in Virtual Worlds: An Ethnography of a Second Life Community," *Space and Culture* 11, 3 (2008): 239–59.

30 Fitting, "Violence and Utopia," p. 94.

31 John Lange, *The Cognitivity Paradox: An Inquiry Concerning the Claims of Philosophy* (Princeton: Princeton University Press, 1970), p. 55.

32 Versions of this argument have been advanced by many authors. One of the best is Rae Langton, *Sexual Solipsism: Philosophical Essays on Pornography and Objectification* (Oxford: Oxford University Press, 2009), pp. 38 ff.

PART II

THE PORNOGRAPHIC MIND
Psychology and Porn

CHAPTER 3

YES. YES! YES!!

What Do Mona's Moans Reveal About Her Sexual Pleasure?

Most research on the topic of pornography has been concerned with some variation of the question (and feel free to sing along), "Porn! . . . Huh! (good God) What is it good for?" and, overwhelmingly, the answer has been "Absolutely nothing! Say it again! Y'all." Research has shown that viewing pornography causes some men to view professional women as sex objects, remembering more of what they look like and less of what they say.[1] Porn viewers are more likely to form erroneous beliefs, such as that women enjoy being raped.[2] Watching violent porn, in particular, can desensitize viewers toward rape victims, leading them to recommend lesser sentences for rapists.[3] Men exposed to pornographic material, such as *Playboy* centerfolds, compared to those in a control group, e.g., who looked at abstract art, report being less attracted to and less in love with their wives.[4] Importantly, high pornography consumption predicts sexual aggression, particularly among men predisposed toward sexual aggression.[5]

Despite the documentation of many pernicious outcomes associated with watching pornography, we believe that one particularly insidious consequence of porn viewing has been overlooked. Specifically, we are proposing that watching porn may make some men bad lovers! Of central relevance to this thesis is that porn movies serve as a salient and accessible basis for social comparison and social learning. People may compare themselves to porn stars and adopt a host of misperceptions.[6] Male porn viewers may conclude that their penis is inadequately small or wonder why their ejaculate does not soar across the room with the propulsion of a Boeing 747. Female porn viewers may see female porn stars appear to have earth-shaking orgasms from intercourse without clitoral stimulation and think there is something wrong with them because they do not respond in this manner during sex with their partner. More centrally, men may learn from watching porn that standard sexual intercourse, without foreplay or emotional context, is enough to send women into the throes of sexual ecstasy. Alas, because, on average, the clitoris is about an inch away from the urethra – a close proxy for the vagina – penile thrusting alone is usually insufficient to bring most women to orgasm.[7]

We coined the term "porngasm" to refer to orgasms depicted within the context of a pornography movie, and our research examined several questions related to perceptions of female porngasm. Our research questions included the following: Do people believe that most female porngasms are real or fake? Do men and women differ in their perceptions of female porngasm? Does frequency of porn viewing predict one's beliefs about female porngasm? We hypothesized that males would be more likely than females to believe in the genuineness of female porngasm. Before describing our research methodology and results it is important that we articulate some of our assumptions.

Female Porngasm is More Interesting to Study than Male Porngasm

Although men occasionally fake orgasm, it is usually easier for men to climax than it is for women. Men take less time to reach orgasm (sometimes less than 30 seconds!) and for most men emotional connection with a partner is not a prerequisite for orgasm. Men are more consistent in their propensity to orgasm across time and partner. Moreover, no one is debating the function of male orgasm. Natural selection has favored men who climax rapidly, readily, and regularly. Additionally, there is usually an obvious cue that men have achieved orgasm. Although there are physiological cues to female orgasm,[7] e.g., vaginal contractions, changes in heart rate and respiration, skin coloration changes, they are not as conspicuous as a man's ejaculation.

𝄢   ANNE K. GORDON AND SHANE W. KRAUS

Most Porn is Designed to Activate and Appeal to Men's Short-Term Sexual Strategies

We rely on theory and evidence from evolutionary psychology to explain why men are usually more interested in watching porn than women.[8] From this perspective, watching porn is enjoyable to men because it activates evolved mechanisms in the brain that are associated with the pursuit of short-term sexual strategies. Over evolutionary history men and women have had to solve a host of problems related to securing short- and long-term mates.[9] For both types of mating, but particularly for short-term mating, men have had to identify and attract women who were fertile. This has meant identifying and attracting women who are young and healthy – two classes of cues that are linked to fertility. A woman's age, health, and fertility can be inferred from visual cues such as waist-to-hip ratio (WHR; a .7 WHR is what most men consider smokin' hot), full lips, smooth skin, long shiny hair, healthy teeth, bilateral symmetry, and high energy level. For these reasons, men's mating psychology is more sensitive to visual stimuli than women's. It is no coincidence that porn is highly visual, and most consumers of porn are male.

Conversely, women's reproductive success has depended less on identifying men who were fertile (because men's fertility is not steeply age graded) and more on attracting men who were able and willing to invest in them and their offspring. Thus, women have had to assess a man's emotional investment, commitment, intelligence, kindness, generosity, dependability, and social status, which are not as closely tied to obvious physical cues. This is not to suggest that women are unconcerned with men's attractiveness. Women generally prefer men who are tall, strong, and athletic, because these traits are associated with health, social dominance, and the ability to protect. Moreover, women consider men's physical attractiveness to be particularly important when pursuing short-term mates.

Importantly, because sperm are cheap, and eggs, internal gestation, and lactation are expensive, men have benefited more than women, on average, from having more sex partners, to whom they are necessarily less emotionally committed. Conversely, women, have benefited more than men, on average, from being selective about whom to mate with and from delaying sex until the aforementioned qualities, e.g., emotional commitment, could be developed and assessed. Thus, differences between men and women in their attitudes toward short-term mating ultimately result from these basic physiological differences. Do not be fooled. Men and women are not equal when it comes to attitudes toward, desires for, fantasizing about, and readiness to engage in casual sex with strangers and acquaintances. In one study, 75 percent of men who were approached on a college campus by a female stranger agreed to have sex with her that night! Not one woman approached under similar conditions by an unfamiliar man agreed to his sexual offer.[10] Porn, of course, is famous for portraying sex between strangers and casual acquaintances.

Most Female Porngasms are Fake

Although the mystery remains unresolved, researchers have accumulated data regarding what predicts female orgasm (guys, get your note pads!). We report a partial list of factors known to be associated with female orgasm: having a mate who is relatively symmetrical,[11] physically attractive,[12] and earns a high income;[13] clitoral stimulation, particularly via cunnilingus;[14] and feeling happy in your marriage, or otherwise being in a stable, long-term, and committed relationship.[15] Conversely, many things interfere with female orgasm. The primary culprits include using drugs (nicotine and anti-depressant medication), being overweight, having cardiovascular disease or poor body image, feeling guilty, thinking sex is dirty or sinful, having low testosterone, being distracted, self-conscious, or anxious, and not focusing on the pleasurable, physical sensations associated with sex. You may notice that all of these predictors of "female sexual dysfunction" are located, perhaps unfairly, within the woman. None refer to the qualities, characteristics, or sexual techniques of the men with whom these women are having sex. Moreover, discussions of female orgasm often erroneously assume that women *should* orgasm as rapidly, readily, and regularly as men.

So, what is the function of female orgasm? Why do women orgasm at all? Several evolutionary explanations have been advanced in response to these questions. Hypotheses include female orgasm as a functionless byproduct of male orgasm, the hedonic hypothesis, the paternity confidence hypothesis, the paternity confusion hypothesis, and the

⨍ ANNE K. GORDON AND SHANE W. KRAUS

sperm-retention hypothesis. We focus on the Mr. Right hypothesis, because it is most relevant to our arguments and is relatively well supported empirically.

A key premise of the Mr. Right hypothesis is that the occurrence of female orgasm is uncertain and unpredictable. Some women never or rarely experience orgasm; others experience orgasm easily and regularly. Importantly, there is substantial variability within women in their likelihood of experiencing orgasm, as a function of sex partner and relationship context. Women may orgasm powerfully with one man and have great difficulty experiencing orgasm with another man. Moreover, the same woman may vary in her sexual response to the same lover, as a function of her current relationship satisfaction. According to the Mr. Right hypothesis, female orgasm functions as a signal that helps women select and retain the best (most caring, sensitive, devoted) mate and dad and/or select the highest-genetic-quality father for her children. From this perspective, a man's ability to bring a woman to orgasm reflects his standing on various dimensions relevant to his being a desirable long-term mate and/or his being a good genetic catch, in terms of health, strength, and masculinity.

Now consider the conditions likely present during the filming of a porn movie, as experienced from the perspective of a female porn star. The director shouts, "Lights! Camera! Action!" There are numerous, possibly dozens of, people in the room. Someone drops a cup of coffee. The director yells, "Cut! Start over with 'Give it to me baby'." There is no privacy. There is a camera in your face and one between your legs. You have to remember your lines. You have to maintain the correct and likely very uncomfortable position so the camera angles are just right. A light bulb goes dead. Again, the director yells, "Cut! Take it from 'Oh Gary, I've always *dreamed* of having sex with you and your buddy Steve'." There is no moonlight piercing through the window; there is no whispering of sweet nothings. There is no soft music or scent of jasmine wafting through the air. Except for when Gary is a pizza-delivery guy arriving with dinner in tow, there is no gift or offering to signal his ability and willingness to invest. Importantly, there is little to no foreplay or emotional context. In sum, Gary is not depicted as the kind of guy who would be Mona's, or many women's, Mr. Right.

Unfortunately, we did not have a group of female porn stars to ask directly about their porngasms or lack thereof (good luck getting that grant funded!). Instead, we rely on the aforementioned arguments and evidence to infer that most female porngasms are fake. Although it is difficult to estimate, we suspect that 5–20 percent of female porngasms are genuine. (Anne's money is on 5 percent; Shane's is on 20 percent.)

Our Study

We designed and administered an online survey to 111 male and 153 female college undergraduates. Volunteers were recruited from introductory psychology classes at a large midwestern university and received course credit for their participaion. Our sample was predominantly Caucasian (86 percent), heterosexual (94 percent), and unmarried (96 percent). Most students (99 percent) were between 18 and 24 years old. A sample of college-aged participants was desirable because this cohort is generally interested in mating pursuits, and they came of age when access to Internet porn was widespread and its use had become mainstream.

Participants were told that they would be asked to answer questions regarding their attitudes and beliefs about pornography and their responses would be anonymous. For the purposes of the study, pornography was defined as sexually explicit material presented in the form of a movie or film designed to create or enhance sexual feelings or thoughts in its viewers. This definition excluded soft-core pornography, in which the sexual activity is simulated. Orgasm was defined as genuine sexual climax.

Participants provided their informed consent and answered a 31-item survey about their attitudes toward pornography, perceptions of female porngasm, and female porn star sexual pleasure. A sample item is included to represent each category of question: "I think that the pornography industry promotes violence toward women; I believe that most orgasms depicted by women in pornographic movies are fake; and, I think that women who star in pornographic movies enjoy their jobs." Response options were as follows: 1 = strongly disagree, 2 = disagree, 3 = neutral, 4 = agree, and 5 = strongly agree.

We also asked participants to estimate the percentage of orgasms depicted by women in pornographic movies that represent genuine orgasm and how much time they had spent viewing pornography, on average, per week, during the past six months. Response options were as follows: had never watched porn, 1–29 minutes, 30–59 mins., 60–89 mins., 90–119 mins., 120–149 mins., 150–179 mins., 180 + mins.

TABLE 3.1   Sex differences in time spent viewing porn

Viewing frequency category	Females	Males
Have never watched	30.7%	1.8%
1–29 minutes	62.7%	55.0%
30–59 minutes	3.9%	25.2%
60–180 + minutes	2.7%	18.0%

Note: The categories 60–89 mins., 90–119 mins., 120–149 mins., 150–179 mins., and 180 + mins. have been combined.

TABLE 3.2   Sex differences in attitudes and beliefs about pornography

Item	Females	Males
I enjoy watching porn.	2.24	3.64*
Porn is demeaning toward women.	3.36	2.97*
Porn is demeaning toward men.	2.51	2.30*
Porn promotes violence toward women.	2.63	2.35*
Porn promotes violence toward men.	2.05	1.79*
It is upsetting that so many people watch porn.	2.69	2.11*
My partner watching porn is a form of betrayal.	2.40	2.03*
Society's views toward porn are too negative.	2.86	3.15*
Many people watch porn to learn sexual techniques.	3.68	3.70

Note: The wording used to describe survey items within the tables is not the wording used in the actual survey. For convenience, we have shortened the survey items and relied occasionally on slang terms. Asterisks in tables 3.2 and 3.3 refer to statistically significant differences between the means for male and female participants, as determined by independent-samples t-tests.

Results

Unsurprisingly, the results indicated marked sex differences in porn view-ing habits (see table 3.1). More females than males had never watched porn or checked the lowest porn-viewing-frequency category. More males than females indicated watching between a half and a full hour of porn during a typical week; and more males than females reported watching over an hour of porn per week. (Three participants indicated watching three or more hours of porn in a typical week. We did not meet these participants, but if we did we would not be enthusiastic about shaking hands.)

Men reported enjoying watching porn more than women (see table 3.2). This sex difference has been documented many times and should surprise

TABLE 3.3 Sex differences in perceptions of female porngasm and sexual
pleasure

Item	Females	Males
Most female porngasms are real.	1.97	2.10
Most female porngasms are fake.	3.85	3.77
At least some female porngasms are real.	3.23	3.55*
Female porn stars enjoy the sex.	2.85	3.15*
Female porn stars enjoy a high degree of pleasure.	3.03	3.57*
Female porn stars enjoy their job.	3.23	3.54*

no one.[16] As noted, porn is more appealing to men than women because it caters to aspects of sexuality that are more characteristic of males' rather than females' evolved sexual psychology. Additionally, women may find porn distasteful because, as our results show, women believe, more so than men, that porn is demeaning toward women (and, to a lesser degree, toward men) and promotes violence toward women (and, to a lesser degree, toward men). Women are also more upset than men that so many people watch porn, perhaps because they are more likely to consider their romantic partner's watching of porn to be a form of betrayal. (To the extent that watching porn makes men believe that there are lots of women interested in having sex *with them*, and, thereby, lowers their commitment to their partner, women's concerns of betrayal may not be baseless.) Men, on the other hand, have more relaxed attitudes about porn. They are more likely than women to think that society's views toward porn are too negative. Importantly, both male and female participants believe that many people watch porn to learn new sexual techniques.

Results depicted in table 3.3 are central to our primary hypothesis. Male and female participants alike disagree with the notion that most female porngasms are real and agree with the notion that most female porngasms are fake. This is good news. Minimally, we know that participants were not snoozing while they completed our survey. Moreover, imagine the gravity of the situation had there been widespread belief that most female porngasms are real!

Although we expected males to provide a significantly higher estimate than females, males estimated that, on average, 38 percent of female porngasms are real, and females estimated that, on average, 40 percent of female porngasms are real. However, as expected, men were more likely than women to believe that at least some female porngasms are real. Moreover, males were more likely than females to believe that female

ANNE K. GORDON AND SHANE W. KRAUS

TABLE 3.4 Relationships between time spent watching porn and perceptions of female porngasm and sexual pleasure

Item	r	p
At least some female porngasms are real.	.19	.003*
Female porn stars enjoy the sex.	.26	.000*
Female porn stars enjoy a high degree of pleasure.	.20	.001*
Female porn stars enjoy their job.	.21	.001*

Note: r refers to the Pearson correlation coefficient. Minutes were coded as follows: 0 = had never watched porn, 1 = 1–29 mins., 2 = 30–59 mins., 3 = 60–89 mins., 4 = 90–119 mins., 5 = 120–149 mins., 6 = 150–179 mins., 7 = 180 + mins. Asterisks refer to statistically significant correlations.

porn stars enjoy having intercourse and other sexual interactions within the context of a porn movie. Highlighting this point further, males were more likely than females to believe that female porn stars enjoy a *high degree* of sexual pleasure via their participation in making porn movies. Males were also more likely than women to believe that female porn stars enjoy their jobs!

Importantly, the *more time* people spend watching porn the *more likely* they were to believe that at least some female porngasms are real, female porn stars enjoy the sex they have within the making of porn movies, female porn stars enjoy a high degree of sexual pleasure from making porn movies, and female porn stars enjoy their job (see table 3.4). Thus, here, as is the case regarding porn watching and other attitudinal and behavioral consequences, *dosage matters*.

But Female Porn Stars Do Love the Sex!

At this point, you (especially if you are a man) may be thinking, "Yes! I, too, believe that female porn stars love having sex during porn movies!" Anecdotally, several of the men we talked with informally about our results stammered, "But . . . but . . . I have heard female porn stars interviewed by Howard Stern, and they *always* say they love the sex!" Even the editor of this volume, Dave Monroe, proffered that *virtually all* of the porn stars he has spoken with have expressed the sentiment that they got into porn precisely because they *love the sex*. There are, however, several reasons to being wary of these porn star claims.

First, in most cases, for self-report data to be considered valid they must be collected under conditions of anonymity and/or confidentiality. Otherwise, these data may be influenced by self-presentation concerns. What people say when their identity is known often reflects the *impression* they want to make rather than what they truly believe. Second, porn stars are paid representatives of a highly lucrative industry. One should believe porn star claims regarding how much they *love* their jobs and the sex they have therein to the same extent as one should believe car salespeople who work for _____ (insert a car company here) claim they *love* the car they drive, which happens to be made by _____ (insert the same car company here). People often say what their jobs require of them.

Finally, even if the porn stars interviewed by Howard Stern or Dave Monroe *really do* love the sex they have during the making of porn movies, we still have the potential problem of biased sampling. It is possible that these women's experiences are honest *but not representative* of the general population of female porn stars. It may be that porn stars who agree to give interviews are precisely those who really do enjoy their jobs. There are numerous reasons for which a young woman may become a porn star, only one of which is the love of sex. For these reasons, female porn star claims of on-the-job sexual bliss should be interpreted with caution.

So, why keep reading?

Most participants reported believing that *most* female porngasms are fake. This could be the end of the story, because it is our position, as well, that *most* female porngasms are fake. Fortunately, we assessed perceptions of female porngasm in a number of ways. Four of our survey items explicitly mentioned the concept of orgasm, and on only one of these four items did we obtain the expected sex difference. In three survey items we asked more generally about perceptions of female porn star sexual enjoyment, sexual pleasure, and job satisfaction. Interestingly, we obtained the predicted sex difference on all of these more subtly worded items. We suspect that respondents did not want to appear gullible. When asked about perceptions of female porngasm they likely answered so as to convey the sentiment, "Of course I don't believe that most female porngasms are real. Only a fool would believe that!" These defenses were likely not activated by questions about general perceptions of porn star sexual enjoyment. Thus, we believe that we have sufficient basis for concluding that people, but particularly men, over-infer the degree of sexual pleasure and the frequency of orgasm that female porn stars experience.

ANNE K. GORDON AND SHANE W. KRAUS

Correspondence Bias

When viewing porn and assessing female porngasm, people appear to engage in what social psychologists call the correspondence bias. According to Dan Gilbert and Patrick Malone, "correspondence bias is the tendency to draw inferences about a person's unique and enduring dispositions from behaviors that can be entirely explained by the situations in which they occur."[17] Put differently, correspondence bias refers to the belief that a person's behavior corresponds to a similar underlying state, trait, attitude, belief, emotion, or feeling, even when this belief is illogical, given the situational constraints on that person's behavior. Applying this concept to female porngasm, it seems as though people see female porn stars moan and groan *as if* they are having an orgasm and infer that genuine sexual arousal is the primary cause of those moans and groans. Viewers seem to temporarily forget that these women are actresses paid to play a role.

Error Management Theory

Correspondence bias, however, cannot fully explain our results, because correspondence bias characterizes human nature (though in Western more than Eastern cultures), not male or female nature, uniquely. Yet, our results indicate that, on several dimensions, men seem more willing than women to infer sexual ecstasy from depictions of female porngasm. It is well known that people often attend to, encode, remember, and accept or criticize information in order to confirm what they want to believe.[18] But *why* would men be more motivated than women to believe that where there are moans and groans there is a person experiencing sexual peak?

Research by evolutionary psychologists Martie Haselton and David Buss on cognitive biases in mind reading is relevant here.[19] Their research shows that men consistently over-perceive sexual intent from a women's friendliness. According to error management theory, men have always faced the daunting task of having to figure out if women were interested in them sexually. Given the difficulty of making such inferences, men are thought to have evolved a cognitive architecture that leads them to make systematic and predictable errors. Namely, men err on the side of inferring sexual interest in women because, even though uninterested women may respond to unwelcome come-ons with surprise, confusion, scoffing, or abject horror, these over-inferences may occasionally yield a sexual encounter. Conversely, erring on the side of under-inferring a lack of sexual interest where lustful intentions may be lurking is more costly, because it may lead to missed sexual opportunities with women.

Of course, inferring the degree to which the friendly woman at the office is sexually interested in you is different from inferring the degree to which porn star Mona is genuinely turned on by porn star Gary's touch. Remember, though, that porn is evolutionarily novel and likely activates ancient evolved mechanisms. Thus, in terms of the brain regions activated within the minds of men there may not be much, if any, difference between judging porn star sexual pleasure, the sexual interests of a co-worker, or the genuineness of your lover's orgasm.

Conclusions

We believe that watching porn may make some men bad lovers. The thrust (no pun intended) of our argument lies in the fact that most porn is suited toward male short-term mating pursuits. Porn is not designed to appeal to the sexual desires of women, which often involve clitoral stimulation and a broader emotional connection. Moreover, porn often focuses primarily on men's sexual pleasure, whereas women's sexual and emotional satisfaction are rarely considered. Nonetheless, our results suggest that men are more likely than women to believe that at least some female porngasms are real, female porn stars enjoy the sex, experience a high degree of sexual pleasure, and like their jobs. Additionally, both male and female participants, on average, agreed with the statement "Many people watch pornography to learn new sexual techniques." To the extent that males' perceptions of female porn star sexual enjoyment are biased or female porn stars are atypical in comparison to most women, these findings suggest that porn movies may misguide viewers about the nuances of female sexual satisfaction. Many adolescents watch pornography,[20] and adolescence is a time for learning sexual scripts, developing sexual techniques, and forming sexual attitudes. Young males who rely on porn to learn about sex may form grossly inaccurate beliefs about how to satisfy a woman.

Clearly, more research is needed to assess the validity of our claims that female porngasms are usually faked, that watching porn may lead men to form erroneous beliefs about the causes of female orgasm, and that watching porn may make some men bad lovers. First, an anonymous and confidential survey of a broad range of porn stars concerning their experiences of orgasm and sexual pleasure is necessary. Second, research could expose male and female participants to the *same* depictions of female porngasm and assess their perceptions of porngasm genuineness. Third, men could be randomly assigned to watch a porn or a non-porn movie prior to having their perceptions of what leads to female sexual satisfaction and orgasm assessed. Fourth, research could examine whether an inverse relationship exists between men's porn watching frequency and the sexual satisfaction of their female partners.

Several caveats, of course, are warranted. First, direction of causality is difficult to infer from correlational studies. Thus, even if watching porn is associated with men's holding inaccurate beliefs about the nature of female orgasm or being relatively poor lovers, it could be that men who hold inaccurate beliefs about female orgasm or are bad lovers are more likely to watch porn. Second, our assumption that most female porngasms are fake is based on a prototypical image of porn movies. There are many types of porn movies and many types of porn stars; consequently, the frequencies of genuine female porngasm may vary widely. A content analysis of porn movies to assess how often female porn stars are depicted having orgasm from intercourse alone and as having multiple orgasms would be helpful in this regard. The more frequent these depictions the more confident we can be that most female porngasms are fake. However, to the extent that female porn stars are atypical vis-à-vis most women it remains problematic if men watch porn and think that what elicits porngasm (genuine or fake) will elicit orgasm in their partners.

Our conclusions may appear to be light-hearted. However, that watching porn may lead men to form erroneous beliefs about the causes of female orgasm, and consequently make them bad lovers, is a serious proposition. Most people consider a satisfying sex life to be an important component of a romantic relationship. Conversely, sexual problems can be a major source of stress within these relationships. Sex that does not fulfill both men's and women's desires can create conflict and undermine relationship satisfaction.

In closing, we think that a warning should appear on porn websites and porn DVDs that reads: "Watching porn may make you feel sexually inadequate, bored with your sex life, and, if you are a man, watching porn may make you a bad lover!" On the other hand, we believe that porn, like violent video games, may be unfairly scrutinized as a cause of society's ills. For example, although it is difficult to find studies concerning the benefits of porn, they certainly exist. Under some conditions porn may enhance people's sex lives or provide an inexpensive source of entertainment. Moreover, we see few studies in the psychological literature on the negative effects of women's reading romance novels!

NOTES

1 Doug McKenzie-Mohr and Mark Zanna, "Treating Women as Sexual Objects: Look at the (Gender Schematic) Male Who Has Viewed Pornography," *Personality and Social Psychology Bulletin* 16, 2 (1990): 296–308.
2 Neil Malamuth and John Check, "The Effects of Aggressive Pornography on Beliefs in Rape Myths: Individual Differences," *Journal of Research in Personality* 19 (1985): 199–320.
3 Dolf Zillmann and Jennings Bryant, "Pornography, Sexual Callousness, and the Trivialization of Rape," *Journal of Communication* 32, 4 (1982): 10–21.
4 Douglas Kenrick and Sara Gutierres, "Influence of Popular Erotica on Judgment of Strangers and Mates," *Journal of Experimental Social Psychology* 25 (1989): 159–67.
5 Vanessa Vega and Neil Malamuth, "Predicting Sexual Aggression: The Role of Pornography in the Context of General and Specific Risk Factors," *Aggressive Behaviors* 33 (2007): 104–17.
6 Mary Roach, *Bonk: The Curious Coupling of Science and Sex* (New York: W. W. Norton, 2008).
7 Cindy Meston, Roy Levin, Marca Sipski, Elaine Hull, and Julia Heiman, "Women's Orgasm," *Annual Review of Sex Research* 15 (2004): 173–257.
8 Neil Malamuth, "Sexually Explicit Media, Gender Differences, and Evolutionary Theory," *Journal of Communication* 46, 3 (1996): 8–31.
9 David Buss, *Evolutionary Psychology: The New Science of the Mind* (Boston: Pearson Education, 2008).
10 Russell Clark and Elaine Hatfield. "Gender Differences in Receptivity to Sexual Offers," *Journal of Psychology and Human Sexuality* 2, 1 (1989): 39–55.
11 Randy Thornhill, Steven Gangestad, and Randall Comer, "Human Female Orgasm and Mate Fluctuating Asymmetry," *Animal Behavior* 50 (1995): 1601–15.
12 Todd Shackelford, Vivian Weekes-Shackelford, Gregory LeBlanc, April Bleske, Harald Euler, and Sabine Hoier, "Female Coital Orgasm and Male Attractiveness," *Human Nature* 11 (2000): 299–306.
13 Thomas Pollet and Daniel Nettle, "Partner Wealth Predicts Self-Reported Orgasm Frequency in a Sample of Chinese Women," *Evolution and Human Behavior* 30, 2 (2009): 146–51.

14 Juliet Richters, Richard Visser, Chris Rissel, and Anthony Smith, "Sexual Practices at Last Heterosexual Encounter and Occurrence of Orgasm in a National Survey," *Journal of Sex Research* 43, 3 (2006): 217–26.

15 David Buss, *The Evolution of Desire: Strategies of Human Mating* (New York: Basic Books, 2003).

16 Donald Symons, *The Evolution of Human Sexuality* (New York: Oxford University Press, 1979).

17 Daniel Gilbert and Patrick Malone, "The Correspondence Bias," *Psychological Bulletin* 117, 1 (1995): 21–38.

18 Ziva Kunda, "The Case for Motivated Reasoning," *Psychological Bulletin* 108, 3 (1990): 480–98.

19 Martie Haselton and David Buss, "Error Management Theory: A New Perspective on Biases in Cross-Sex Mind Reading," *Journal of Personality and Social Psychology* 78, 1 (2000): 81–91.

20 Shane Kraus and Brenda Russell, "Early Sexual Experiences: The Role of Internet Access and Sexually Explicit Material," *CyberPsychology and Behavior* 11, 2 (2008): 162–8.

CHAPTER 4

PORNOGRAPHY AS SIMULATION

Consider the following scenario:[1]

Mr. Crane and Mr. Tees were scheduled to leave the airport on different flights, at the same time. They traveled from town in the same limousine, were caught in a traffic jam, and arrived at the airport 30 minutes after the scheduled departure time of their flights. Mr. Crane is told that his flight left on time. Mr. Tees is told that his flight was delayed, and just left five minutes ago.

Now answer the following question: Who is more upset, Mr. Tees or Mr. Crane?

Like 96 percent of people, I suspect your answer to this question is Mr. Tees. In this chapter I aim to convince you that the cognitive process you just underwent in order to generate this answer is the *very same* cognitive process that one employs in order to engage pornographic material. In fact, the parallel between what your brain is doing when it contemplates Mr. Tees' scenario and what your brain is doing when it watches, say, *Debbie Does Dallas*, offers the only plausible explanation for how the porn industry managed to gross $97 billion in 2006.

Here is a more detailed description of the plan of this essay. In part one I discuss the everyday activity of "folk psychology" with particular emphasis on what cognitive scientists term "mental simulation." In part two I describe how the consumption of pornographic material places the simulation heuristic in the service of a purpose that is radically different from that for which it was designed. The final part of the essay explores the implications of the pornography-as-simulation model and offers comparisons to actual sexual experience.

The Tools of Folk Psychology[2]

Human beings are prolific psychologists. By this I am not suggesting that individuals typically interpret one another in clinical terms such as "projection," "avoidant disorder," or the "phallic stage." The sense in which humans are psychologists is rather more pedestrian. What it means is that people have an ability to interpret others in terms of beliefs, desires, intentions, emotions, etc., and people also understand something about how these mental states interact and cause behavior. For example, suppose you are in a betting parlor and witness Jones shake his head, crumple his betting stub, and toss the stub in the trash. Quite automatically you explain this behavior by attributing to Jones the desire that a certain horse win the race and also the belief that this horse did not win. Or, suppose you select for your Aunt Ginger a birthday card filled with puppy pictures because, attributing to your aunt the belief that all small cuddly creatures are wonderful, you *predict* she will enjoy it (note the recursive structure of folk psychology: Aunt Ginger will later *explain* why you chose this card by attributing to you the belief that she would like it).

Two competing proposals for how we perform this mind-reading activity are prominent in the literature. The first maintains that individuals mentalize on the basis of a *theory* about psychology. According to one version of this view, "beliefs" and "desires" are theoretical entities that we posit in order to explain behavior – in the same way that astronomers posit black holes to explain gravitational forces – and we know a set of theoretical principles that causally link these entities to one another and overt behavior. A common example of such a principle is the "belief-desire law": if you desire x (beer), believe that doing y (going to the fridge) will bring about x, then all things being equal, you will do y (go to the fridge).

Mental simulation

Many philosophers and psychologists find the above "theory-theory" approach to folk psychology a bit too, well, scientific. This group favors what they believe is a more natural and parsimonious explanation of folk-psychological ability. Applying this second proposal – broadly called "simulation theory" – we simply imagine what *we* would do in another's situation and then use the results of this exercise as the basis for a prediction or explanation of behavior. For example, if I want to figure out how Holmes will react to a decrease in the size of his pension, I simply "put myself into his shoes" in order to see how *I* would feel about it. After discovering that *I* would not be happy about a loss of retirement funds, I project the result back onto Holmes and predict that *Holmes* will not be happy. Note that I do not need a theory about how people react to decreases in pensions; I just need to figure out how I will react (and to do this I just *react*, I don't have a theory about reacting that tells me when and how to do it).

The most widely accepted account of mental simulation is the "off-line" heuristic.[3] The heuristic begins with feeding "pretend inputs" into one's practical reasoning system in order to engage the target's perspective. The reasoning system then processes these inputs according to whatever principles and laws govern the functioning of the system, e.g., the belief-desire law. The process is off-line in the sense that the interpreter will ascertain the output of the reasoning process but stop short of converting this output into overt action. Instead, the interpreter projects the outcome onto the target in order to predict or explain the target's behavior. Returning to the example of Mr. Tees, the process might go something like this: (1) generate pretend inputs for Mr. Tees' situation (caught in traffic, arrived 30 minutes late to the airport, flight was delayed by 25 minutes); (2) feed these inputs into your reasoning system; (3) determine your reaction to this situation – e.g., recognize that you would be upset; (4) project this attitude onto Mr. Tees.

This process will yield accurate mind-reading data about Mr. Tees because your mind and Mr. Tees' mind operate roughly the same. But more important for our purposes, the process is accurate because there is a correspondence between your mental states during an actual experience and your mental states when you simulate that experience. Off-line reasoning on the basis of *imagined* states produces approximately the same sequence of cognitive and affective states as on-line reasoning on the basis of actual experience.[4]

The origin of simulation

Before we examine the pornographic appropriation of mind-reading skill, it is worthwhile to remark on the origin and purpose of mentalizing ability. Animals, with possibly the exception of a few primates, do not have the ability to think theoretically or simulatively about other minds.

𝄞 THEODORE BACH

While it is true that many species are social (just think of ants and bees), the interpretive skill that underlies this sociality is *behavior* reading and not mind reading.

Probably, natural selection favored the development of mind-reading skill for two reasons. First, it was advantageous for our ancestors to predict each other's behavior more accurately than what was possible by behavior reading alone. Second, it was advantageous for our ancestors to avoid deception from adversaries and have the ability to return it in kind. Because deception involves exhibiting behavior that is at variance with true intention, a special "Machiavellian" mind-reading ability may have developed for the purposes of detecting deception. Supporters of the simulation account fill in the details of this story by claiming that natural selection first targeted forms of emotional contagion and empathy, and these basic abilities later developed into the cognitive simulation routine that we examined in reference to Mr. Tees. The implication is that the biological purpose of simulation – its *raison d'être* – is to predict behavior and avoid deception.

Enter the porn industry, which is perfectly yet unintentionally crafted to take advantage of mind-reading capacities. The porn industry, I'm quite sure, could care less about the phylogenetic history of porn-processing neurons.

The Modern Perversion of Mental Simulation

Why porn is like NutraSweet

It is not altogether uncommon for there to be some mechanism (M) that was designed for a job (J) but now regularly performs some different job (X). For example, the broken-down Ford Escort in my front yard was designed for traveling paved roads, but now it provides safe harbor for several mice and at least one nest of bees. More interesting is when a mechanism "runs normally" – functions mechanically as it ought to – but systematically achieves an end for which it was not designed. Technology is a regular manipulator of mechanisms in this respect. Consider what happens when you sip a Diet Coke. The biological purpose of your "sweet-taste mechanism" is to indicate and encourage the ingestion of high caloric foods. How it does this is by sending pleasurable sensations to your brain in response to a sweet taste. However, non-caloric substitutes such as aspartame (NutraSweet) are specifically designed to trigger this same orosensory operation. Thus, when you drink Diet Coke your orosensory mechanism operates normally but works in the service of an end for which it was not designed.[5]

I propose that something very similar occurs when the mind processes pornographic material. Pornographic material is designed to co-opt the simulation heuristic in the same way that aspartame is designed to co-opt the sweet-taste mechanism. This does not imply, of course, that porn-film directors have detailed theoretical knowledge about the simulative process. The creators of porn may have considerable know-how when it comes to invoking viewer simulation, but they need not have propositional knowledge about the process through which their films successfully highjack the specialized cognitive routine (similarly, the folk-psychological prowess exhibited on MTV's *The Hills* does not command an advanced academic degree in psychology).

The idea that a medium of communication could act to stimulate an audience's simulative involvement is not entirely new. Several researchers have advanced a simulationist approach to fictional engagement.[6] On a strong version of this view, when someone watches a film they simulate the perspective of the protagonist. This thesis has come under considerable fire, however.[7] A more tempered claim is that viewers simulate the perspective of a "hypothetical observer" of the narrative rather than the perspective of an actual participant in the narrative.[8] So instead of simulating Luke Skywalker, for example, we simulate someone who currently observes the inter-galactic events that comprise *Star Wars* (like some futuristic, quasi-omniscient news reporter).

How not *to watch porn*

Whatever the outcome of the debate over viewers' simulative relationship to films rated by the Motion Picture Association of America, I maintain that the status of viewers' simulative involvement in *pornographic* films is clear and definite. Before providing detail on the simulative model of porn consumption let's first consider a non-simulative way to watch porn. For the remainder of this essay my discussion of the consumption of pornographic material will focus on the target porn audience and the dominant pornographic medium – *men* and *videos* (Internet and DVD format), respectively.

One method for watching porn is to objectively admire naked body parts and the sexual configurations and rituals they execute. This would be similar to the manner in which an artist thinks about a figure model. Such an artist might contemplate the relationship between a glancing shadow and the curvature of hips, or the angle at which hair falls across a back. In all probability the artist does not imaginatively reconstruct the perspective of the model or the perspective of someone interacting with the model. It is possible that a porn viewer could achieve a similar objectivity by taking a third-person perspective on the sexual players and events depicted on-screen. On this construal, there is no sense in which porn viewers think or imagine that *they* are involved in sexual activity.

Maybe some people watch porn this way. Or maybe most people occasionally watch porn this way. As with many psychological processes, individual differences must be taken into account. Any attempt to discover necessary conditions for porn consumption is therefore misguided. Instead, researchers should target a theory that explains the staggering popularity of pornographic videos. Such a theory would explicate the central dynamic between porn and its audience rather than the necessary dynamic. In this respect, the third-person explanation of porn consumption fails. It fails for the simple reason that people would rather have sex than watch sex. When people watch porn they do not actually have sex, of course. But if they *simulate* having sex then they recreate (to some degree) the cognitive and affective states that occur when they actually do have sex. Even if the simulated experience lacks complete verisimilitude, it is vastly closer in its approximation to actual sex than passive sex watching. I now develop this idea in more detail.

Simulating a day at the office

In the popular video series "Naughty Office," corporate executives discover that the true desire of their demurely dressed secretaries is not to provide administrative assistance but to engage in heroic sessions of on-the-job fellatio and vaginal/anal penetration. Said bosses are themselves eager to indulge the sexual appetites of their secretaries.

Suppose in rural Nebraska somewhere a dude named Max is watching *Naughty Office 8*[9] from his couch. Max has never had a secretary – he's never even worked in an office before. But he can *simulate* being a boss with a secretary, and he can *simulate* the things that bosses and secretaries like to do in the "Naughty Office." For example, Max can simulate the activity of hastily clearing his desk of official documents so that he and his secretary can more comfortably perform sexual maneuvers.

It is helpful to compare Max's simulation of the Naughty Office to the simulation of Mr. Tees. The first step for the simulation of Mr. Tees is the generation of pretend inputs. While the script about Mr. Tees that prefaced this essay *prompts* our imagination, it does not do the actual imagining for us. Cognitive capacities such as visual imagery (e.g., seeing ourselves in a limo stuck in traffic) and memory recall (e.g., that particular anxiety we've experienced in past traffic jams) are used to produce the facsimile mental states that locate the simulator "in the shoes" of Mr. Tees. On the other hand, one of the tricks of pornographic video is to eliminate the cognitive work and creativity that is typically required for this initial imaginative step. While engaging porn the viewer does not have to visualize a secretary because the secretary is *right there* on the screen. Nor does the viewer strain to imagine the secretary seducing him because again, she is *right there*, ostensibly disrobing and discussing her carnal intentions.

When Max feeds the pretend secretary-seduction inputs into his reasoning system the system will run off-line and produce further mental states. For instance, Max may believe that he is receiving fellatio, that the secretary desires him, that their behavior is risky, and so on. Certainly, Max sees these things to some extent, but he also *believes* them and believes they are a consequence of his behavior. Also, Max's beliefs are about *himself* (and the secretary), but nowhere is Max presented on-screen. These cognitive states, then, must be explained by simulation and do not reduce to mere audio-visual stimulation. On the other hand, it is the visceral power of pornographic video that most directly explains how the off-line process is enforced. If Max's mind were left to its own resources (provided no sensory stimulation) it is unlikely that Max could maintain the off-line succession of mental states that occurs during a secretary-seduction. Fortunately for Max, the audio-visual narrative of *Naughty Office 8* functions to continuously enforce the off-line processing and suppress potentially contradictory beliefs (e.g., the belief that the secretary's desire for him is grossly implausible).

Simulation can also produce affective states, or mental states that have an emotional component. Perhaps during a production of *Romeo and Juliet* we simulate the lovers and generate an emotional state that replicates (to some degree) the genuine emotional state that accompanies love-loss. Now, to the extent that Max is able to simulate surrogates of the cognitive states that attend a secretary-seduction, he should also experience affective states (i.e., desire, lust, affection, disregard) according to the way that his affective system responds to his beliefs. As I discuss below, this is a potentially worrisome result.

So far I have discussed the simulation of cognitive and affective states. But perhaps the most intriguing modes of simulation that underlie the consumption of pornographic video are a form of mirroring called "tactile empathy" and the production of motor imagery. Tactile empathy occurs when someone views another person being touched. Keysers et al. performed functional magnetic resonance imaging (fMRI) studies of subjects in two different conditions.[10] In the tactile condition, subjects' lower legs were brushed back and forth with a glove. For the visual-stimulation condition, subjects viewed videos of actors having their lower legs brushed. The results of the fMRI indicated that being touched and watching someone being touched produced a similar pattern of activation in the secondary somatosensory cortex. Additional evidence indicates that tactile empathy generalizes to other body parts and other types of tactile stimulation. Quite plausibly, watching pornography produces activation patterns in this somatosensory cortex that are similar to patterns produced during actual sexual activity. (No doubt porn consumers also deploy auto-erotic behavior in order to more accurately replicate genuine tactile sensations).

I suggest that porn consumption also involves the closely related but distinct cognitive production of motor imagery. Motor imagery is the imaginative reproduction of mental states that accompany bodily action. For example, before a foul shot, basketball players often "make the shot in their head." Several empirical studies show that the neurological regions activated during actual bodily movement are also activated during the imaginative enactment of bodily movement.[11] Putting this all together, we return to Max. Not only is Max's somatosensory cortex mirroring the somatosensory cortex of the porn actor, but Max is also actively imagining himself executing the motor movements of the porn actor. These subconscious forms of mental mirroring likely anchor the more controlled cognitive reenactments as described above.

One clear difference between the uses of simulation during mind reading versus porn watching is that only the former employs the final projective step. In no sense does Max want to exit the simulation heuristic ("come back to reality") in order to ascribe a mental state to the naked stranger on the screen! Rather, Max wants to maintain the affective, imagistic, and cognitive states that encode *him* as that person (the boss), with that person's attributes, and undergoing that person's activities.

Money, lesbians, and woodsmen

I submit that the simulation model of pornography has a number of explanatory merits that are not available on other accounts. First, I believe that it offers a highly plausible explanation for why pornography is staggeringly popular. We *already know* that actual sex is very appealing and that the attainment of the mental and physical states that accompany sex is, to put the matter mildly, highly motivating. If pornography serves as an audio-visual prop that allows viewers to create surrogate mental states that are phenomenologically and cognitively similar to mental states experienced during actual sex, then it follows that pornography should also be very appealing and highly motivating.

The pornography-as-simulation model also explains the central importance of the "money shot" – the literal and figurative climax of nearly every porn scene. The money shot is the successful filming of the male's ejaculation, where said ejaculation always occurs visibly and directed towards some female body part. It is curious why the money shot is so important to the structure of a porn scene. After all, the porn industry is constantly experimenting and changing existing forms. Yet the money shot persists, unwavering and unrestrained. This all makes sense if the money shot is an essential audio-visual prop for viewer simulation. If the money shot is absent, then the viewer may question whether the sexual activity is "really" happening. But in order to question the authenticity of the sexual behavior, the viewer would first have to *exit* the simulative mode (inhibit their off-line processing) so that they could make an objective analysis. The invariable inclusion of the money shot, then, functions to preserve the simulative connection between viewer and video.

More generally, an account of porn consumption should be able to explain why, given a largely male and presumably heterosexual viewing audience, porn exhibits a preponderance of penises and male ejaculate.[12] It is easy to draw the wrong inferences from this fact. Take, for instance, the following author's claim: "Pornography highlights the penis; men watch pornography; therefore, men must be watching the penis."[13] From this the author concludes that "pornography exists as a conduit for male homoerotic interaction,"[14] and that "porn's central taboo is homosexuality."[15] This gets it completely wrong, completely backwards. The author's argument assumes that people watch pornography objectively, in the third person. If this were the case, then perhaps it is reasonable to wonder why so many presumably heterosexual men are watching so many penises. But it is not the case, because viewers are simulating the actor rather than watching the

ᴧ THEODORE BACH

actor. From the simulative perspective, the viewer is watching *their own* penis and the sexual contact it receives/provides. This is also why large endowment is common in the porn industry: *ceteris paribus*, men prefer to imagine themselves as well endowed and to simulate the effects thereof.

During lesbian scenes there is no male actor that serves as a location to which the viewer can imaginatively project himself. This may seem like a potential problem for the simulation approach to porn, but several responses are available. First, recall that I am not advancing any necessary condition for porn consumption because I don't think there are any. Second, it is possible that men are simulating the women's perspective. Third, and most likely I think, the viewer is simulating the perspective of a "hypothetical observer" to the women. The fact that many lesbian scenes are set up such that it is possible for there to be a secret observer (e.g., the women are in tall grass somewhere) supports this claim.

Conclusions and Assessments

I now examine some of the implications of the simulative model of porn consumption. I hope to show that there are some clear benefits for the porn viewer and perhaps society at large, but also some significant worries. I end on a theoretical note, arguing that the model advanced here opens up new directions for empirical research.

Even better than the real thing?

The world of actual sexual relationships can be a dangerous and cruel place: sexually transmitted diseases are more common and lethal than ever; sexual rejection and unfulfilled sexual desires are par for the course for just about everybody; acts of intimacy interact unpredictably and sometimes undesirably with other non-sexualized elements of people's lives; and so on. The world of pornography offers an escape from many of these unwanted contingencies. If pornographic experience *qua* simulation approximates actual sexual experience, then why bother with any of the problems that are only endemic to the actual sexual world? Sure, there is the argument from Nozick that people want to be *actual* people with *actual* experiences.[16] But in the context of sexual experience this is often the very problem, namely, that the activities which exist in the pornographic milieu are not readily available in the actual world.

Two worries

Here are two concerns that arise if porn viewing is simulative. (I have several other concerns, but I've been given a word limit). First, the disconnect between pornography and actual sex is exacerbated by the remarkable proliferation of porn categories. Internet sites can have literally thousands of alphabetized categories of sexual fetishes and interests that range from *Braces* to *Anal Fruitshakes*. Many of the activity types and partner types featured in these categories are unavailable in the (relatively speaking) prosaic world of real sex. However, I do not believe that the growing population of porn categories exists in response to people's antecedent desires. Rather, these categories *create* desires, and these new desires may conflict with standards of wellbeing and moral behavior.

What I have in mind here is similar to what Ian Hacking calls "dynamic nominalism," in which a category is initially empty but eventually comes to exist on the basis of labeling practices.[17] My specific worry is that through simulative exposure to obscure porn categories, during which people vicariously experience the satisfaction of these desires, they will actually develop these desires in reference to non-simulative and non-pornographic contexts. Such desires then create unrealistic expectations in the non-pornographic world that are potentially harmful for real relationships.

Second, the content of mainstream (as opposed to fetish) pornographic material is increasingly defined by aggressive and degrading behavior towards women. This suggests that porn viewers are simulating aggressive and degrading behavior. Given the layers of simulative reenactment described in the previous section, the concern is not only that viewers simulate the belief that, for example, they are dominating women, but also that they experience the attendant affective states (e.g., derision) in reference to women. If the simulative character of these mental states causes them to persist or have any efficacy in the non-simulated world, then that is a deep problem.[18] Note also that this problem interacts with the problem just described. Even where there is no antecedent desire for domination and degradation, simulated experience of actions on the basis of such desires may foster their development.

Simulation as a research program into the effects of pornography

The vast majority of empirical research on pornography is directed at the *effects* of viewing pornography. In particular, researchers investigate possible correlations between exposure to pornography and violent behavior

𝕸 THEODORE BACH

towards women. To date, this empirical data is inconclusive. But researchers have largely neglected the cognitive processes that occur during the consumption of pornographic material. This is an important oversight because a model of consumption will make specific predictions about the effects of consumption.

Simulation theory is an established empirical research program. Thus the model of porn consumption set forth in this essay has important empirical implications. Consider that researchers have converged on a pattern of data that links the simulation of an action to future performances of that action. Here are two examples. Yue and Cole compared subjects who physically trained (contracted their muscles) to subjects who only mentally trained (no muscle contraction).[19] Subjects who actually trained increased muscle strength by 30 percent and those who simulated training increased strength by 22 percent! In another study, Coffman determined that the mental rehearsal of a piano chordal piece was effective in improving the speed at which performers could subsequently play the chordal piece.[20] This study is consistent with the general finding that mental simulation can improve one's performance in the *conceptual* demands of a task in addition to the motor demands.[21]

Given this body of research, the simulation model of porn consumption offers a mildly amusing prediction and also a generally disturbing prediction. The mildly amusing prediction is that the school-yard notion that watching pornography will improve physical, sexual skill may actually have some merit. The disturbing prediction is that the motor and conceptual processes that occur during engagement with mainstream, aggression-themed pornography will likely facilitate one's ability to transfer these processes into the real world.

NOTES

1   Originally from D. Kahneman and A. Tversky, "The Simulation Heuristic," in D. Kahneman and A. Tversky (eds.) *Judgment Under Uncertainty* (Cambridge: Cambridge University Press, 1982), p. 203.

2   Throughout this essay I will use the expressions "folk psychology," "mind reading," and "mentalizing" interchangeably.

3   See A. Goldman, *Simulating Minds* (Oxford: Oxford University Press, 2006); S. Stich and S. Nichols, "Psychology: Simulation or Tacit Theory?" *Mind and Language* 7 (1992): 35–71.

4   Folk-psychological ability *qua* simulative skill is a mundane and often unconscious process rather than an expert proficiency. This is an important point

because it helps makes plausible the claim that we unwittingly and effortlessly bring this skill to bear in other areas (i.e., pornographic consumption). To get a feel for the degree to which folk psychology penetrates our lives, consider the phenomenon that is reality television. Here is a sample piece of dialogue from MTV's *The Hills* (Season five, Episode five), replete with mental attributions and behavioral explanations/predictions:

Brody:	Listen man, I messed up. I cheated on my girlfriend
Frankie, Doug:	[Laughing, clapping encouragingly]
Doug:	I would have put that down like a sick dog! [meaning: he also would have cheated] Come on, dude! Come *on!* So how do you think Jade is going to feel?
Brody:	How's she going to feel?
Doug:	I mean, do you think she's going to be upset? Do you think you're going to have to like tell her?
Frankie:	[interjecting] Of course she's going to be upset!
Doug:	Are you gonna call her today and be like "hey you know I . . . I . . . [trails off]
Brody:	[stumbling over words]: No man! There's nothing to . . . What?! Are you kidding?
Frankie:	I wouldn't doubt Audrina going and telling the other girls that something happened.
Doug:	She wouldn't do that, I don't think.
Frankie:	How do you know?
Doug:	I mean I don't . . .
Frankie:	Dude, girls are evil.

To the extent that folk psychology is simulative, Brody, Frankie, and Doug are inexhaustible simulators. It is also quite plausible that the *reason* people tune in to watch this drivel is because they want to see folk psychology in action – to see how other people do it and to determine if they themselves are deviant (but this is another story, perhaps better left for "Reality TV and Philosophy").

5   The calorie ratio of Coke Classic to Diet Coke is 97:1.
6   See S. Feagin, *Reading with Feeling: The Aesthetics of Appreciation* (Ithaca: Cornell University Press, 1996); A. Goldman, *Simulating Minds* (Oxford: Oxford University Press, 2006).
7   See N. Carroll, *The Philosophy of Motion Pictures* (Oxford: Wiley-Blackwell, 2008).
8   See G. Currie, "The Paradox of Caring: Fiction and the Philosophy of Mind," in M. Hjort and S. Laver (eds.) *Emotion and the Arts* (Oxford: Oxford University Press, 1997), pp. 63–77.
9   Produced by Naughty America, 2007.

10   C. Keysers, B. Wicker, V. Gazolla, J.-L. Anton, L. Fogassi, and V. Gallese, "A Touching Sight: SII/PV Activation during the Observation of Touch," *Neuron* 42 (2004): 335–46.

11   See J. Decety, "Neurophysiological Evidence for Simulation of Action," in J. Dokic and J. Proust (eds.), *Simulation and Knowledge of Action* (Amsterdam: John Benjamins, 2002), pp. 53–73.

12   The insider slang of the porn industry reflects the central role given to the male performer's erection. As David Foster Wallace decodes in his essay *Big Red Son*: "*Wood* is a camera-ready erection; *woodman* is a dependably potent male performer; and *waiting for wood* is a discrete way of explaining what everybody else in the cast and crew is doing when a male performer is experiencing *wood trouble*, which latter term is self-evident." See David Foster Wallace, *Consider the Lobster and Other Essays* (New York: Little, Brown, 2005), p. 23, n. 18).

13   S. Strager, "What Men Watch When They Watch Porn," *Sexuality and Culture* (Winter 2003): 50–61, p. 58.

14   Ibid., p. 55.

15   Ibid., p. 60.

16   The objection comes from Robert Nozick's analysis of why people would choose not to live in an "experience machine" that could give them any experience they desired.

17   Ian Hacking, *Rewriting the Soul* (Princeton: Princeton University Press, 1995).

18   What I am suggesting here is an elaboration of MacKinnon's well-known criticism of pornography, but I am developing that criticism in the theoretical and empirical context of simulation theory. See C. MacKinnon, *Feminism Unmodified: Discourses on Life and Law* (Cambridge, MA: Harvard University Press, 1987).

19   G. Yue and K. Cole, "Strength Increases from Motor Program: Comparison of Training with Maximal Voluntary and Imagined Muscle Contractions," *Journal of Neurophysiology* 67 (1992): 1114–23.

20   D. Coffman, "Effects of Mental Practice, Physical Practice, and Knowledge of Results on Piano Performance," *Journal of Research in Music Education* 38, 3 (1990): 187–96.

21   For a review, see D. L. Feltz and D. M. Landers, "The Effects of Mental Practice on Motor Skill Performance and Learning: A Meta-Analysis," *Journal of Sport Psychology* 5 (1983): 25–57.

CHAPTER 5

BROTHERS' MILK

The Erotic and the Lethal in Bareback Pornography

Why is it that when boys play, they always play at killing each other?
(Marge Sherwood in *The Talented Mr. Ripley*)

In an anthology with a title as provocative as *Porn – Philosophy for Everyone*, with such kinky intellectual offerings as bondage, domination, girl-on-girl action, role-playing, orgasm, and so forth, it may seem rather pointedly an erotic buzz-kill to bring up the subject of AIDS. Indeed, for over a quarter of a century now, the AIDS virus has killed much more than buzzes. Yet its arrival on the national and global scenes has had an enormous, and often unpredictable, impact on erotic identities, subcultural sex practices, and the pornography industry. It is here I want to begin, with a focus in particular on the ways that AIDS has both constrained and enabled different sexual practices and fantasies within the gay community. While AIDS has clearly had far-reaching effects outside of the US gay population, I take a portion of this community as the focus of this study to explain a particular response to the epidemic, and how that response has been expressed and aestheticized in the world of gay porn.

Specifically, I address the subculture and pornographic portrayal of barebacking, the erotic celebration of condomless anal sex. Despite, or perhaps because of, compelling scientific information that defines unprotected anal sex as a high risk activity in the spread of HIV, a small but substantial minority of gay men in the US have developed a sexual sub-culture centering on the risk of viral transmission, the circumvention of medical advice surrounding "safe sex," and the formation of an outlaw sexuality that defies social convention and legal parameters.

In this essay I intend neither to defend nor to wholeheartedly condemn the practice and the pornographic representation of bareback sex; instead, I seek to account for the emergence of the bareback genre by exploring its potential pleasures and its attendant "seductive" qualities. I begin with a brief history of AIDS in the US and its semiotic ties to the gay community. I then explore some salient features of the bareback porn. I end by examining some of the psychic motivations that undergird the success of this medium.

AIDS as a Gay Disease?

It is a significant though often forgotten fact in the deeply sad history of AIDS in America that the virus, within the first two years of its appearance in the US, was (mis)labeled the Gay-Related Immunodeficiency Disease. In 1982, when reported cases still numbered in the triple-digits, the virus was given the name GRID, despite the fact that nearly half of its sufferers were not homosexual. It took several years for virologists to adjust the terminology to reflect scientific fact, whereupon it was given the name Acquired Immune Deficiency Syndrome. It took much longer for the virus itself to lose its cultural associations with homosexuality; arguably, in some circles, it never has.[1]

There are some understandable reasons for the initial impulse to see the AIDS virus as largely a "gay disease." For years, the Center for Disease Control thought it had isolated the *primum mobile*, the first carrier of the disease to the United States, in the form of Gaetan Dugas, a promiscuous gay French-Canadian flight attendant, who was sexually linked to forty or so of the first reported cases. And in fact the initial infected population reflected a highly disproportionate number of homosexual men, almost all of whom resided in large urban areas – mostly Los Angeles and New York City.

It was not until the later 1980s, when a critical mass of heterosexuals were sero-converting – a number too large to ignore – that the Reagan administration brought the epidemic to national attention. By then, tens of thousands of US citizens had died. To this day, the Reagan administration bears much of the burden of guilt for waiting so long to inform the general public of the growing epidemic; its decision to sit on the information it had regarding the virus was based, in part, on the disease's apparent ghettoization within the gay community – a portion of the American citizenry that Reagan had clearly relegated to second-class status at best.

Yet there exist other reasons for the persistent association of homosexuality with the AIDS virus. For the greater part of the twentieth century, homosexuality in America bore the status of a medical illness. Michel Foucault, in his *History of Sexuality*, remarked persuasively that the homosexual was "invented" as a social category in the Victorian era. Before this time, homosexuality was not seen as a condition, but as a criminal act. Therefore, homosexual sex was punishable as a discrete offense. Foucault argues that a paradigm shift occurred that saw homosexuality as an individual condition, rather than simply criminal behavior. Thus, for the past 100 years or so, homosexuality has been incorporated into medical discourse as a "deviance." When AIDS arrived on the scene in 1981, it had only been eight years since the American Psychiatric Association had removed homosexuality as pathology from its diagnostic manual, the DSMR-III. Thus, the equation of homosexuality with disease had long been entrenched in the American imaginary.

Lee Edelman, in his brilliant book *No Future: Queer Theory and the Death Drive*, delineates another pathologizing tendency in mainstream American culture concerning homosexuality. Edelman maintains that the Symbolic order is supported and naturalized through the valorization of a procreative sexuality that guarantees the social and biological reproduction of the same. Legitimate subjecthood, he argues, is assumed through taking on the mandatory cultural labor of reproduction. This procreative identity ensures the stability of the subject through the fantasmatic marriage of identity to futurity. Queer sexuality, in its noncompliance with this political futurity, registers as outside the Symbolic order, as a deathly shadow of the stable subject. In short, queer sexuality reads as the death of the subject, the end of a name and a bloodline. At the risk of sounding glib or reductive, I posit that, with the advent of AIDS, there came to be a truism that fed the straight/queer dichotomy: *Heterosexuals breed babies. Homosexuals breed viruses.* Later in the essay, I will return to this pervasive association of homosexuality with mortality.

As the evidence linking unprotected sex to HIV transmission became more persuasive, the gay community as a whole responded to the epidemic through large-scale campaigns for safer sex practices. Condom companies worked together with gay publications and other media outlets

CASEY MCKITTRICK

to put out the word on safer sex. They even tried, for a period of time, to advance the idea of eroticizing latex. In an attempt to align condom use with a sort of fetishism, they hoped to minimize the association of condoms with a restricted, sanitized, and prophylactic regulation of sexual practices. The gay pornography industry stood at the vanguard of this safer sex movement, both by requiring condom use in its depiction of anal sex (and less frequently, with oral sex) and by including a warning at the beginning of gay porn videos that identified the risks involved in the practice of gay sex. An analogous safety measure in the straight porn industry was, by and large, not to be found. While some production companies began requiring condoms for vaginal and anal sex, most companies remained condomless, perhaps further indicating the mentality that AIDS was not a heterosexual concern.

However, by 1997, a gay subculture began to emerge on the Internet advocating condomless sex.[2] Concomitant to the presence of websites and message boards devoted to discussions of bareback sex, amateur pornography depicting barebacking came into circulation. Many online barebackers and producers of bareback porn had simply grown tired of the restrictive measures taken to police gay sex after the onset of AIDS. They saw the closing of bathhouses in urban areas, the lingering criminalization of gay sex in the form of sodomy laws, and the ubiquitous reminders of the mandate to wear rubbers during sex as part and parcel of the regulatory regime that seeks to contain and constrict sexual practices outside the realm of social normalcy. This "condom fatigue," coupled with the recent medical innovations regarding treatment of the AIDS virus, cleared a space for the growth of bareback sex, both as a subcultural practice and as a commercially viable pornographic genre. For some, the renunciation of safer sex practices constituted a powerful statement of political dissent surrounding the policing of gay male desire. For others, advancements in anti-viral medication allowed a new perspective on the AIDS virus that no longer saw the disease as a death sentence, but as a manageable illness akin to diabetes.

While major gay porn producers such as Falcon Video, Pacific Sun, Vivid, Titan, and Jocks have refrained from depicting condomless sex since the late 1980s, bareback porn has its roots in smaller, often amateur, production companies which were either downloadable online or offered for sale online through the mail. In 1998, production companies began offering their wares through their own websites, with pretty extensive advertising web space, advanced systems of credit card payment, and elaborate design. By that time, three major producers and distributors of bareback porn existed on the web: Treasure Island Media, Hot Desert Knights, and Gas Lamp Video. All three are thriving today (Gas Lamp now incorporated by SX Video) and comprise a large portion of bareback distribution and online exhibition; however, many smaller enterprises are currently their competitors. The product of these distributors ranges from amateur productions with hand-held cameras depicting real-time sex, to medium-scale productions with professional lighting, scene editing, and sound track. As of now, roughly 30 percent of gay adult videos within video stores are bareback productions.

Features of the Bareback Video

The typical bareback video is remarkable not only in its graphic depiction of sex deemed highly risky by health officials, but in its persistent focus on the visible exchange of semen in the act of anal intercourse. A salient feature of the bareback video is the *money shot*, the moment of visible ejaculation discussed in Linda Williams' famous work *Hardcore: Power, Pleasure, and the 'Frenzy of the Visible'* and elsewhere; however, bareback videos, unlike contemporary mainstream gay video, as well as what we now call pre-condom classics, are distinguished in large part by their depiction of a money shot followed by a reinsertion of the still-ejaculating penis into the submissive sex partner. This reinsertion, followed often by a display of the anus filled with semen, typifies the culmination of many sex acts in the bareback video.

It must be noted that many bareback scenes do end in a manner similar to mainstream gay porn, where the active partner ejaculates on the chest or face of the passive partner. However, a substantial number of bareback scenes employ this reinsertion shot to assure the spectator of his/her having witnessed the transmission of semen from one partner to the other.

The typical bareback video enacts many of the fantasies defined by online users – the transmission of semen, either in a one-on-one or group scenario. Like other forms of gay porn, there are between three and six scenes involving oral and anal sex. The word "bareback" is usually fore-grounded in the title. *Bareback Buddies, Bareback Boys, Bareback Lovers* are some of the inspired titles to be bought online or through magazine advertisements. Big-name gay porn performers are mostly absent in condomless productions, although a "star system" of its own is emerging in the bareback genre; there are several notable exceptions – Jeff Palmer and Jackson Price, once quite prominent in mainstream gay porn, crossed over into bareback video and have since been blacklisted by the larger companies for which they formerly performed. Both are also admittedly HIV-positive.[3] While new bareback actors are constantly being introduced to the viewing public, certain bareback production companies, like Hot Desert Knights, employ a core group of actors who can be seen in many of the company's productions.

Mise-en-scène is typically at a minimum in these videos. There are almost never gestures towards plot or characterization (not even a perfunctory pizza delivery guy or gym buddy in need of spotting). The scenes are often very quiet, with no musical enhancement (there are some exceptions); the only recurring setting with any sort of elaboration is a dungeon; within bareback porn, there is some cross-over with leather, bondage, and fisting, although, to be sure, there is a large contingency within the leather culture that would disavow any affiliation with barebackers.

Tim Dean, in his provocative book-length study *Unlimited Intimacy: Reflections on the Subculture of Barebacking*, remarks that the bareback porn is shot in a manner closer to documentary realism than the more theatrical and stylized productions of mainstream porn. Dean finds that bareback porn is more likely to reveal the presence of another camera in bareback porn, whereas mainstream productions tend to minimize intrusions that foreground the constructedness of the scenario. In Dean's reasoning, the unpretentious style of filming, including shots of another camera and similar "mistakes," foregrounds the spectator's status as witness to an actual event. The viewer is thus implicated in the intimate exchange taking place on the screen. In dispensing with props, plot lines, musical accompaniment, and sophisticated editorial flourishes, the bareback porn emphasizes the fucking as a real-life event to be witnessed. While I would temper Dean's reading of the standard bareback scene as "documentary realist" by suggesting that even these signifiers of "authenticity" and "realness" are, to some degree, performative in nature, containing an element of less recognizable theatricality, he makes a legitimate distinction between the tone of bareback scenes and that of mainstream gay porn.

Rehearsed dialogue in the bareback video is also practically non-existent; we often begin the sex scenes *in medias res*. Verbal exchanges are typically monosyllabic and sparse. What is striking about bareback scenes is the intensity of eye contact often involved among performers. While not much is uttered in a typical scene, visual contact is palpable. The scenes, which end in single or multiple ejaculations into the submissive performer/performers, often witness the bottom partner thanking the dominant one for the "gift" he has given or the "seed" he has scattered. After ejaculation, the top often either digitally or orally extracts the semen as visible proof of the fluid transmission. Overall, the scenes come across as heavily ritualistic, often reverent, with an air of religiosity.

Bareback porn frequently employs a more diversified profile of actors. We have a wider range of ages among the performers; often a middle-aged man will be paired with one in his late teens or early twenties. Mainstream gay porn tends to value very young performers (so-called "twinks," who are usually between 18 and 22 and have idealized fit, slightly muscular bodies); when mainstream porn does employ older actors, there is usually an explicit "daddy" theme in the film. In addition to including a wide range of ages, much bareback porn contains a racially diverse cast of characters,[4] and the body types of the actors are much more varied than the hyper-body-conscious mainstream porn product.

One often-employed format of the bareback video consists of one bottom, in essence the "star" of the production, who takes the semen of multiple partners over a period of time. Whereas mainstream gay porn, when it features an orgy scene, usually has several tops and several bottoms who may or may not switch positions (known as "versatile" performing), bareback porn is more likely to take the form of a gangbang, where one bottom functions for the pleasure of many tops. In an extreme version of this format, we have the title *Dawson's 50-Load Weekend*, which is not an exaggeration, but a visual document of 50 different ejaculations, with the performer Dawson as a bottom in all of these acts. Sometimes, the number of fluid transmissions is used in the title, or a tally is kept within the filming itself (for instance, the performer, once he has ejaculated, may make a hash mark with a marker on the back or ass of the bottom, and these hash marks are tallied at the end of the performance).

In introducing a new star and a new release from Treasure Island Media, Paul Morris describes the process by which he procured his newest "ingénue" bottom. He writes:

> Ian Jay, a smooth and boyish 20-year-old, isn't my usual kind of obsession. . . . [B]ut he wrote to me and told me he was ready to take a big step: he wanted to be irrevocably bred. I knew what he meant, and I took him at his word. So I flew him to San Francisco and put him through a deep-boning weekend that would do the job. Before he came to me, he'd

been dabbling in raw sex, but he was still naïve. By the time the weekend was over, his hole was fuckin' insatiable, ready and willing and available to any man.

Because Morris cannot explicitly announce his intention to get his "star" infected, he uses the above oblique language to make it clear to an audience who is "in the know." Clearly, the "big step" that Ian envisions is his sero-conversion. The next sentence is interesting in its implications: "I knew what he meant, and I took him at his word." Obviously, knowing "what he meant" indicates Morris's recognition that infection is what Jay desires; the clause "I took him at his word" seems to indicate that Morris felt no need to examine his request in depth, in terms of his motivations or desires. His declaration, as far as Morris is concerned, is simply an admission of consent to the orgy, where sero-conversion might take place, an exhortation to "do the job."

Tim Dean makes a valuable observation concerning the prominence of the bareback gangbang scenario in gay porn that has both an aesthetic and a practical dimension. Scenes like these clearly depict a common sexual fantasy of many gay men – that of submitting to and being dominated by a group of men. Thus, the gangbang scenario offers a vicarious satisfaction of the multiple-top fantasy. However, the presence of multiple tops has a strategic element as well. If a bottom does in fact sero-convert as a result of being fucked in a bareback video, the top – provided it is a one-on-one scene – can be charged with manslaughter in many states, and the recorded act constitutes the proof. However, if a bottom sero-converts as a result of a multiple-top orgy, it becomes much more difficult to prosecute, given the various permutations of sex partners.

Cultural Responses to the Bareback Video

Obviously, this subcultural practice, as well as its enactment in this subgenre of porn, has come under vicious attack from AIDS activists, public health officials, and many other cultural and political groups. It has been discussed heatedly among medical practitioners, gay outreach organizations such as the Gay Men's Health Crisis, and by journalists in both gay-centered and more mainstream media outlets. In 1997 the gay and lesbian publication *The Advocate* included a feature about the unwelcome resurgence of unprotected sex in gay culture. *POZ* magazine, a publication dedicated to HIV-positive issues, published a feature in 1999 as well; however, it was not as much a condemnation of the practice as it was an exoticizing take on a new fad. In 2001 the issue of barebacking came to greater public prominence when *Rolling Stone* magazine chose to run a feature profiling two out-and-proud barebackers.

Reaction to the publicization of condomless sex has been predictably vitriolic. To many, its emergence signifies a kind of cultural amnesia around the issue of AIDS or a naïve or delusional complacency regarding the status of AIDS as a manageable illness, given the pharmaceutical advances (the drug cocktails, etc.) over the last few years. Still others blame the outbreak of publicized barebacking on the always popular notion that gay men act in self-destructive ways that are rooted in internalized homophobia and self-loathing. I should make the distinction here that condomless sex has, without a doubt, been a practice before AIDS, at the onset of AIDS, and ever since. I do not intend to demarcate a particular cultural moment where this particular activity came into being; I am, rather, interested in tracing the emergence of a discourse around barebacking and the accretion of cultural meanings around the term as it began to be deployed by the subculture itself, which of course was formed by the very naming of the act, and by those in opposition to the subculture. Primarily, my interest lies in how, why, and at what cost the subculture founds its expression in the production of condomless video.

The Language of the Bareback Experience

It is not surprising that the bareback video has become so successful, given its online "grassroots" origins. It is on the web that people have met, organized, and produced a formidable virtual community, with hundreds of chat rooms and websites (like bareback.com and barebackrt.com) dedicated exclusively to barebackers (or online browsers who claim their identity as a barebacker). A new vocabulary has surfaced on the web to describe the multifarious identities, desires, motives, and activities of the subculture. HIV-positive individuals looking for sex with one another use monikers like Poz4Poz; likewise, users who identify as negative use names like Neg4Neg. Perhaps the more disturbing appellations involve those who are looking to be infected or to infect someone else. The name "bug-chasers" has been adopted by those looking to sero-convert, while users intent on spreading the virus frequently call themselves "gift-givers." Solicitations of fluid exchange and viral transmission have taken on a rhetoric strikingly similar to that of the Aryan brotherhood. Users looking to "spread the power" and finding "brothers to unite" abound in online personal ads. Condom use is explicitly stigmatized in these online environments; those advocating safer sex are repeatedly labeled "latex police" or "condom Nazis."

Other operative metaphors show a co-opting of the language of heterosexual reproduction; exhortations to "knock me up," "give me your seed," or "breed me" liken viral reproduction to human reproduction. Other parlance reveals a less veiled relation to aggression, danger, and death; users looking for "poison cum," a "lethal load," or the "hot virus" foreground the perils and risks involved in unprotected anal sex. Many online are seeking a mythic moment they call the "Fuck of Death," where they rhetorically ritualize a hoped for sero-conversion experience.

Before trying to account for the ways in which the bareback video as a cultural form might be compelling and desirable for some queer audiences, I would like to summarize a few of public intellectual Michelangelo Signorile's astute observations about why barebacking and the infection rate among gay men particularly has reached such a critical mass at this cultural moment. He cites the "glamorization" of barebacking and its portrayal as an outlaw sexual fad, the sense of entitlement among gays to have the most pleasure in sex possible, the ads for protease inhibitors which portray buff, sexy, and healthy-looking men with AIDS, the often-heard yet dubious claim that "AIDS is over," young gay men's lack of firsthand experience with AIDS-related deaths, and the already transgressive nature of gay men's sexuality as factors contributing to the popularity of unsafe sex. I would suggest that these are also substantial reasons for the continued marketability of bareback video.

Plenitude and the Death Drive in Bareback Porn

Undoubtedly, Signorile's explanations for this sea-change in attitudes and sexual practices ring true. In closing, I would like to propose some more psychically oriented descriptions of the pleasures intrinsic to the practice of unsafe sex and the visual representation of it. The AIDS crisis brought about unfathomable loss in gay culture and in American culture in general. Not only has it heralded the deaths of millions and the challenging illnesses of many more to come; it has brought other forms of devastation. Accompanying those material, bodily consequences are countless manifestations of loss that are less tangible. The ongoing association of gay sex with impending peril has generated a profound loss of perceived intimacy among gay men. What many perceive to be the consummation of gay sex – the exchange of semen – has been associated with the most reckless form of human endangerment.

Bareback porn producer and owner of Treasure Island Media Paul Morris emphasizes the importance of fluid exchange in the sex act as the ultimate guarantor of intimacy; he laments the presence of condoms in mainstream gay video. He argues, "Condoms in this context – a context of stylized and commercially driven political correctness – actually say little about safe sex or personal responsibility. They become instead the final sign for the absolute unavailability to the viewer of the communion and connection that the entire well-practiced language of the video had promised."[5]

Freud's insights into the psychic registering of loss and the desire for the lost object become valuably descriptive here of the desires evoked (but never, of course, fulfilled) by bareback video. I would argue that semen operates as the fundamental lost object in post-AIDS gay male sexuality. It becomes, in essence, the mother's milk that, once denied to the child, shatters a sense of original plenitude and belonging. The exchange of what I term "brothers' milk" signifies a fantasy of restored intimacy, of essential sharing of the self with another. Just as the advent of AIDS installed a radical sense of alienation and displacement in the gay psyche, the condom becomes a barrier to this intimacy, a place where feelings of separation and radical incompletion are cathected. Bareback video provides a fantasy space in which viewers can access an image of fullness and completion, however vicarious or metaphorical. The nature of desire, after all, is its inability to be fulfilled; the condomless video becomes a dream screen whereby desire is glimpsed and renewed.

Finally, the bareback video is a potent condensation of the struggle between eros and thanatos. AIDS has forced gay men to confront the inextricably entwined notions of sexuality and mortality. Freud has argued that the death drive permeates, even constitutes, sexual impulse, and that no attempt to dispel aggression from the psyche or from sexual relations is possible. The visual representation of imperiling sex makes visceral, explicit, and palpable the many shifting feelings of aggression, anger, frustration, intimacy, attachment, and identification that infiltrate gay eroticism, particularly since the onset of AIDS. Survivor guilt, the need to blame and scapegoat, the need to annihilate vengefully, to be annihilated psychically – all of these motives oppose themselves violently to the also-present instincts of self-rebuilding, of moving forward, of forging

ᴍ CASEY MCKITTRICK

meaningful and loving relationships. This struggle between hostility and affection, between estrangement and reunion, is animated by the spectacle of unsafe sex.

Jonathon Dollimore, in his book *Death, Desire, and Loss in Western Culture*, echoes Freud in his pithy remark: "Death inhabits sexuality: perversely, lethally, ecstatically." It is not hard to succumb to the romantic notion of the epic battle waged within between eros and thanatos, just as it is easy to romanticize a sense of fullness and wholeness before the ravages of AIDS. It becomes crucial, then, to understand the importance of fantasy in the negotiation of these desires. Bareback pornography nostalgically houses and nurtures these fantasies, for better or for worse. Equally important are the social repercussions of what we do with these fantasies in the realm of the social, the interpersonal, and the communal. The demonization of gay barebacking practices will not make them disappear. Future dialogue will be crucial to discern the many nuanced ways we may have of letting desire and pleasure speak to personal responsibility and accountability to the futures of others and ourselves.

NOTES

1   I am thinking of jokes and mantras that persisted well into the 1990s, such as "AIDS Cures FAGS."
2   I use "gay" and "queer" interchangeably throughout the essay. When I use "gay," "I generally intend to describe male same-sex orientation and sexual acts. When I use "queer," I emphasize same-sex practices as consciously oppositional to heterosexual identity.
3   Jeff Palmer admitted his HIV-positive status, and then retracted the statement, insisting that HIV and AIDS are not medically linked, and that whereas he formerly had AIDS, his illness was a product of drugs and negativity. He claims to now be free of disease.
4   I use "racial diversity" here only in the sense of its being relative to mainstream porn. While the number of black and Latino performers is much higher than mainstream porn, the genre is still predominantly white. There are, however, mainly explicitly racialized bareback porns like *Barrio Bareback Gangbang* and *Black & White Bareback*.
5   Paul Morris, "No Limits: Necessary Danger in Male Porn," *Treasure Island Media* (July 15, 2009). www.treasureislandmedia.com/TreasureIslandMedia_2007/paulsPapers.php?article=noLimits.

PART III

BETWEEN THE SHEETS
Porn Ethics and Personal Relationships

CHAPTER 6

STRANGE LOVE, OR

How I Learned to Stop Worrying and Love Porn

Going Deep

Pornography has a long history, but perhaps it was the 1970s that saw the beginning of the massive industry it has become, with films such as *Deep Throat* (1972), *Behind the Green Door* (1972), and *Debbie Does Dallas* (1978). And let us not forget the influence of magazines such as *Playboy* and *Penthouse*, as well as pornography on the World Wide Web. Pornography has its fans, but it also has opponents. It has faced legal, moral, and religious opposition. Our focus here is to examine the case for the censorship of pornography. We will see that in accordance with the Harm Principle, censorship is unjustified. The Harm Principle protects pornography against censorship despite concerns about sexual morality, concerns that pornography causes violence against women, or concerns that it supports the patriarchal domination of women.

The Porns of Our Lives

Any philosophical examination of pornography ought to begin with a clear understanding of what exactly it is that is under examination. We will regard as pornographic any sexually explicit representation intended to produce sexual arousal in its audience. Pornography may serve as an instrument for obtaining a sexual catharsis. It may be a substitute for a sexual partner. Not all sexually explicit material counts as pornography – that it be intended to cause sexual arousal is a necessary feature. So-called "slasher" films that depict naked women in sexual situations – and who usually meet a violent end – do not count as pornography. In *Hostel: Part 2* (2007), for example, several American college girls traveling throughout Europe become the victims of a gruesome torture club. Violence and sexuality are mixed in a way that pushes boundaries, but the film does not cross the line into pornography. It may be intended to offend and frighten, but it is not intended to sexually arouse. In fact, "slasher" films have sometimes served as warnings for the young against promiscuity or premarital sex. In films such as those in the *Friday the 13th* series it is often the sexually active teenagers who are the first to die. The audience of such films may be seeking something with graphic depictions of sex and violence, but they are not seeking sexual catharsis or a sexual substitute. Whatever criticisms may be raised against such films, they are not pornographic.

Sexually explicit material that is intended to cause arousal comes in many forms. The pornography found in *Playboy* magazine, for example, does not typically contain explicit themes of domination or sexism – we will refer to such pornography as non-sexist erotica, or just erotica. Some pornography, while not containing explicit domination themes, is nonetheless sexist. For example, sexually explicit films in which women are portrayed as conforming to an insulting, derogatory stereotype – the silly, stupid, and servile "empty-headed bimbo," for example – would fall into this second category. So, too, would films portraying women in positions of socioeconomic subordination happy to provide sexual services on command – the female secretary eager and ready to perform fellatio on her male boss in his office, for example. Of course, not only pornography may be sexist in this way – non-pornographic films, for example, may contain the same portrayals of women. A third category of pornography includes explicit domination themes, such as photos of naked women on their hands and knees while wearing dog collars and leashes. The final category of pornography contains depictions of violence – women being tied up, tortured, or raped, for example. In violent pornography the victims may be depicted as enjoying and consenting to the sexual acts or as being unwilling and terrorized.

We must be careful when identifying material as pornographic – whether some material counts as pornography will not always be obvious or uncontroversial. The film *Secretary* (2002), for example, contains a portrayal of a female secretary who engages in a submissive sexual relationship with her dominant male employer. On the surface, the film may appear to be a sexist, sexually explicit film containing themes of male domination, but a closer viewing reveals an exploration of the boundaries of human sexuality and love. The film received an *R* rating from the MPAA and is not generally regarded as pornographic. Perhaps we have missed a distinguishing feature of pornography in our analysis of it above which would allow us to distinguish pornography from films such as *Secretary*, or perhaps *Secretary* ought to be regarded as pornographic after all. Rather than become weighed down in definitional matters, however, we will proceed as follows. Along with the distinctions explained above, we will trust ourselves to recognize pornography when we see it. Also, we must not have a definition of pornography that is so broad that everything counts as pornography or so narrow that nothing does. Where there is controversy as to whether some material ought to be regarded as pornographic, we will not concern ourselves with it. We will avoid the controversy, because if it can be shown that even material that is regarded as pornographic without controversy – especially material that is sexist, degrading, and violent – should not be censored, then we need not concern ourselves with material that would be even less troubling.

All that having been said, let us remind ourselves that not all pornography is identical. The wide scope of pornography is an immediate reminder that we should not necessarily expect to draw the same conclusions about all pornography. Child pornography is wrong and ought to be legally prohibited. Pornography produced without the consent of the people being subjected to sexual violence – as in so-called "snuff" films, for example – is also wrong and ought to be legally prohibited.[1] These claims are taken as uncontroversial and without need of justification. But we may agree about the status of child pornography and snuff films without agreeing that pornography involving consenting adults is similarly objectionable and ought to be similarly censored.

Dial M for Missionary

Why are we concerning ourselves with all these distinctions and definitions? Of what concern is sexism, domination, or violence? That may all be problematic, but perhaps we do not need to get that far into it – the trouble with pornography is the sex! Sex is supposed to be part of an emotional relationship, isn't it? Porn stars engage in sex for money. The sex in pornography is not a reciprocal expression of loving desire, but rather the consenting to sexual acts with the consolation of payment. Sex for money? Porn stars are prostitutes! Prostitution is wrong – at least that may be the common opinion – and it is legally prohibited just about everywhere.[2] And if porn stars are prostitutes, then pornography should have the same moral and legal status as prostitution.

Let's slow down a moment. That objection seems too obvious to have gone unnoticed – and it hasn't. The objection was the subject of an importantly relevant court case, *California v. Freeman* (1989).[3] According to the court decision, porn stars are not engaged in prostitution, because their genitals do not come into contact for the purpose of causing each other sexual arousal in return for payment. The prostitute, through genital contact, intends to cause sexual arousal in the client. The porn star, on the other hand, is an actor or actress, portraying sexual arousal. The porn star, in other words, is paid not for causing sexual arousal through direct genital stimulation, as the prostitute is, but rather for acting out sexual activity and arousal. This is an important difference as far as the courts are concerned.

Why doesn't this settle the matter for us? First, even if pornography is not regarded by the law as equivalent to prostitution, there may be independent reasons to censor it. Second, even if pornography were regarded as equivalent to prostitution, this would only push the question back a step – we would have to examine whether prostitution ought to continue to be legally prohibited. Nevertheless, while we will not be able to rely on the simple argument that porn stars are prostitutes, there still may be a sufficient argument for censorship. That argument may not need to depart far from where we began this section. Porn stars may not be prostitutes, at least not in the eyes of the law, but they are engaged in loveless sex, and that's still wrong – isn't it?

Let us examine that idea. Just what is wrong with loveless sex? Even if lovemaking – which is what we will call sex that involves the mutual expression of love – is better than loveless sex, loveless sex might be quite good! Consider an analogy: a well-aged red wine from Napa Valley may be better than boxed wine from New Jersey, but some people may happen to like boxed wine from New Jersey – especially if the alternative is no wine at all! Furthermore, even if loveless sex is worth less than lovemaking, or even if it is valueless without love, it does not follow that engaging in it, filming it, photographing it, and so on ought to be prohibited. Finally, if pornography were objectionable on these grounds, the same case could be made about other sorts of sexual activity, such as premarital sex and promiscuity. This objection may justify legally prohibiting all sexual activity that is not part of a loving relationship. While this may appeal to some opponents of pornography, it likely will not appeal to all of them, and is a much harder position to maintain. The objection is far too broad.

Perhaps the problem is not about relative value, but rather that loveless sex undermines – or diminishes the value of – lovemaking. For example, if pornography were widely available, then fewer people would have an incentive to be in a committed, loving relationship in order to obtain sexual catharsis, and thus fewer people would be engaging in sexual activity that involves the mutual expression of love. If we think that it is a good thing that there are mutual sexual expressions of love, then we might want to remove from society those things of lesser value that present obstacles to achieving more of this higher value. If, for example, an increasing availability of boxed wine had the result that fewer and fewer people enjoyed superior wine, then we may have a reason for decreasing the availability of boxed wine – assuming at least that we think people would be happier drinking bottled wine and that we ought to be enacting policies to maximize people's happiness. But wait right there – what about those assumptions? What if some people are really happier drinking boxed wine? If so, then we would be making them worse off by taking away their boxed wine. If we want to claim that their preferences are mistaken – that they do not know what is good for them, for example – then we are imposing a value judgment upon them, and that may be something we should not do.

For Your Thighs Only

The context for considering the censorship of pornography is a context of political liberalism. We are citizens of a liberal democratic republic, of which one of the fundamental guiding principles is the Harm Principle, explicated by John Stuart Mill in *On Liberty*:

> The sole end for which mankind are warranted, individually or collectively, in interfering with the liberty of action of any of their number, is self-protection. That the only purpose for which power can be rightfully exercised over any member of a civilized community, against his will, is to prevent harm to

others. His own good, either physical or moral, is not sufficient warrant. . . . The only part of the conduct of any one, for which he is amenable to society, is that which concerns others. In the part which merely concerns himself, his independence is, of right, absolute. Over himself, over his own body and mind, the individual is sovereign.[4]

What this means is that the only good reason to restrict conduct, including speech or expression, is to prevent harm to others. Harmless conduct – even if it is regarded as immoral – should not be restricted. Even some harm should be permitted, such as some harms to which a person consents. Persuasive speech may create a risk of harm, but this alone is also insufficient to justify restricting that speech. On the other hand, some speech is very likely to cause harm directly through its persuasive effects. The Harm Principle affords no protection to speech that, for example, contains a specific and immediate incitement to criminal conduct. Nor does the Harm Principle afford protection to shouting a false cry of "fire" in a crowded theatre.

But why should we accept the Harm Principle? Why not, for example, censor immoral speech or false speech? According to Mill, one reason why we should never suppress speech is that an expressed opinion might be correct.[5] Or, even if we are quite certain that an opinion is wrong, its presence reaffirms our own opinions – keeping them from degrading into mere dogma. Freedom, or autonomy, in general is valuable at least in part because it allows individuals to experience and observe a variety of experiments in living. A diversity of experiments in living allows people to learn from one another, and thus contributes to long-term progress for society as a whole, while also allowing people to develop their individuality as human beings. Ultimately, individuals are the best judge of what is best for them. Individuals have unique access to information about what makes them happy.

According to this principle, then, pornography should not be restricted – or censored – unless it causes harm. In accordance with respect for individual autonomy and freedom of expression, the state ought to allow individuals to live according to and express their own values, rather than imposing values upon them and restricting their conduct – unless the conduct causes harm to others (and even then the state ought to consider whether restricting the conduct will result in greater harm than the harm that the particular conduct might cause). The consumption of pornography may be seen as merely a matter of private morality. Pornography produced by consenting adults for private adult consumption causes harm to no one else, and thus is not the state's business.

Nevertheless, while the intention of pornography is to arouse, not to harm or persuade people to cause harm, it may actually cause harm or implicitly endorse a viewpoint that leads to harm. For example, it may be that violent pornography endorses violence against women, and that consumers of such pornography are thereby more likely to commit acts of violence against women. In this case, pornography may not be protected by the Harm Principle. Indeed, this is just the right approach to attack pornography and support censorship within the context of political liberalism – namely, to show that pornography either constitutes a harm itself or directly leads to harm. The remaining sections address these kinds of attempts to support censorship of pornography within this context.

A Clear and Present Stranger

If violent pornography directly causes harm or alters its consumers' desires or beliefs by non-persuasive or non-rational means, then censorship of it would not violate the Harm Principle. What is meant by "non-persuasive" or "non-rational" means? We may distinguish between two ways of influencing people.[6] Non-rational influence would include speech of a certain pitch that excites the aggression center in the brains of its listeners, causing in them strong urges to act violently even if they do not understand what is being spoken; or a command that affects your behavior only if you understand its meaning, but which is given to you while you are drugged or under hypnosis. Persuasive or rational influence would include, for example, articles written by academics, speeches made by campaigning politicians to voters, or the speech of fundamentalist ministers to their congregations. The important difference is whether the influence allows the listener to shape his or her response or whether the influence renders the listener powerless in responding. Non-rational, persuasive speech, if it incites the listener to violence, for example, is not protected by the Harm Principle.

Does pornography have a kind of non-rational influence on its consumers such that they are compelled to violence? Of course, arousal itself is harmless. What needs to be shown is that violent pornography causes violence against women through a substantial non-rational means. If it were shown to instill in its consumers an ideology of violence toward women through a process similar to subliminal suggestion or hypnosis, for example, then censorship of it would not violate the Harm Principle.[7]

A ban on violent pornography to reduce male violence against women may in fact be consistent with the Harm Principle. The principle does not protect speech insofar as it non-rationally affects its hearers' mental states, and perhaps violent pornography affects its consumers in just that way.[8]

Even if it could be shown that pornography has this affect on its consumers, it may be difficult to argue that it is any more influential in this way than misogynistic jokes or songs, or other non-pornographic speech that condones sexual violence. We must also consider whether pornography's negative effect is greater than that produced by other professions in which women largely service men (for example, secretarial labor). There may be some differences.[9] First, people might believe that it is especially wrong, so it will then disproportionately fuel negative images. Second, the particular image of women in pornography is more of an image of inferiority than that of women secretaries. Nevertheless, a policy of censorship would not only fail to promote the wellbeing of women, but also exacerbate associated wrongs.[10] It would render women who work in the pornography industry more vulnerable (by pushing it "underground" rather than eliminating it), raise the dilemma of the "double bind" (i.e., it would deprive some poor women of one way to improve their economic condition), and reflect a view of women that contributes to their inequality (for example, the view that sex makes women dirty). This concern may be grounds for some moral condemnation, but not for censorship. Various kinds of speech (for example, sexist jokes), books, television, cinema, and video games may also have similar influences on their consumers, but this is insufficient reason to legally ban them.

Another possibility is that pornography reinforces preexisting desires or urges to harm women by conditioning, in which behaviors or desires are reinforced. A consumer of pornography may desire to commit acts of sexual violence against women, and this desire is reinforced by pornography through the strong, rewarding pleasures of arousal, masturbation, and orgasm. Reinforcement of such desires increases the likelihood that the consumers will act according to those desires against real women. But does pornography reinforce harmful desires? Perhaps the desire that gets reinforced is, for example, a desire to masturbate to violent pornography. In fact, if this use of pornography is a kind of self-reinforcing catharsis, then censoring it could be counterproductive, increasing rather than decreasing actual violence.

Perhaps pornography conditions its consumers to be sexist – to desire to control women or seek out submissive sexual partners. Perhaps arousal through pornography reinforces a desire to keep women politically and

⚡

economically subordinate in the real world. Even if this is the case, however, sexist pornography may not be alone in contributing to these desires. Traditional Judeo-Christian-Islamic teachings about women, marriage, and family, for example, may play a similar role. If such teachings are protected by the Harm Principle despite their contribution to sexism, then pornography, to the extent that it contributes to sexism, is also protected.

On the other hand, violent pornography may be a far more potent conditioner than anything else we have compared it to in this section, including sexist, but non-violent pornography.[11] Consumers of sexist pornography likely do not fantasize about keeping women at home to raise children, but consumers of violent pornography might fantasize about committing the very acts that they are viewing. While the arousal caused by sexist pornography may give it no greater ability to reinforce sexism than that of sexist jokes, religious teachings, and the like, the arousal caused by violent pornography may have a much greater effect. It may reinforce a desire to sexually assault women. If consumers of violent pornography act on these desires, then violent pornography is contributing to an increased number of sexual assaults. Censoring pornography with the goal of reducing its availability may then reduce the total amount of sexual violence against women.

Nevertheless, as we have seen above, evidence is needed to support the claim of a direct link between the consumption of pornography and acts of violence – rather than merely the reinforcement of desires, which may or may not be acted upon. If consumption of pornography may only possibly contribute to harm, then it is still protected by the Harm Principle. Finally, even if satisfactory evidence was shown that violent pornography directly causes sexual violence, only a very specific type of pornography would be in trouble. Erotica and sexist, but non-violent, pornography would not be included in the objection – not unless it were shown that they too directly cause sexual violence. The objection that pornography should be censored because it directly leads to sexual violence is on shaky ground.

Enema of the State

An opponent of pornography might claim that the liberal approach to pornography fails to understand it in the context of women's subordination and inequality. The liberal approach excludes the patriarchal dimension of our society from scrutiny. In our society, relations between men and women are unequal. They occur in a context in which women are in a state of social, political, economic, and personal subordination to men, i.e., a patriarchal context. Seen in that context, pornography will be seen as playing a role in maintaining that subordination and inequality. Pornography may be seen as the portrayal of women as sexual objects for the satisfaction of male desires. The Harm Principle, insofar as it protects pornography in this context, is protecting expression that perpetuates the subordination of women. Or, perhaps censorship of pornography is consistent with the Harm Principle if we understand the concept of harm widely enough. The harm of pornography, on this view, is that it makes the patriarchal context arousing. The harm is in eroticizing subordination, and this is contrary to the value we all place on autonomy – a value which grounds our interest in the Harm Principle in the first place. We must consider whether limiting some freedom of expression may better serve the protection of autonomy overall.

One of the important differences we have pointed to between child pornography and other pornography is that other than in child pornography the people involved are consenting to their role in its production. Also, except perhaps in some of the most explicitly violent pornography, women portray women who consent to and enjoy their role in satisfying male sexual desires. The appearance of consent seems to let this pornography off the hook, especially in light of the Harm Principle. But consensual pornography allows for the eroticization of subordination. Pornography eroticizes this patriarchal context, but gives it the air of legitimacy by showing it in a context of consent. Pornography is thus playing a special role in sustaining a patriarchal regime. While censoring pornography may appear on the surface to be contrary to the value of autonomy, on closer inspection we may see that doing so actually promotes more autonomy overall – by restricting one means by which the patriarchal regime is perpetuated. What seems like a context of consent is really a disguised context of coercion – hidden perpetuation of patriarchy. The consent of women in pornography – both in the portrayals and in their participation in its production – is manufactured. Even if women themselves complain that they are consenting and thus no harm is being done, they are simply taken in by the patriarchal social context in which they are immersed.[12]

The failure of the liberal approach to recognize this objection to pornography is a result of failing to recognize that not only the state wields coercive power over individuals. Classes and groups also have and exercise this power. The Harm Principle limits the coercive power of the state, but fails to address – and may perpetuate – other pernicious social relations. Social oppression may be at least as powerful as political

TAIT SZABO

oppression, and is more easily disguised, such as by the appearance of consent. Pornography exerts a social coercion over men and women, a coercion that is masked by the appearance of consent. Not only does pornography target men – reinforcing the patriarchal regime in which they live – but also succeeds in getting women to cooperate in their oppression.

The problem with this objection is that it is difficult to demonstrate that pornography does this to any greater degree than many other elements of our social lives. We may agree that to make a complete determination of the moral status of pornography in our society we must consider the fact that in our society pornography happens to play a role of entrenching the beliefs that oppress women. We can agree that we ought to work to subvert patriarchal and oppressive beliefs and attitudes, but this is not best accomplished by censorship of everything that contributes. Literature directed at women that supports the subordination of women is perhaps far more objectionable on these grounds than pornography. For example, romance novels, insofar as they eroticize the subordination of women, may have a greater effect than pornography at sustaining a patriarchal status quo. Furthermore, there may be far more effective ways to sustain inequality than eroticization, especially for private consumption. Inequality pervades our social context in a variety of ways; why regard pornography as especially problematic? Literature or films that contain themes of domination of women, which are far more widely consumed, and which are presented in a much more familiar context, seem more problematic. So, too, with children's literature that aims at directing children to eventually adopt unequal adult roles (consider *Cinderella*).[13] To support censorship of pornography on these grounds would seemingly justify and require censoring far more than pornography – indeed, whatever supports male fantasies of domination or encourages women's fantasies of subordination. The objection really amounts not to an objection to sexually explicit materials, but rather to institutionalized inequality of men and women, in any medium.

Good Will Humping

The concerns above remind us to be careful to avoid false consciousness. While, for example, a female porn star may appear to be consenting to, benefiting from, and possibly even enjoying the activity, this may be because cultural forces have made her inadvertently complicit in her oppression. Her consent may be an illusion. Nevertheless, we must also be wary of other social forces, such as religious teachings and traditional sexual morality. Our objections to, rather than our approval of, pornography may be the greater culprit in upholding a patriarchal status quo with its traditional gender roles and rules for sexual morality. Additionally, whatever harms may be associated with pornography under the best of conditions may be outweighed by the potential goods of pornography – among other possibilities pornography may be beneficial as sexual education (for anyone from beginner to the highly experienced), provide otherwise unavailable economic opportunities, and, let us not forget, provide hours of carnal enjoyment. So, stop worrying and enjoy your pornography, or, if it is not for you, at least leave your neighbors alone while they enjoy it.

NOTES

1   If the existence of snuff films is mere myth, it is just as well.
2   Except in some counties of Nevada.
3   www.caselaw.lp.findlaw.com/scripts/getcase.pl?court=us&vol= 488&invol=1311.
4   John Stuart Mill, *On Liberty* (Cambridge: Cambridge University Press, 2000), p. 13.
5   Ibid., chapters 2 and 3.
6   Danny Scoccia, "Can Liberals Support a Ban on Violent Pornography?" *Ethics* 106, 4 (1996): 785.
7   Ibid., pp. 786–7.
8   Ibid., p. 777.
9   Debra Satz, "Markets in Women's Sexual Labor," *Ethics* 106, 1 (1995): 81.
10 Ibid., pp. 81–5.
11 Scoccia, "Can Liberals Support a Ban on Violent Pornography?" p. 794.
12 David Dyzenhaus, "John Stuart Mill and the Harm of Pornography," *Ethics* 102, 3 (1992): 534–51.
13 Robert Skipper, "Mill and Pornography," *Ethics* 3, 4 (1993): 726–30.

CHAPTER 7

CHEATING WITH JENNA
Monogamy, Pornography, and Erotica

 Kelly was supposed to be out all evening, but her book group was cancelled at the last moment. She is secretly a bit relieved; it will be nice to relax with her boyfriend, Zach, and a glass of wine. When she gets home, she can hear Zach in the study. As she opens the door, Zach turns towards her, clearly startled, his face bright red and guilt-stricken. She takes one look at the computer screen and runs out of the room.

Kelly walked in on Zach masturbating while looking at pornography. She is very upset by this. She feels like Zach has betrayed her and their relationship. Using pornography, on his own, behind her back, seems almost like cheating. Kelly's reaction may be a little extreme, but it is not completely off the wall. Many people would feel betrayed if they found their partner using pornography alone. This essay will consider whether this reaction is reasonable: do partners have the right to forbid this kind of behavior, to feel wronged or betrayed by it?

I focus on the solo use of pornography by a person who is in a monogamous relationship. I consider cases like that of Zach and Kelly, where two partners have agreed, implicitly or explicitly, to be faithful to each other and yet one partner uses pornography on his or her own. There are many interesting issues about the use of pornography in general. However, I think that the solo use of pornography within monogamous relationships raises some special questions. When Kelly is upset by

Zach's masturbation in front of the computer, she feels that Zach has wronged *her*, betrayed *their relationship*. I want to explore whether there should be relationship-based restrictions on the use of pornography.

I will look at two different objections that a partner might make to the solo use of pornography. The first objection suggests that sexual activity using erotic material depicting another person is a kind of infidelity. I will argue against this suggestion. Although Kelly may feel betrayed, she has not been cheated on. I will then consider the suggestion that solo use of pornography by a partner is objectionable because it displays or involves attitudes, usually attitudes towards women, which are incompatible with a loving relationship. I will suggest that this objection holds against some, but not all, erotic material. The upshot of my discussion will be that whether Kelly's outrage is reasonable or not will depend upon the nature of the material Zach has been using.

Let us begin with the thought that by using pornography on his own Zach is being unfaithful to Kelly; he is "cheating with Jenna." After all, they are supposed to be in a monogamous relationship. Zach has been indulging in sexual activity that has involved another person – or at least the representation of another person. Isn't this a kind of cheating?

Zach and Kelly might have made some explicit agreement about the rules of their relationship. They may have agreed that solo use of pornography should count as cheating. However, very few couples actually do this. We assume that our partners will implicitly understand what is forbidden. Additionally, the way we govern our relationships is a *normative matter*: we can ask what rules a couple *ought* to accept, as well as what rules they actually accept. A couple might agree not to eat chocolate-chip cookies with anyone else. This is one of the rules of their relationship and breaking it would involve "cheating." We can evaluate this rule; barring special circumstances, it is a silly rule. It is unreasonable to forbid extra-marital cookie eating. In general, any relationship-based rule that restricts the partners' access to something valuable, such as cookies or sexual pleasure, requires some justification. Would it be a good idea for a couple to have a rule about monogamy that restricted the use of erotica? I shall suggest that the reasons that support adopting a rule of monogamy in the first place do not support an extended rule of monogamy which forbids the solo use of erotica. In fact, there are good reasons to permit the solo use of erotica within a monogamous relationship.

As I and my co-author Bryan R. Weaver have suggested elsewhere, the rules of monogamy involve two restrictions: sexual activity is restricted to relationships with a certain feature and the number of others with whom one can be in a relationship with that feature is restricted to one.[1] A monogamous person is only permitted to have sex with another if he is in a loving relationship (a relationship of erotic love) with that person; he is only permitted to be in such a relationship with one other person at a time.[2] Clearly, only the first of these restrictions will be relevant to the permissibility of solo use of pornography within a relationship. The consumer of pornography is not forming an additional relationship of erotic love. Thus, I shall focus only on the part of monogamy that restricts sex to loving relationships.

We argue that some, but not all, couples have good reason to be monogamous; that is, they have good reason to accept, and to keep faith with, each of the restrictions involved in monogamy. Again, in this essay I will focus on the first restriction: the restriction of sexual activity to loving relationships. Why does this make sense?

The nature of sex makes it natural for a couple to see sex as a significant activity. Sex is deeply connected to intimacy. It goes without saying that sex involves a high degree of physical intimacy. But sex also involves another kind of intimacy. It is a shared experience of intense pleasure. This pleasure is a product of the partners' interaction – it is pleasure found in and with the other. This intimate activity can be both symbolic of and partly constitutive of the love in the relationship. Thus, it is reasonable to attach great significance to sex – to see it as something that plays an important role within the relationship. I will call sex that has this kind of significance "lovemaking." It is reasonable (although not obligatory) to attach significance to all sexual intercourse involving either partner: the actions involved in sexual intercourse are special because they are seen as the things that the partners do as part of the intimate relationship. Once either partner sees sex as significant in this way, it will be hurtful if one partner has sex with someone outside the relationship with whom he or she is not in love. In having sex without love, the cheater implicitly denies that sex has the kind of significance that his partner understands it to have. The hurt partner sees the performance of those actions by either partner as lovemaking; the cheater is able to have sex without making love. This can undermine the partners' understanding of previous episodes of sex within the relationship. This will be deeply hurtful to the other partner. If loveless sex would cause reasonable hurt to one or both partners, it makes sense to restrict sex to loving relationships.[3]

If our argument is correct, it can make sense for partners to be monogamous and to see their commitment to the relationship as excluding non-loving sexual encounters. What does this imply about solo use of pornography? Should the rules of monogamy be extended to exclude solo masturbation using pornography? Should solo masturbation count as cheating?

This rationale for monogamy might appear to lead to restrictions on solo use of pornography. Like a one night stand, masturbation might be seen as loveless sex. Engaging in this kind of sexual activity could be seen as an implicit denial of the partners' understanding of sex as symbolic of and partly constitutive of the intimacy that they share.

However, I do not think that this argument goes through. For solo use of pornography to undermine the significance of sex within the relationship, it must be relevantly similar to the sex within the relationship. Unless solo use of pornography and sex with one's partner involve the same kind of act, solo use of pornography without love cannot be a denial that the partners' performance of acts of the kind is significant. Unless solo use of pornography involves having sex, it cannot undermine the connection between sex and the love in the relationship. Eating jelly-beans in September does not challenge the special connection between chocolate eggs and Easter.

We should draw a distinction between sex between partners and solo use of pornography. Solo use of pornography typically involves auto-masturbation. We *could* describe pornography based masturbation as a sex act that involves another person: the image of the model (let's call her Jenna) stimulates arousal and she will often play a role in the masturbator's fantasies. However, Jenna is involved in an attenuated sense. There is no real interaction between Zach and Jenna. This makes masturbation significantly different from lovemaking. Masturbation is clearly a *sexual* activity, guided by sexual arousal and usually leading to orgasm. However, it does not involve what we might call "sexual intercourse," referring not to penetrative sex but to sexual interaction between two or more persons. Unlike a casual affair, solo masturbation does not involve sexual intercourse without love, physical intimacy without emotional intimacy. The significance of lovemaking comes from the fact that it is a deeply pleasurable and highly intimate interaction between partners. Thus the absence of interaction in masturbation means that this solo activity need not be seen as undermining the significance of lovemaking.[4] Partners may see sexual *intercourse* as the significant activity. This would lead to a norm of monogamy that restricts only sexual intercourse, not auto-masturbation, to loving relationships.

Kelly might respond that although there has been no actual sexual interaction between Zach and Jenna, Zach has been fantasizing about

₥ FIONA WOOLLARD

Jenna, perhaps picturing himself having sex with Jenna, and he has used this fantasy to bring himself to orgasm. So Zach has been fantasizing about loveless sexual intercourse, endorsing the idea of sexual intercourse without love and thereby implicitly denying that sexual intercourse is something significant connected to the love in their relationship.

This response treats fantasy as a type of wishful thinking. It assumes Zach wants to take the place of the hero of his fantasy. However, fantasies need not be this way. People fantasize about situations they would find very uncomfortable in real life, for example, fantasies about sex in public seem to be common. I suggest that we should understand Zach as imaginatively taking the viewpoint of a person who has casual sex with Jenna. His enjoyment in this imagined viewpoint does not imply that *he* wants to have sex with Jenna. The character in the fantasy may be called "Zach" and may even look a little like Zach (although probably better looking). Nonetheless, he is not Zach. Zach can imagine this situation while still maintaining that sexual intercourse is something significant for him because of its role in his relationship with Kelly, so that he would not want to have sex with someone he did not love.

There is all the difference in the world between fantasizing about sex with Jenna and having sex with Jenna. If Zach had actually had sex with Jenna he would by this act have threatened the significance of sex for him and Kelly. He would be performing an act in which sex is separated from love. In fantasizing about sex with Jenna, Zach merely imagines being a person for whom sex and love are separable. There is no separation for him in fact. This has two aspects: first, Zach is not involved in an actual case of loveless sex, but merely an imagined one. Secondly, it is not Zach but "Zach" who has loveless sex. For Zach himself, sex is still bound up with his love for Kelly. This means that sex can continue to play a significant role, expressing and constituting the love in their relationship.

The key thought behind the constraint against loveless sex is that when the partners have sex this is both a way of expressing their intimacy and partly constitutive of that intimacy. When they have sex, they make love. For one of the partners to have sex with someone he does not love undermines the significance of sex within the relationship because it involves *him* performing the usually significant act without its usual significance. If he has sex without love, then his actions in lovemaking no longer have the same meaning, they no longer express or constitute loving intimacy. But merely imagining or fantasizing about loveless sexual intercourse does not involve either having loveless sex or seeing loveless sex as a real possibility for him. It remains true that when he has sex, this is a way of making love.

It is a crucial part of my argument that Zach can see sex as bound up with love *for him* without condemning all casual sex. He can imagine, and even enjoy the thought of, casual sex between "Zach" and Jenna. This directly contradicts John Finnis's claim that attaching the appropriate significance to marital sex requires "one's conscience's complete exclusion of non-marital sex acts from the range of acceptable and valuable human options."[5] Finnis argues that viewing casual sex as permissible involves "a present, albeit conditional willingness" to engage in casual sex. If casual sex is good for others, then universalizability implies that it would be good for me if I were in the same circumstances.[6] But my monogamous relationship involves seeing sex in a particular way, which rules out any willingness, even conditional willingness, to have casual sex. Finnis concludes that monogamous partners must see casual sex as *generally* impermissible, impermissible for all.

Nonetheless, I think it is possible for monogamous partners to attach significance to sex, the kind of significance that rules out casual sex *for them*, while seeing casual sex as acceptable, or even good, for others. For a monogamous couple, sex is connected to love *because* of the role it plays in the relationship. For those who are not in such relationships, sex need not be connected to love. The monogamous couple can recognize and endorse these other approaches to sex, without undermining their own understanding of sex as something emotionally significant *for them*. The ground for the partners' rejection of casual sex is their relationship. Willingness to engage in casual sex that is conditional on the absence of this ground is very different from current willingness to have casual sex. Current willingness to have casual sex involves being willing to have casual sex while in a relationship in which sex is understood as an act with deep emotional significance. This implicitly undermines the significance of the sex in the relationship in a way that can be deeply hurtful to the other. Conditional willingness to have casual sex does not undermine the significance that the relationship bestows upon sex.

I have argued that solo use of pornography, even if it involves fantasizing about sex with the model and even if it is utterly loveless, need not undermine the emotional significance of sex within the relationship. However, masturbation, with or without pornography, may not be quite as loveless and lacking in significance as some might think. As Woody Allen's Alvy Singer puts it, "Hey, don't knock masturbation. It's sex with someone I love."[7]

We have, I hope, left behind the days when masturbation was feared to be physically harmful, turning boys blind and causing hairy palms, but there is still a tendency to look down on masturbation. Some still see it as emotionally harmful, fostering a selfish or base attitude to sex. At best, it is seen as a method for releasing sexual tension when the preferable option – sex with your partner – is unavailable. However, I claim that masturbation has a valuable role to play in a person's sexual life and that solo use of pornography is a particularly effective type of masturbation for playing this role.

Masturbation, particularly when coupled with fantasy, is a personal sexual exploration. It enables one to make discoveries about both one's body and one's mind. By exploring one's body, one can find out what sensations one enjoys, which areas of one's body are particularly sensitive. Fantasy allows us to explore the sexual side of our minds, which ideas and images we finds arousing.

Pornography or erotica can be a great resource for such exploration. First, and most obviously, pornography can provide the stimulus to get things started – the erotic image is a springboard from which one's imagination can leap. Additionally, pornography might make accessible sexual alternatives which one had never thought about before. Wendy McElroy observes, "Pornography provides women with a real sense of what is sexually available to them: masturbation, voyeurism, exhibitionism, sex with a stranger, in a group, with the same sex. . . . It has been called 'The Hitchhiker's Guide to the Sexual Galaxy.'"[8] It increases the range of options available for fantasy, so the woman is not limited by her own imagination. As well as simply increasing the available options, pornography also helps to make the fantasy more vivid. We can vicariously experience the depicted situations. We acquire a sense of how the situation feels and of our response to it.

Such sexual exploration can be good for relationships. As magazines for young women often remind us, a good groundwork of solo sexual exploration makes it far easier to know what to do and what to ask for during sex with a partner. Masturbation brings with it an understanding of the physical stimuli to which each partner's body responds best, which can be used to help the partners please each other. Partners may also try out ideas suggested to them by erotic material. For this, it is important that the partners be given space to perform such explorations on their own. Solo exploration allows us to discover our reactions to certain fantasies without commitment. We are able to stop whenever we wish, or to continue as far as we want, without worrying about disappointing or discomforting our partner.

But more than this, personal exploration and enjoyment of one's own sexuality is valuable in itself. Masturbation is an important part of a person's proper relationship to their sexuality. In part, this is a matter of self-knowledge and self-understanding: how can a person truly endorse their sexuality if they have not explored it fully? In part, it is a matter of lavishing positive attention on one's own body, focused on one's own pleasure. Masturbation will never be a substitute for sexual intercourse. It lacks the shared intimacy, the action and reaction that characterises sex with a partner. Nonetheless, masturbation has its own good points. In sexual intercourse, when done properly, each partner is always at least partially focused on the other, concerned to ensure the other's pleasure, responsive to the other's needs. In masturbation, the agent focuses on their own pleasure. This licence to be totally self-centered (without being selfish) can enable the agent to find a type of satisfaction that may not be available with a partner. Additionally, the acceptance that it is alright to focus on one's own pleasure in this way, that one's own pleasure is something worth pursuing, is part of self-acceptance.

Masturbation plays an important role in a cluster of aspects of a healthy sexuality: self-focused sexual pleasure, understanding and acceptance of one's sexuality, the exploration of new sexual techniques and experiences. Pornography is a useful tool, helping masturbation to fulfil these various roles. We thus have reason to reject the extended version of monogamy which forbids the solo use of pornography. As I argued above, there are significant differences between solo use of pornography and casual sex. Forbidding casual sex need not imply forbidding solo use of pornography. The fact that solo use of pornography can play a valuable role in a person's sex life gives us reason to choose the weaker version of monogamy – monogamy that forbids casual sex but not pornography.

However, Kelly might object to Zach's use of pornography for reasons other than a supposed violation of monogamy. She might say that Zach's use of pornography reveals something about Zach that undermines their relationship. Zach is not the man that she thought she knew. She is hurt by the attitude towards women that is displayed by his use of pornography.

Zach is supposed to be in a loving sexual relationship with Kelly, a relationship based on equal respect. Even if, as I argued earlier, we do not necessarily wish to act out our fantasies personally, sexual enjoyment is a kind of endorsement. It involves seeing what is depicted as desirable. Thus, if Zach is turned on by degrading pictures of women, if his sexual enjoyment is rooted in the mistreatment, subjugation, or objectification of women, his relationship with Kelly is undermined. This is in part

FIONA WOOLLARD

because, as Thomas Scanlon notes, there is something unsatisfactory about a personal relationship, be it love or friendship, with someone who does not recognize your independent moral standing.[9] A truly loving relationship with a woman requires appropriate respect for women in general. If Zack sees women as less than persons, he must see Kelly as less than a person. He may think that as *his woman* she should be treated with respect, but he does not recognize her status as a person in her own right. In the case of degrading pornography, there is an additional threat. Sex plays an important role in Kelly and Zach's relationship. As his lover, she has particular reason to be concerned with the way Zach relates to women sexually. If Zach finds sexual enjoyment in the degradation of women, this casts a disturbing light on his sexual intercourse with Kelly. She may find it impossible to forget, impossible to relate to him in the same way.

Alice Walker's protagonist in "Porn" has this kind of reaction to her lover's pornography collection of "page after page of women . . . bound, often gagged. Their legs open. Forced to their knees." Later, the couple try to make love. Walker describes the woman's visceral reaction in two words: "She gags." After seeing this other side to her lover's sexuality, his enjoyment of material she finds "disgusting," "sleazy," and "depressing," she can no longer make love with him.[10]

Some people enjoy sadomasochism or bondage and dominance, often as part of a loving relationship. They claim that, when properly understood, these activities need not involve objectionable attitudes to others. For the purposes of this essay I do not need to debate this issue. All I want to argue is that *if* the pornography used endorses objectionable attitudes to women *then* this will have significant ramifications for the supposedly loving sexual relationship. Some types of pornography are objectionable in this way; anyone who finds them sexually arousing has failed to recognize women as persons. Andrea Dworkin describes a series of photographs of "a woman slicing her breasts with a knife, sticking a sword up her vagina."[11] Erotic pleasure based on serious harm, on terror, on torture, is incompatible with a loving relationship. Whether more nuanced forms of dominance and pain-play have the same implications, I leave a deliberately open question. Nonetheless, where it is reasonable for the consumer's partner to interpret pornography as misogynistic, it is reasonable for her to object, to challenge the consumer to explain why things are not as they appear. There is a tension in the requirement that the consumer defend his turn-ons to his partner; part of the value of private sexual fantasy is as a safe place to explore one's sexuality without fear of consequences. Unfortunately, this tension, this compromise of sexual freedom, seems an inevitable result of the fact that in forming a loving sexual relationship with someone we give them a stake in our sexuality.

Does all pornography consumption involve objectionable attitudes towards women? Anti-porn feminists sometimes incorporate the mistreatment of women into the definition of pornography. According to Dworkin and MacKinnon, pornography "means the graphic sexually explicit subordination of women through pictures and/or words."[12] Subjugating pornography is contrasted with empowering erotica. However, this does not seem to fit with ordinary language, in which almost any explicit "naughty" picture or book will be called "porn." The word "erotica" has overtones of sepia photographs or prints, porn with pretentions of grandeur rather than a particularly good attitude to women. I think that we need a new term, a term for violent pornography, so that condemnation of this type of material is not taken to imply condemnation of all erotica. Whatever words we use, we should understand that erotic material can fully recognize, and be fully compatible with, the robust autonomous personhood of its subject. A woman (or a man) can be depicted as a sexual creature, in a sexual pose, without being degraded. Unless we think sexuality is itself degrading, why should we see sexual depiction as degrading?

I have argued that using pornography is not a form of cheating. The most reasonable norm of monogamy will not forbid the solo use of pornography. Solo use of pornography is not a kind of casual sex. It does not undermine the significance of sex within a relationship. Additionally, we have reason to adopt a norm that permits the solo use of pornography, because solo masturbation and fantasy play an important role in a good sexuality and pornography can be an important tool for this. Nonetheless, the use of some types of pornography can be a betrayal. The erotic endorsement of the degradation of women can undermine the supposedly equal loving sexual relationship. Some, but not all, pornography is objectionable in this way. Some erotic material portrays women as sexual subjects, enjoying and controlling their own sexuality. The use of such material is compatible with, and may indeed contribute to, a monogamous loving sexual relationship.

NOTES

1 We originally stated that the norm of monogamy restricts the number of loving sexual relationships to one. I have modified this to avoid ruling out masturbation prematurely. For as Dave Monroe pointed out to me, the restriction

FIONA WOOLLARD

to a single loving relationship seems to rule out being in a loving relationship with oneself and in a loving relationship with another at the same time. Some relationship-based norms may forbid masturbation, but the common-sense norm of monogamy does not do so. Restrictions on masturbation would be based on the inappropriateness of self-directed sexual activity, rather than on the claim that loving oneself and loving another involves too many relationships of erotic love.

2 Bryan R. Weaver and Fiona Woollard, "Marriage and the Norm of Monogamy," *The Monist* 91, 3–4 (2008): 507.

3 Ibid., pp. 515–17. Weaver and Woollard argue that whether loveless sexual activity undermines the significance of sex within the loving relationship will depend upon how partners see the significance of sex. They may see sex within the relationship as significant, but not see all sexual intercourse involving either partner as significant. Our argument for monogamy depends on the claim that some partners reasonably attach significance to all sexual intercourse involving either partner.

4 There is a difference between the cheater who claims that casual sexual inter-course is different from lovemaking and the solo masturbator who claims that auto-masturbation is different from lovemaking. Casual sexual inter-course is still sexual intercourse – still the same physically intimate interac-tion to which a partner can reasonably attach significance. Although a partner might attach significance to sex in general (including auto-masturbation), the important differences between auto-masturbation and sexual inter-course and the important role masturbation can play in a person's sex life (which I will defend below) suggest that this understanding of the signifi-cance of sex is not reasonable.

5 John Finnis, "The Good of Marriage and the Morality of Sexual Relations: Some Philosophical and Historical Observations," *American Journal of Jurisprudence* (1997): 123. Finnis classifies as non-marital, and condemns, sex between unmarried or homosexual partners in committed relationships as well as masturbation and casual sex. I wholly disagree with this condem-nation, but will not discuss this here. These aspects of Finnis's argument are not relevant to the point at issue.

6 Ibid., pp. 122–3.

7 Woody Allen (dir.) *Annie Hall*, Rollins-Joffe Productions, 1977.

8 Wendy McElroy, *XXX: A Woman's Right to Pornography* (New York: St. Martin's Press, 1995), p. 130.

9 Thomas Scanlon, *What We Owe to Each Other* (Cambridge, MA: Belknap Press, 1998), p. 165.

10 Alice Walker, "Porn," in *You Can't Keep a Good Woman Down* (New York: Harcourt Brace, 1981), pp. 77–84. Reprinted in Drucilla Cornell (ed.) *Feminism and Pornography* (Oxford: Oxford University Press, 2000), pp. 600–5.

11 Andrea Dworkin, "Pornography and Grief," in *Letters from a War Zone* (London: Martin Secker and Warburg, 1987). Reprinted in Cornell, *Feminism and Pornography*, p. 43.

12 Andrea Dworkin and Catharine A. MacKinnon, *Pornography and Civil Rights: A New Day for Women's Equality* (Minneapolis: Organizing Against Pornography, 1988), p. 138.

CHAPTER 8

CELEBRITY SEX TAPES
A Contemporary Cautionary Tale

 That the Internet has played a significant role in the development and viewing of pornography goes without saying. One surprising area of pornographic evolution stems from the availability of privately recorded pornography online, perhaps the most popular and influential being celebrity sex tapes. Since the release of the Pamela Anderson and Tommy Lee sex tape in 1998, celebrity sex tapes have garnered a stronghold in pornography, specifically on the Internet. As interest in celebrity sex tapes rises so does availability as well as acceptability by the consumers and participants. The celebrities involved in such tapes are as diverse as the field of their profession. Celebrities such as Pamela Anderson, Paris Hilton, Vern Troyer, Dustin Diamond, Kelsey Grammar, Kim Kardashian, Amy Fisher, Collin Farrell, Chyna Doll (Joanie Lauren), John Edwards, and Jessica Sierra represent only a small sample of celebrities involved in some way with sex tapes. In some cases, the tapes are recorded and released without the knowledge or permission of the celebrity. In other instances, the scandal consists only of the celebrity's blocking the release of the tape, or the denial of an alleged tape. Some others, however, have intentionally recorded and released tapes to further their careers.

While filming oneself can provide a means of extending sexual expression and exploration, these examples may provide poignant lessons. On the one hand, these tapes have encouraged others to explore the thrill or intimacy that private taping can offer. Yet, on the other hand, these celebrity sex tapes provide a more cautionary tale. They remind us that there are risks associated with filming one's sexual activities. While the act of taping may enhance sexual experiences in one way or another, the public release of the tape may be quite traumatic. What seems to be forgotten is that private sexual intimacy takes on different meaning when exposed to public eyes, especially when it is done without permission. Furthermore, the demand for private tapes, celebrity or not, is rising. The market of home recorded or even amateur porn is expanding exponentially for several reasons, only one of which is the low cost and high availability of privately recorded porn. This ought to bring up considerations about trust, privacy, and distribution when thinking about filming one's sex acts. However, the increased amount of personally filmed pornography indicates that either these considerations are not often made or are not compelling enough to dissuade individuals from filming themselves.

Defensible Taping

People's sex lives may be recorded for a variety of reasons. Before discussing the impact and consequences of private pornography or home porn, it is necessary to first identify when it, and/or its release, may be justified. The first and perhaps most obvious criterion is that the participants must be consenting adults. In order for the tapings to be justified all involved parties must have autonomously chosen to engage in the act. This means that the people involved must have consented to do so voluntarily. Furthermore, they must be as fully informed about the circumstances as possible. Under this model, the taping of an individual without her or his consent would not be ethically justified because it is a violation of the individual's privacy rights and autonomy. For example, hiding a camera to tape someone without her or his knowledge would not be an example of justified taping; nor would be telling your partner that the tape recorder is off, or does not have a recording medium installed (such as tape, a DVD, memory card, and so on), or any other similar deception. However, if consenting adults agreed to tape themselves having sex there would not (at this juncture) be a strong moral objection to the recording.

In addition to consenting to taping the involved individuals must establish the conditions under which the tape is made and/or distributed. They must establish and agree upon whether the tape is intended only for private use or if it may be distributed publically. In the former case, the agreement makes any release of the tape unjustified in that it violates privacy rights, self-determination, and trust – all features that are essential to sex. However, in the latter type of agreement the tape can be released under the conditions that the involved parties agreed upon. Wrestling personality Chyna and her partner allegedly brought their sex tape to a porn production company for distribution. In such a case, both the recording and distribution would be justified on the grounds that they have consented to, established, and agreed upon terms of release.

The Public Appeal

For many, the appeal of watching celebrity sex tapes comes not just from sexual interest but from a celebrity obsessed culture. In the United States, for example, paparazzi follow celebrities non-stop, documenting every behavior from the mundane to the more salacious. While magazines that sport a celebrity's latest trip to the grocery store *sans* makeup will sell some copies, magazines that show celebrities in compromising situations will sell in droves. It seems all the more so that documentation of celebrities having sex will appeal to a considerable audience. This interest can stem from two basic elements. First, we have created a culture that glorifies celebrities and has elevated them to a level of importance above and beyond other cultural or social figures. Entire enterprises have been created to connect the lives of celebrities to the lives of regular people.

Second, as a result, people feel a connection to the celebrities. The more the public knows about a celebrity, the closer they feel to that person (even if it is still in a distanced voyeuristic manner) and this connection creates higher levels of interest. Reconsider the previous statement about going to the grocery store. Every day, millions of women go to the grocery store without makeup in their least flattering outfits, yet this garners no national attention. However, if that woman is Eva Longoria Parker the outing will get attention from magazines, webzines, and perhaps even news or TV coverage. Likewise, if a sex tape of a no-named couple is released the public interest will probably be relatively low (unless the tape shows something of interest beyond being homemade porn) in the absence of an impetus to garner interest. However, if the tape is of someone familiar or known, personally or distantly, the interest in the tape rises. If, for example, the no-named couple are colleagues, neighbors, or friends of yours, you may have an increased desire to see the tape. People have curiosity about the lives of others that is intensified by relationships, which creates an appeal to seeing others (especially others we have relationships with) in compromising situations. Since we live in a culture where we feel like we "know" celebrities, this desire extends to them as well. Compound that with our obsession with celebrity behaviors and there is a clear explanation for the public demand for celebrity sex tapes; we're obsessed with them and are intrigued by seeing people we know (or have an interest in) caught in inopportune situations.

Sexual Appeal

For others, though, the intrigue is not just a desire to look into the lives of celebrities. Several of the reasons people give for watching porn in general give insight into why there is a social interest in celebrity sex tapes. One such reason is that there is an erotic appeal to voyeurism. People have expressed that the sheer act of viewing others engaged in sexual acts is arousing.[1] In this vein, celebrity sex tapes fulfill a sexual desire to see others in sexual scenarios.

Another appeal to pornography is that it elevates one's ability to fantasize. Porn provides viewers with the means to expand their sexuality by offering a variety of new sexual images and possibilities. This enables the viewer to fantasize that she or he is engaged in the displayed acts. Additionally, the viewer is able to imagine that she or he is engaged in the acts with the porn stars. For some, this provides an opportunity to "have sex with" someone who would otherwise be out of her or his league.[2] However, celebrity sex tapes have additional elements that may be absent in traditional pornography.

First, celebrity sex tapes have additional voyeuristic appeals beyond traditional porn. This is closely related to the earlier claim that we are obsessed with celebrities. With celebrity sex tapes, you're not just seeing people having sex, you're seeing famous people having sex. In our culture, this may be the penultimate form of celebrity watching: viewing them in their most intimate moments. Additionally, a person not only gets to view the sex but can also become engaged in it. By viewing celebrities having sex one can become involved (granted, in a very distanced and removed way) in the act; it is an opportunity to participate in sex with a celebrity. Celebrity sex tapes strengthen and elevate the ability to imagine oneself having sex with a celebrity. When watching the tapes, one can engage in a sexual encounter with a celebrity and can imagine oneself as participating in what has been recorded. For most, this is the closest they will ever get to having sex with a celebrity. Furthermore, with the idealization of celebrities, this provides the opportunity to imagine oneself having sex with what has become the most coveted class of society, an opportunity that would be impossible outside of pornography.

The Allure of Taping

Why people are compelled to watch celebrity sex tapes may seem obvious. However, given the public demand for celebrity sex tapes, one may question why a celebrity would make a sex tape. The allure of making a sex tape is that it may add to the excitement of sex. Taping oneself adds elements of the taboo and intensifies the voyeurism; it creates a visual stimulus wherein oneself and one's partner(s) are the ones being seen. For some, the idea of being watched can be as arousing as watching others. However, many hesitate to experiment with actually being watched. Taping oneself mimics the allure of being watched with presumed controls over who will actually be able to view the tapes.

Furthermore, taping oneself extends the porn experience. When one merely watches porn, involvement in the sex is entirely fantasy. There is no real connection, engagement, or participation. However, if you tape yourself your involvement is real and is at the highest level possible. Watching your previous sexual encounters can be more arousing than watching professional porn because you will be drawing on, and reliving, the acts. But, given the demand for celebrity sex tapes, a certain level of risk is involved in this type of sexual exploration; the likelihood that the tape will be released is phenomenally high.

For those who voluntarily tape themselves (that is, those who are aware they are being taped), there are a variety of additional motivations. For some, the taping occurs while within a long-term or serious relationship. In these instances, the celebrity may honestly believe that the tape will be made for private use only. In such circumstances there is a high level of trust. The celebrity honestly believes that the tape will not be leaked and that only the couple will view it. In such scenarios, the taping is an extension of that trusting relationship; it is a means of expressing the intimacy, trust, and respect in their sex life. This extension of trust can be sexually enticing and may contribute to the motivation to tape. The celebrity does not believe the risk of the tape being released is high. She or he believes that the trust within the relationship creates control over the viewing of the tape and that it is relatively safe from public access.

Motivations for Release

For others, however, sex tapes have been a lucrative career move. Paris Hilton may not have taped her evening with then-boyfriend Rick Saloman with the intention of public distribution. However, when a porn distribution company acquired the tape, Paris opted to permit the tapes to be sold. As a result, Paris saw a boom in her career.[3] For celebrities like Paris, the release of a sex tape can accelerate a person from a barely known into a household name. In such cases, a sex tape can create an elevation to celebrity status.

Others have picked up on the PR magic of sex tapes and have opted to record and release tapes to boost a dwindling career. Some celebrities, such as Kelli McCarty, have opted to fully immerse themselves into venturing into a career in pornography.[4] Other celebrities with whom the public has lost interest feel that a scandal can bring back the public attention and can revive their careers. Sex tapes tend to provide the perfect scandal opportunity. The public has an interest in sex tapes of celebrities past and present. Moreover, sex scandals no longer carry the penalty of social ostracism they once did. General acceptance of sexuality and sexual expression has risen. As a result, the social stigmas associated with the revelation that a person has had sex are not as strong as they used to be. Thus, while there are still some taboos and associated concerns with the release of a sex tape they no longer guarantee the end of one's career. Instead, a celebrity sex tape tends to bring more public attention to the celebrity, which usually increases career opportunities *even if* the response to the tape is negative. Because of this potential career boost, filming a sex tape may seem like a quick and easy way to put oneself back in the limelight.

The Complications of Releasing a Sex Tape

However, while some people may choose to film a sex tape with the intention of releasing it for career opportunities, this is not always the case. The fact that people enjoy celebrity sex tapes and are generally more accepting about sexuality does not guarantee that a sex tape will have desirable outcomes. The release of a sex tape can be damaging in several different ways. The first is the means by which the tape is released. If the tape was filmed without one's knowledge or consent the existence and release of the tape can be psychologically traumatic. Additionally, the release of a tape can be damaging to a public image; for celebrities, one's image can often determine one's career. For example, in 2006 the courts ruled on the side of Colin Farrell, who wanted to stop the distribution of a sex tape on the grounds that the content would jeopardize his career.[5] Likewise, celebrities may rely on an image that does not correlate with the image sex tapes portray. In such cases tapes could undo years of image building and could hinder one's career. Moreover, more than career considerations may be at stake. A sex tape could be harmful to one's family life and other private relationships. The courts have often ruled in favor of the victims of released tapes, recognizing potential damages such as emotional distress and invasion of privacy.

Avoidance of these consequences is precisely why some celebrities do not consent to taping themselves, or agree only under the condition that the tapes will remain private. However, even within a trusting relationship, wherein a tape is made with the intention of privacy, the tape may still be released. There are three common ways this can happen: theft, accident, and betrayal. In the case of theft, an outside party in some way learns about the tape, steals it, and releases it. Since the person has acquired it by theft and violation of the celebrity's rights, the thief will probably be unable to make long-term profit from the tape. Instead, the thief will either have to settle for a one-time payment from a company that wants to distribute the tape (again, probably without serious compensation because the distribution company would not be the legal copyright holder) or would have to release it on the Internet with little or no compensation. When theft is involved, it may be difficult for the celebrity to keep the tape from being released due to the absence of sales. If a tape is freely distributed on the Internet it may be problematical to identify the source, and thus it may be difficult to seek legal action and compensation for damages. Furthermore, by the time the tape is discovered it may be too late to do anything about it. The damage has been done and there is not much to do by way of suitable compensation once one's private life has been exposed; once a reputation has been tarnished, it is hard to remove it from the court of public opinion or perception. Additionally, with the versatility of the Internet, once something has been posted and distributed online, it can be nearly impossible to remove.

Accidental releases have similar consequences. If a celebrity accidentally posts a video or pictures the damage to her or his reputation could be irremediable. The main problem this brings up is that individuals often forget the possibility of unintended release or the consequences (positive or negative) of released sex tapes. Once the world is shown a glimpse of a person in coitus it is nearly impossible to forget that image; from that moment on public perception of that individual will involve knowledge about her or his sex life. When a person decides to make a sex tape she or he may not be considering the fact that the tape may be released and that the associated consequences may not be desirable. The person most likely has an elevated sense of safety and control of the situation, assuming that the tape will only be used in the intended capacity and viewed only by the intended audience. Similarly, the person may assume total control of the material and may also be in denial about the likelihood of an accidental or unplanned release.

When Trust Fails

An additional level of denial comes from assumptions about trust. It is easy to put utter faith in one's partner when deeply in love and in the throes of passion. When the person one loves and trusts suggests filming sex, it is unlikely that one will consider long-term contingencies. However, a common way for home porn to be released is out of revenge or some other form of betrayal. Although we may argue that it's wrong, when a couple separates it is common for the partners to go back on promises made while in the relationship. Under these circumstances a jilted lover may decide to release a sex tape that was supposed to remain private. The ex-lover is likely motivated by pure spite. It could also be from a desire to make money; since the partner participated in the film, she or he may hold copyrights, and thus compensation is possible. The partner may also see this as an opportunity to improve her or his reputation. If the celebrity's lover has aspirations of being famous, a sex tape may help put the lover's name on the map. Finally, the partner may merely want the social bragging rights associated with having sex with a celebrity; being seen as a person who has slept with a celebrity may be ample, though illegitimate, cause for breaking one's promise not to release a tape.

A Failed Career Move

An additional concern for those considering releasing a tape is that tapes do not always improve one's career. If it seems like the celebrity is too eager, is fishing for attention, or is filming the tape out of desperation to be in the public eye, the level of scrutiny increases. Vanessa Hudgens, for example, has been under scrutiny for her most recent scandal (commonly referred to as "scandal 2009" to avoid confusion with the pictures leaked in 2007); critics speculate that the timing of the leaked nude pictures too closely corresponds with her latest movie release. Moreover, the act too closely mimics the previous scandal which was timed between the releases of her "High School Musical" movies.[6] The public does not often respond well to obvious ploys and crafted maneuvers. Additionally, any positive press that may come from a sex tape is likely to be fleeting. The sex tape may get one a quick advance in stardom but it will only sustain interest for a limited time. As the adage goes, fame has a half-life of 15 minutes. If a celebrity relied on a sex tape for a career boost, she or he may see a quick influx of opportunities. However, those opportunities will soon dwindle as well. The individual is then in a bit of a conundrum; releasing a sex tape probably will not be as effective the second, third, or fourth time around. As much as people enjoy watching celebrities, half of the allure is seeing the celebrities in new circumstances and vantage points. Once the public has seen a celebrity in a sex tape, future tapes would have to have escalated content in order to recreate high levels of public interest. After all, the intrigue is seeing a celebrity out of her or his public element, getting a glimpse of her or his private life. If the sex tapes become too frequent, it begins to appear merely as an extension of her or his career and she or he begins to share more in common with a porn star. Once this similarity is drawn, the arousal of curiosity begins to wane. For this and all of the above listed problems, it should be clear that recording a sex tape is a gamble and deciding to release the tape can be equally risky.

Why We Still Tape

Given the complexities of the consequences of celebrity sex tapes, it is questionable why non-celebrities may feel compelled to make their own sex tapes, especially in light of the potential damages. Many of the things that motivate celebrities also motivate non-celebrities. On the most basic level, taping sex with one's partner may be an extension of intimacy and trust. It may be an activity that helps a couple bond and expand their borders of trust. It is a means of showing one's vulnerabilities, but more so of showing comfort in entrusting one's partner with those vulnerabilities. The potential of this closeness has provided sufficient motivation for several couples.

Non-celebrities may not see celebrity sex tape scandals as cautionary tales because of the assumption that while there is a market for celebrity sex tapes, there is no comparable market for non-celebrities. Individuals assume that their personal tapes are safe from unwanted public viewings because the public would not be interested in the tapes. Without a market, the risk of release seems slim. Granted, it may be possible that tapes or pictures could be accidentally posted online, or that someone could accidentally come across the material. Perhaps an individual may even concede that in a worst-case scenario one's partner may show the video to others without permission. However, many assume that the people to whom the video will be shown will be small in number. So perhaps one may experience some embarrassment and a violation of privacy, but it would be on a small scale and the damages would be manageable. Operating under this assumption, individuals see the possible benefits as highly outweighing the possible risks.

This, however, ignores the vast markets in porn. Amateur and first-time porn has gathered a significant following. Individuals are willing to pay to access sites that feature homemade porn, and sites that are dedicated to non-celebrity girlfriends have a massive following as well. While celebrity sex tapes may generate more interest generally, private porn is quickly becoming a major segment of the porn industry. One reason is that home porn elevates the voyeuristic element; it is not a person who has sex as a profession, it is a normal person engaged in real, unstaged sex, unlike typical porn.

A rising issue, however, is not necessarily the fact that one's home porn may be released without one's consent. A growing concern is that with the increased acceptance of sex tapes, with our "pornified" culture, displaying one's sex life publically is almost becoming a status symbol among the young. Junior and high schools are finding themselves struggling to address the problem of sexually explicit content featuring their students. Young girls are taking nude pictures of themselves and texting them to groups of their classmates (often colloquially referred to as "sexting"). Explicit pictures and videos are posted online. The justification students give in these circumstances is that "porn is cool," that "this is what one has to do to be popular," and so on. This presents a new set of problems. Individuals are consenting both to the creation and distribution of sex tapes. However, in the case of minors, this brings up added concerns such as accusations of child pornography, and an absent ability to seriously consider the long-term consequences of the actions.

While porn may seem like the popular thing to do, the responses to it can be varied and unpredictable. This is true as well concerning adults. In both cases, a sex tape may sound like a great way to fit into certain circles, or to express one's sexuality. However, once a sex tape has been released it may be nearly impossible to "un-release" it. Once the content is out there and gets online, it is accessible for an indefinite amount of time and to an indefinite number of people. While porn is acceptable in some circles, it is not gladly received in all venues. It is not uncommon for people to be fired from their jobs for the posting of obscene personal material. Likewise a person could be denied a job, acceptance to schools and other opportunities for growth. While adults may have a better concept of the negative consequences of sex tapes, young adults or minors may not. No matter one's age, it may be difficult to grasp the full scope of potential or to fully understand the psychological effects of having others see oneself engaged in sex. Individuals are often incapable of truly predicting how she or he will feel after this material is shared. Nor may she or he be able to comprehend the actual scope of the act and associated consequences.

In a society that encourages sexual autonomy and sexual exploration, it is easy to see the appeal of sex tapes. On the personal level, the excitement of sexual enhancement and exploration associated with taping one's sex life is clearly alluring. On a more social level, the fact that individuals have often profited (financially, socially, or emotionally) from the release of a sex tape is undeniable as well. However, it is easy to be misled by these positive results, forgetting that there may be undesirable consequences as well. When a person consents to make a sex tape she or he needs to remember that there are no guarantees in this venue; release and social or professional fallouts are an all too real possibility. While celebrity sex tapes remind us of the appeal of sexual autonomy and voyeurism, they also warn us to act thoughtfully and carefully in this avenue. A person considering her or his own tape should thoughtfully and seriously consider the consequences before taping. Perhaps more importantly, as a culture, we should cultivate different habits regarding sexuality. We ought to remind people that in order for a sexually positive environment to exist, we need to maintain our promises and protect trust in the bedroom. Without trust, sex, or sex tapes, cannot be a fully enjoyable, or morally justified, experience.

NOTES

1 It should be noted that this applies specifically to people who are aroused by porn; there are without a doubt a large number of people who are not aroused, and may in fact be disturbed, by viewing others in sexual situations. For some of these accounts, see Pamela Paul, *Pornified: How Pornography is Damaging Our Lives, Our Relationships, and Our Families* (New York: Times Books, 2005), or Alan Soble, *Pornography, Sex and Feminism* (Amherst: Prometheus, 2002), or any of Soble's several related works.
2 For further discussion of this, see Soble, *Pornography, Sex and Feminism.*
3 Lola Ogunnaike, "Sex, Lawsuits and Celebrities Caught on Tape," *New York Times*, March 19, 2006. Online at www.nytimes.com/2006/03/19/fashion/sundaystyles/19tapes.html?_r=1 (accessed July 19, 2009).
4 Hollie McKay, "Pageants to Porn: Kelli McCarty Suffering 'Creepy' Treatment Since Launching XXX Career," *Fox News*, February 12, 2009. Online at www.foxnews.com/story/0,2933,491426,00.html (accessed August 25, 2009).
5 Ogunnaike, "Sex, Lawsuits and Celebrities Caught on Tape."
6 Saul Relative, "Vanessa Hudgens Naked Pictures Scandal: Is It a Box Office Draw?" *Associated Content*, Auguest 18, 2009. Online at www.associatedcontent.com/article/2076775/vanessa_hudgens_naked_pictures_scandal.html?cat=40 (accessed August 25, 2009).

PART IV

TALKING DIRTY

Legal Issues and Free Speech

JACOB M. HELD

CHAPTER 9

ONE MAN'S TRASH IS ANOTHER MAN'S PLEASURE

Obscenity, Pornography, and the Law

If the First Amendment guarantee of freedom of speech and press is to mean anything . . . it must allow protests even against the moral code that the standard of the day sets for the community.
(Justice William O. Douglas,
Roth v. United States, 354 US 476, 513, 1957)

Censors are, of course, propelled by their own neuroses.
(Justice William O. Douglas,
Ginsburg v. New York, 390 US 629, 655, 1968)

When most people think about our freedom of speech they recall the First Amendment: "Congress shall make no law . . . abridging the freedom of speech, or of the press."[1] People often take this to mean that anything we can utter or print is protected, that is, the government cannot prevent me from saying or writing whatever I want. There are obvious exceptions, such as yelling "fire" in a crowded theatre, or utterances that otherwise pose a "clear and present danger."[2] But barring these limited restrictions, we do seem able to say what we please. However, when the issue of pornography is raised, the Supreme Court has been of a different opinion. Although they are quick to distinguish pornography from obscenity, claiming that not all sexually explicit material is obscene, they have maintained that obscene speech is not protected by the First Amendment.[3] This position has led to a half-decade of contentious court cases.

The scope of the following essay is immense. As the title implies, this essay is going to attempt to cover the relationships between pornography and obscenity, obscenity and the law, and pornography and the law. Any one of these topics could and has filled books. So I will apologize in advance for any glaring omissions and the quick gloss some important issues receive. But let us begin at the beginning, with a brief history of obscenity laws.

Defining "Obscenity"

The history of obscenity laws in the United States is long. The first federal law restricting obscene material was the so called Comstock Act, 17 Stat. 598 (1873). Passed in 1873 by the 42nd Congress, this act restricted the trade, possession, manufacture, and distribution of "obscene" materials and materials of an "immoral nature," including information on contraception and abortion. The ability of the government to regulate such material went unquestioned until in *Roth v. United States*, 354 US 476 (1957) the Supreme Court considered the constitutionality of 18 USC 1461, which made punishable the mailing of "obscene, lewd, lascivious, or filthy" materials. The issue was not whether Congress had the authority to regulate the mail, since the court recognized this right under Article I, 8, cl. 7 of the US Constitution. Rather, if these laws are to be enforceable, then "obscenity" must be clearly defined.

In a contentious statement of principle, Justice William Brennan, delivering the opinion of the court, made the claim that the First Amendment does not protect obscene speech.[4] As justification he offered a brief history of state and federal laws that prohibited various forms of speech, from obscenity to blasphemy. Brennan concluded that the First Amendment was never meant to protect every utterance. Its ostensible purpose is to assure the "unfettered interchange of ideas for bringing about political and social changes desired by the people."[5] Thus, exceptions to First Amendment protections apply to those ideas or expressions that do not possess "redeeming social importance."[6] Obscenity is unprotected according to Brennan since it is not the kind of valuable speech that the First Amendment was meant to protect. So unless the court could find redeeming importance in Jenna Jameson's oeuvre – work which would be defined as obscene according to the definition below – it would not be protected under the First Amendment. This is a bold conclusion to draw, and a significant reframing of First Amendment law. Therefore, one effect of the *Roth* opinion was that it carved out an exception to First Amendment protections which up to that point were unacknowledged: obscene speech is not protected. Thus, it became paramount to define "obscenity." If obscene speech is not protected, then it is necessary in order to protect our free speech that the court clearly outline the parameters of obscenity so as not to infringe on legitimate, protected speech.

Justice Brennan offered the following definition of obscenity: "The standard for obscenity . . . is whether, to the average person, applying contemporary community standards, the dominant theme of the material, taken as a whole, appeals to prurient interest."[7] Brennan's intention was to offer a definition that was neither too broad nor too narrow. After all, if you are going to delineate a previously unacknowledged area of unprotected speech, that is, speech that can be suppressed at the whim of local legislators, then you are going to want to be precise to protect legitimate speech. Brennan wanted to include all and only obscene material. The problem is that any definition of "obscene" creates the class of utterances it picks out. What is "obscene" is determined by the definition, since obscenity is not something objective that is discovered in the natural order of things; it is a value judgment. Only after the criteria of evaluation have been enunciated and applied can the "obscene" be determined. Thus, the evaluation of the justices determines how broad "obscene" will be insofar as it is their interpretations that determine the scope of the obscene. Brennan's definition is thus as broad or narrow as the minds of those justices applying it, and therein lays the fatal flaw of obscenity laws. Since the law is applied at the discretion, or according to the discriminating tastes of, the justices, the application of obscenity laws is unpredictable and erratic, the ultimate effect being that people will be prosecuted for committing crimes they could not know were crimes beforehand. This will have a chilling effect on the literary, artistic, and scientific community. If you are the producer or distributer of a potentially "obscene" work, rather than risk criminal prosecution you are more likely to avoid any contact with potentially inflammatory materials. Thus the free exchange of ideas, the purpose of the First Amendment, is compromised. Brennan tried to ameliorate these negative side effects by being as precise as possible. He was clear that obscenity and sex are not synonymous. Material is not obscene merely in virtue of dealing with sexually explicit themes; it is obscene when it does so appealing to prurient interests.[8] He did not want to allow the suppression of legitimate contributions to the arts that may be simply risqué, only those that were "obscene." Brennan strove to make the law clear so it would be predictable and temperate, so it would not have a chilling effect on our intellectual culture.

Will We Know It When We See It?

The problems the *Roth* decision created were numerous. One of the most common was the fact that the justices had to assess each "obscene" work to see if it was truly obscene. Consider having to determine whether a particular work has "redeeming social importance." The court held that to be classified as obscene materials must be "utterly without redeeming social importance."[9] But is anything without any redeeming social importance? Is this even determinable? As one justice remarked, "Redeeming to whom? Importance to whom?"[10] Obviously, people do find importance and value in some works others might deem obscene, and they produce, distribute, and/or consume them. Is it the government's role to determine the value of literary, artistic, political, or scientific works and thus prescribe which attitudes or tastes are valuable and which utterly lack social importance? Frustrated, one justice finally claimed, "I know it when I see it."[11] And herein lies the problem; we may see the same thing, but evaluate its merit differently.

In addition to problems with the definition itself, there were problems with the very idea of obscenity laws. First, there was the notion that the First Amendment allows an exception for obscene material. Several justices vehemently disagreed with this notion, most notably Justice William O. Douglas, who saw this exception to be a fabrication without justification.[12] Second, the problem of applying evaluative criteria such as the obscenity standard made the application of obscenity laws difficult to say the least. As is recognized by the court, in order for a law to be legitimate it must offer "fair notice" to all those accountable to it. People have to know what behaviors are proscribed so that they may refrain from them. If one does not and could not know that one's behavior was forbidden by law, then the law cannot justly be applied against one. As one justice notes:

JACOB M. HELD

I think that the criteria declared by the majority of the court today as guidelines for a court or jury to determine if . . . anyone . . . can be punished as a common criminal for publishing or circulating obscene material are so vague and meaningless that they practically leave the fate of a person charged with violating censorship statutes to the unbridled discretion, whim, and caprice of the judge or jury which tries him.[13]

Barring the gift of premonition one could not determine beforehand how a judge or jury would bring these vague standards to bear on any particular work. If as a publisher you produced and distributed works by the Marquis de Sade, will a judge or jury applying contemporary community standards find them to be without redeeming importance? Are you a criminal? The history of the courts on this matter demonstrates this is a legitimate concern, as circuit courts overturn local courts and the Supreme Court overturns circuit courts, all using the same criteria. Disagreement is not the exception, it is the rule. Obscenity laws do not afford fair notice, and the court eventually recognized the problems it had created. So in 1973 the court redefined obscenity in an attempt to alleviate these problems.

Here We Go Again

In 1973 the court revisited the issue of obscenity in a pair of rulings, *Miller v. California*, 413 US 15 (1973) and *Paris Adult Theatre I v. Slayton*, 413 US 49 (1973). In *Miller* the court, recognizing the problems with the *Roth* standard, offered new guidelines for the determination of obscenity. The new guidelines consisted of three criteria for the determination of obscenity:

(a) whether "the average person, applying contemporary standards" would find that the work, taken as a whole, appeals to the prurient interest . . . (b) whether the work depicts or describes, in a patently offensive way, sexual conduct specifically defined by the applicable state law; and (c) whether the work, taken as a whole, lacks serious literary, artistic, political, or scientific value.

This new standard, far from solving the previous problems, exacerbated them by expanding the scope of "obscenity." This new standard rejected the notion that a work must be utterly without redeeming social importance and instead merely required that the work lack "serious" value. Given the problematic nature of determining the value of a literary, artistic, political, or scientific work, this new criterion, just as the old, demanded that judges function as critics, assess the value of a work and rule against it if they do not see the serious value in it. Judges had to function as aesthetes. As Justice Antonin Scalia would later remark:

> [I]n my view it is quite impossible to come to an objective assessment of (at least) literary or artistic value. . . . Since ratiocination has little to do with esthetics, the fabled "reasonable man" is of little help in the inquiry, and would have to be replaced with, perhaps, the "man of tolerably good taste" – a description that betrays the lack of an ascertainable standard.[14]

We ought to be wary of handing over our right as mature adults to discern what is and is not of value to a committee of judges.

In response to *Miller*, Justice Brennan, who had previously been the author of the court's obscenity standards, had a change of heart. In his dissent in *Paris Adult Theatre I v. Slayton*, Brennan emphasizes several problems with obscenity standards in general and the new *Miller* standards in particular. First, he claims that this new standard, particularly the claim that a work merely needs to be shown to lack "serious" value, causes the statute to be over-broad, that is, it includes too much speech and so suppresses a great deal of what ought to be protected expression.[15] This is due to the fact that "none of the available formulas . . . can reduce the vagueness to a tolerable level."[16] These standards fail "to provide adequate notice to persons who are engaged in the type of conduct the statute could be thought to proscribe . . . [and invite] arbitrary and erratic enforcement of the law . . . [thus] . . . in absence of some very substantial interest in suppressing such speech, we can hardly condone the ill effects that seem to flow inevitably from the effort."[17] The problems inherent in regulating obscene speech and the potential abuses and negative repercussions of doing so poorly should not be tolerated, barring some weighty countervailing interest. However, Brennan and the other dissenters were in the minority. Although historically the courts have dealt with pornography only insofar as it fell within a narrower definition of obscenity, there has recently been a movement towards the legal proscription of pornography itself. It is towards this trend that we now turn.

Anti-Porn Feminists, or the Best Answer to Bad Speech is Less Speech

When it comes to reasons for censoring, prohibiting, or otherwise suppressing pornographic material there are various rationales. Some claim that pornography leads to sexual violence or other forms of deviance. Ultimately, these accounts are only as successful as the connection between the two is strong. This connection is contentious at best, and some maintain that these arguments are doomed to failure insofar as they fail to show a causal connection between porn and violence.[18] Others, with whom the rest of this section will be concerned, claim that pornography promotes inequality by depicting women in an unflattering light, perpetuating harmful stereotypes, and ultimately discriminating against them. Thus, instead of the classic and problematic argument that porn harms society by leading to criminal behavior, namely that porn should be proscribed since it may lead to bad tendencies in some consumers, these theorists argue that pornography is a civil rights issue. Two of the most vocal and well-known proponents of this view are Catharine MacKinnon and Andrea Dworkin.

MacKinnon and Dworkin's basic claim is that pornography "eroticizes hierarchy, it sexualizes inequality. . . . It institutionalizes the sexuality of male supremacy, fusing the eroticization of dominance and submission with the social construction of male and female."[19] As a practice, pornography reinforces a hierarchy of inequality and perpetuates a culture that excuses and rationalizes sexual aggression and male dominance. Pornography thus bolsters sexual discrimination. Some have made the additional claim that the mere existence of pornography is discriminatory insofar as it presents as authoritative a ranking of women as inferior.[20]

MacKinnon's case is simple: women's right to equality is hampered by the culture promoted through pornography and thus women have a right against the consumers, producers, and distributors of pornography. Thus, women's Fourteenth Amendment protections to equal protection under the law take priority over anyone else's right to pornography.[21] MacKinnon has used this line of reasoning to pursue a legal attack on pornography.

In 1983, MacKinnon and Dworkin drafted an amendment to the Minneapolis Civil Rights ordinance that would construe pornography as discrimination. Then in 1984 the Indianapolis City and County Council adopted a similar law. It was quickly challenged in court and ruled unconstitutional by the Seventh Circuit Court of Appeals. The ordinance in question contained prohibitions on trafficking pornography, coercing others into performances, and forcing porn on anyone. In order to be applied, the ordinance thus needed a working definition of pornography, and I think the reader knows where this is going.

Pornography was defined as:

> The graphic sexually explicit subordination of women, whether in pictures or in words, that also includes one or more of the following: (1) women are presented as sexual objects who enjoy pain or humiliation; or (2) women are presented as sexual objects who experience sexual pleasure in being raped; or (3) women are presented as sexual objects tied up or cut up or mutilated or bruised or physically hurt, or as dismembered or truncated or fragmented or severed into body parts; or (4) women are presented as being penetrated by objects or animals; or (5) women are presented in scenarios of degradation, injury, abasement, torture, shown as filthy or inferior, bleeding, bruised, or hurt in a context that makes these conditions sexual; or (6) women are presented as sexual objects from domination, conquest, violation, exploitation, possession, or use, or through postures or positions of servility or submission or display.[22]

You have to love lawyers! This law was clearly directed at more than obscene speech as defined by the Supreme Court, and it left out the restraints adopted by the court, such as considering a work as a whole, not just a part, and weighing its merits against its contribution to political, artistic, literary, or scientific discourse. The language in this law is broader. A work may be considered just in part, and its other redeeming values are irrelevant. But as with obscenity laws in general, the most problematic element of this law is the use of vague evaluative criteria. Consider the definition of pornography: "the graphic sexually explicit subordination of women." This standard is faulted with the same interpretative problems of which previous obscenity laws were guilty. Who determines if a representation is "subordinating"? Whether or not a depiction represents an inappropriate power relation is very much open to debate and one's conclusion ultimately rests on one's views of sexuality and interpersonal relationships. To illustrate the problem this standard raises, consider MacKinnon and Dworkin's own view on the matter. Dworkin and MacKinnon each hold a view of sex that is particularly jaded. Dworkin has claimed, "It's very hard to look at a picture of a woman's body and not see it with the perception that her body is being exploited."[23] It is not a stretch to conclude that the definition above – if interpreted in light of Dworkin's own perceptions of female sexuality – would determine all sexually explicit material to be porn. Likewise, "MacKinnon has condemned pornography specifically because it shows women 'desire to be fucked.'. . . MacKinnon also echoes Dworkin's thesis that women who believe they voluntarily engage in, and enjoy, heterosexual sex are victims of 'false consciousness'."[24] This type of attitude brings me back to the wisdom of Justice Douglas and a quotation with which I opened this essay: "Censors are, of course, propelled by their own neuroses."[25] This view of sex is idiosyncratic to say the least, and to apply this standard to the law as the interpretative yard stick would have disastrous effects on free speech. In fact, in 1992 the Canadian Supreme Court in *Butler v. The Queen* interpreted Canadian anti-obscenity laws to apply to "degrading" and "dehumanizing" depictions of women, and although MacKinnon lauded the decision it led ironically to the seizure of Andrea Dworkin's own work at the border.[26] All laws as applied are applied by judges, and judges use their own judgment in adjudicating the meaning of the law. So we must rely on their interpretations and discretion, and in the case of anti-porn laws we must rely on their interpretation of "subordinating." If the judge is as jaded as the authors of these laws, then a great deal of speech is going to be subject to prosecution. To author an insufferably vague law is to hand over great power to the judiciary. Vague laws are not problematic because a few erratic judges may abuse the indeterminacy, they are problematic because by their nature it is implied all applications are equally justifiable. The idea that any interpretation can be justified betrays the fact that there is then no actual standard by which to adjudicate matters. Thus, even though there are myriad problems that can be raised with this style of law, the fatal flaw is indeterminacy, the fact of which renders it impossible to predict how the law will be applied, since we cannot predict how the neuroses of the judges/censors will play out in each case.

Conclusion

Obscenity and anti-pornography laws attempt to either carve out an area of non-protected speech and thus suppress what is not protected, or limit our freedom of expression by bringing other interests to bear against the freedom to produce, distribute, and consume pornographic material. Yet all such attempts seem to possess the same fatal flaw: the wording of the statutes is necessarily vague given the nature of the material they seek to regulate, and the specification of the meaning of these vague terms is susceptible, in fact probably necessarily so, to competing equipollent interpretations. The fact that these laws are susceptible to varying and at times capricious interpretations means that no one can be given fair notice regarding the application of them. Thus, these laws are indeterminate, due to the material held proscribe, and because of this they lack the form of law demanded by a rule of law.

Our rights are protections against governmental power, as the history of the Bill of Rights attests. So we should be wary of giving government the power to circumvent the protections guaranteed by the First Amendment, or any other amendment for that matter, especially when the scope of the exceptions is left to the discretion of a few judges. If we allow courts to haphazardly determine what speech is and is not protected based on how valuable they deem it, as has been the case with obscenity laws, and if we allow the court to continually redefine obscenity and base that definition on indeterminate evaluative criteria, then our liberties are held hostage to the peccadilloes of a handful of judges. Regardless, whatever the rationale, whether that of the early Brennan or the anti-porn stance of MacKinnon and Dworkin, the fact is that these laws are impracticable. The only censor a mature adult needs is his or her own taste.

NOTES

1   "Amendments to the Constitution of the United States of America," in *The Declaration of Independence and the Constitution of the United States of America* (Washington, DC: Cato Institute, 1998), p. 43.
2   *Schenck v. US*, 249 US 47, 52 (1919) (Holmes, J.).
3   *Roth v. United States*, 354 US 476, 484–7 (1957) (Brennan, J.).
4   *Roth v. United States*, 354 US 476 (1957).
5   Ibid., p. 484.
6   Ibid.
7   Ibid., p. 477.
8   Ibid., pp. 477, 487.
9   *Jacobellis v. Ohio*, 378 US 184 (1964).
10 *Ginzburg v. United States*, 383 US 463, 490 (1966) (Douglas, J. dissenting).
11 *Jacobellis v. Ohio*, 378 US 184, 197 (1964) (Stewart, J. concurring).

12 See *Memoirs v. Massachusetts*, 383 US 413, 428 (1966) (Douglas, J. concurring).

13 *Ginzburg v. United States*, 383 US 463, 478 (1966) (Black, J. dissenting).

14 *Pope v. Illinois*, 481 US 497, 504–5 (1987) (Scalia, J. concurring).

15 *Miller v. California*, 413 US 15, 47 (1973) (Brennan, J. dissenting).

16 *Paris Adult Theatre I v. Slayton*, 413 US 49, 84 (1973) (Brennan, J. dissenting).

17 Ibid., pp. 86–103 passim.

18 For a discussion of these issues, see Nadine Strossen, *Defending Pornography: Free Speech, Sex, and the Fight for Women's Rights* (New York: New York University Press, 2000), chapter 12.

19 Catharine A. MacKinnon, "Frances Biddle's Sister: Pornography, Civil Rights, and Speech," in Susan Dwyer (ed.) *The Problem of Pornography* (Belmont: Wadsworth, 1995), pp. 59–60.

20 For a good discussion on these points, see Rae Langton, *Sexual Solipsism* (Oxford: Oxford University Press, 2009), chapters 1, 4, 8 passim.

21 MacKinnon does offer other arguments as well. Her full case against pornography covers issues from First Amendment rights and the claim that women are silenced by porn, to equal rights, to the claim that porn causes violence. I cannot deal with all of them here, so I am focusing on the case from equality. It is in my opinion the strongest case she can make, and it seems to motivate her legal case against porn, so it is the most relevant to the present discussion.

22 *American Booksellers Association, Inc. v. William H. Hudnut, Mayor, City of Indianapolis*, 771 F.2d 323, 324 (7th Circuit, 1985).

23 Andrea Dworkin, "Where Do We Stand on Pornography?" Roundtable, *Ms.*, Jan./Feb. 1994. Cited in Strossen, *Defending Pornography*, p. 23.

24 Strossen, *Defending Pornography*, p. 111.

25 *Ginsburg v. New York*, 390 US 629, 655 (1968).

26 Strossen, *Defending Pornography*, p. 237.

CHAPTER 10

WHAT'S WRONG WITH PORN?

 I have heard that women watch porn films through to the end (if we watch them at all) because we don't want to miss the wedding. Funny or not, this familiar joke highlights a real or perceived mismatch between what women want from pornography and what it actually delivers. It seems clear that the vast majority of pornography fails the vast majority of women. After all, men, not women, are the primary consumers of porn. It seems less clear, however, that this failure should be attributed to the stereotype that women are interested in sex only as an expression of romantic love between monogamous life partners. If the problem with pornography is not marriage, or rather the apparent lack thereof, then what is the problem with pornography? To put it another way: *What's wrong with porn?*

Following a tradition that was framed by anti-pornography feminists, most notably Andrea Dworkin and Catharine MacKinnon, feminist analyses of porn tend to divide into two camps.[1] In one camp, there are those who believe that pornography perpetuates (perhaps even creates) negative attitudes toward women, which in turn perpetuate (perhaps even create) the negative treatment of women, most notably in the form of sexual violence, particularly rape. Officially, both Dworkin and MacKinnon oppose censorship, but their equation between porn and rape transfers pornography from the realm of free speech to the realm of action. Thus, the Dworkin-MacKinnon thesis, if not Dworkin and

MacKinnon themselves, justifies the censorship of pornography by blurring the boundary between thought and action. In the case of pornography, censorship is warranted in the interest of harm prevention. In the other camp, feminist advocates of free speech, particularly Nadine Strossen, remind us that, "In the free speech context, once the government is granted the power to censor one unpopular or controversial type of expression, it can and will grab the power to censor another."[2] In other words, the censorship of unpopular or controversial expression in the case of pornography is equivalent, in some meaningful sense, to the censorship of unpopular or controversial expression in other cases, such as the expression of feminist ideals.

I am not unconcerned about the prevalence of hostile representations of and attitudes toward women, nor do I deny that pornography often presents such images and fosters such attitudes. Nevertheless, because my position as a feminist is consistent with and supportive of my stance against virtually all forms of censorship, I am picking up where the debate over censorship, itself a relic of the Dworkin-MacKinnon thesis, usually ends. The censorship debate creates a false division between those who would criticize pornography, either in general or in particular instances, and those who would defend the freedom to produce, distribute, and consume pornography. For those of us with feminist interests, as well as interests that are decidedly "prurient," the problem of pornography is much more complex. I am taking for granted that the representations of women within pornography, like the representations of women within our culture more generally, often betray an underlying misogyny that warrants scrutiny and criticism. At the same time, I am also taking for granted, first, that censorship is not a viable response to this problem and, second, that this problem is neither unique to nor constitutive of pornography.

Pleasure as Power

Given that there are women for whom various forms of pornography represent a source of sexual pleasure, it is worth exploring the potential role of pornography in service of Audre Lorde's notion of the erotic as power. Lorde regards the erotic as "a resource within each of us that lies in a deeply female and spiritual plane, firmly rooted in the power of our unexpressed or unrecognized feeling."[3] For Lorde, the erotic is the "measure between the beginnings of our sense of self and the chaos of our strongest feelings," which permeates all aspects of existence:

> The aim of each thing we do is to make our lives and the lives of our children richer and more possible. Within the celebration of the erotic in all our endeavors, my work [*sic*] becomes a conscious decision – a longed-for bed which I enter gratefully and from which I rise up empowered.[4]

"Of course, women so empowered are dangerous,"[5] and Lorde associates the suppression of female erotic power with patriarchal oppression. She differentiates pornography and eroticism as "two diametrically opposed uses of the sexual,"[6] however, and maintains that pornography bears only superficial resemblance to the erotic:

> We have been taught to suspect this resource, vilified, abused, and devalued within Western society. On the one hand, the superficially erotic has been encouraged as a sign of female inferiority; on the other hand, women have been made to suffer and to feel both contemptible and suspect by virtue of its existence.[7]

"Pornography emphasizes sensation without feeling," claims Lorde, and therefore stands in "direct denial of the power of the erotic."[8] At the same time, she advances the casual assessment "It feels right to me" as a testament to the deep, inner knowledge that is born of the erotic:

> Beyond the superficial, the considered phrase, "It feels right to me," acknowledges the strength of the erotic into a true knowledge, for what it means is the first and most powerful guiding light toward any understanding. And understanding is a handmaiden which can only wait upon, or clarify, that knowledge, deeply born. The erotic is the nurturer or nursemaid of all our deepest understanding.[9]

It seems to me that Lorde should invite individual women to determine, in individual cases, whether and why pornography does or does not "feel right." It seems to me that the unreflective dismissal of all instances of pornography, both actual and potential, serves only to diminish the power of the erotic that Lorde encourages us to explore and expand. While there is no denying that particular representations of sexuality through pornography do, indeed, feature "the confused, the trivial, the psychotic, the plasticized sensation"[10] with which Lorde equates all pornography, there is also no denying that pornography does, or at least could, at times, meet the "feels right" criterion that she associates with the erotic. In other words, while pornography and eroticism are by no means identical, they are not mutually exclusive, either.

Individual reactions to pornography are as idiosyncratic as the personal histories and corresponding sexualities by which those reactions are conditioned. I do not pretend that it would be possible or desirable to develop a universally normative distinction between pornography that is empowering, or potentially empowering, and pornography that is oppressive, or potentially oppressive, solely on the basis of what "feels right" to *me* – or to anyone *else* for that matter. I do acknowledge, however, that what "feels right" to me, from an explicitly feminist perspective, is an indispensable source of insight when addressing my own concerns at the intersection of feminism and pornography. Moreover, because I also acknowledge that my own sense of what "feels right" has been informed by insights from others, particularly other feminists, my disregard for universally normative feminist standards should not be mistaken for unmitigated relativism about the potential role of pornography as a source of sexual or erotic empowerment. For the sake of comparison, consider, for example, that despite the widespread agreement among feminists that sexual harassment of women by men is a real and pervasive problem, particular feminists would disagree about what does and does not "feel right," and hence what does and does not constitute sexual harassment, in our day-to-day interactions with men. In the case of pornography, as in the case of sexual harassment, what "feels right to me" functions, not as the defining criterion, but as an entering wedge into an analysis that is simultaneously reflective of and relevant to our lived experiences.

A subtle but significant distinction can be drawn between what "feels right" in the context of pornography and what "feels right" in real life. Consider the possibility that the label "pornography" accurately applies only to sexually explicit material that strikes us, for lack of a better term, as "naughty." This suggestion is captured quite effectively in the following passage from the futuristic fiction of Stanislaw Lem:

> For pornography is not directly obscene: it excites only as long as there is a struggle within the viewer between lust and the angel of culture. When the devils carry off the angel; when, as a result of general tolerance, the weakness of sexual prohibitions – their complete helplessness – is laid bare;

when prohibitions are laid on the rubbish heap, then how quickly pornography betrays its innocent (which here means ineffective) character, for it is a false promise of carnal bliss, an augury of something which does not in fact come true. It is the forbidden fruit, so there is as much temptation in it as there is power in the prohibition.[11]

Given this assessment, it comes as no surprise that we frequently are disinclined to participate in various activities that nevertheless "feel right" as pornography. This distinction is of critical importance. Pornography promises to promote the power of the erotic only insofar as it permits women to explore our most private fantasies without thereby committing or consenting to enact those fantasies. As Amber Hollibaugh notes, the prohibition on sexual fantasy is so powerful that many women have explored only a limited, and predominantly masculine, range of sexual possibilities.[12]

Feminist Porn

Insight into the range of what some women deem "naughty" in a way that "feels right" can be obtained through an examination of the emerging designation of "feminist porn." Even a cursory tour through this category will reveal intersections, first of all, between feminist porn and lesbian porn and, second of all, between feminist porn and couples porn. Although the connection between lesbian porn and feminist porn invites a discussion of why representations of lesbian sexuality, or at least some such representations, "feel right" from a feminist perspective, it would be a mistake to draw a hasty or straightforward equation between feminist and lesbian porn for at least two reasons. First, depictions of lesbian sexuality are readily available outside the fairly narrow domain of feminist porn. Often enough, the mainstream depiction of lesbian sexuality is virtually indistinguishable from the mainstream depiction of women's heterosexuality. Second, drawing the hasty equation between lesbian sexuality and women's empowerment, like drawing the hasty equation between heterosexuality and women's oppression, means dismissing the erotic desires of heterosexual women, bisexual women, and even many queer women – including many feminists.

An alternative to the equation between feminist and lesbian porn can be found in the tendency to use the designations "couples porn" and "feminist porn" interchangeably. For example, Candida Royalle, who was motivated to create Femme Productions because she "wanted to make films that say we all have a right to our own pleasure, and that women, especially, have a right to our own pleasure,"[13] describes her films as pornography for couples to watch together. I have already rejected the equation between lesbian sexuality and feminism, thus acknowledging the possibility of particular expressions of heterosexuality, including pornographic expressions, that participate in the power of the erotic. Because I also acknowledge the possibility of pornographic expressions of lesbian sexuality that participate in the power of the erotic, and because the content of couples porn seems geared primarily, if not exclusively, to heterosexual couples, I am as reluctant to equate feminist porn with couples porn as I am to equate it with lesbian porn. Moreover, the characterization of feminist porn as porn for couples limits women's sexuality by suggesting, albeit subtly, that women would not, or perhaps should not, have use for pornography outside of romantic relationships with men. In addition, either the equation between feminist porn and couples porn implies that a given example of pornography – be it a snuff film or one of Candida Royalle's films – is empowering when viewed by a heterosexual couple and disempowering when viewed by an individual or a larger group, or it implies that pornography should be regarded as feminist, not in consideration of its content or style, but in consideration of its intended manner of use.

Facile equations between feminist porn and lesbian or couples porn, like those between feminist porn and its actual or intended manner of use, do not invite an exploration of the particularities of what does and does not "feel right" about particular examples of pornography. Insofar as the discussions of feminist pornography by advocates of feminist lesbian porn[14] and advocates of feminist couples porn[15] do explore the particularities of what "feels right," they thereby suggest that the feminist character of feminist porn derives from something separable from and more fundamental than either its depiction of lesbian sexuality or its orientation toward heterosexual couples. In order to illustrate what I take to be a fundamental feature of both feminist lesbian porn and feminist couples porn that conforms to my personal, yet explicitly feminist, sense of what "feels right," I will turn, by way of contrast, to an example of the sort of pornography that does not "feel right." I refer specifically to what is generally termed "fuck machine porn."

Fucking machines are mechanical gadgets with the ostensible function of fucking women (or, less often, men). On the face of it, fuck machine porn seems capable of transcending the limitations of both lesbian porn and couples porn by replacing the gendered sexual partner with an ungendered mechanical partner designed for *her* pleasure. Regarded in this manner, fuck machine porn would seem like the ultimate expression of woman-centered sexuality! Even so, fuck machine porn does not "feel right" to me.

The fact that fucking machines "feel wrong" is not merely a consequence of their exaggerated size and speed, nor is it just my reaction to the names of the various machines. The website fuckingmachines.com,[16] for example, features machines bearing such names as Annihilator, Chopper, Drilldo, Fuckzilla, Hammer, Hatchet, Intruder, Monster, Predator, Trespasser, and so forth, many of which betray an underlying impulse toward domination. Exaggerated penis size is a common element within pornography, and the extent to which size or speed correlates with a woman's pleasure is largely a matter of personal preference. Representations of sexual domination are another common element within pornography. The sexual domination of women by men is not without feminist critics, of course, but serious conceptual difficulties arise in connection with efforts to delineate the boundary between sexual acts of domination and ordinary sexual acts. This is especially clear in consideration of the radical feminist suggestion that all acts of penetration, and hence all "vanilla" sex acts, amount to the domination of a woman by a man. I accept this characterization, not as a criticism of particular sex acts, but in recognition of the fact that sex and power are intimately entwined. The wholesale suppression of desire, including the desire to dominate or be dominated, diminishes the power of the erotic. Just as pornography featuring missionary position sex, or even pornography featuring women in bondage, does not necessarily "feel wrong" simply in virtue of its display of domination, the fact that fuck machine porn does "feel wrong," at least to me, must derive from some other source. Indeed, the fact that the vast majority of mainstream pornography "feels wrong" to me must also derive from some other source.

Pornography often centers on decontextualized sex acts. In many cases, it centers even more directly on some specific portion of the decontextualized sex act. Consider, for example, the position of prominence occupied by the "money shot" in mainstream porn. Also consider video loops, a mainstay of cyber porn, in which specific portions of decontextualized sex acts are edited into an endlessly repeating cycle. By narrowly focusing on particular acts and portions of acts, much pornography seems like an effort to reduce human sexuality to its essential core for quick and convenient consumption. In contrast, Luce Irigaray suggests that women's sexuality is not limited to a single sex organ and, as a result, lacks the boundaries that would allow us to clearly delineate a discrete point at which sex begins and ends.[17] Indeed, Irigaray claims that "woman has sex organs more or less everywhere"[18] and that "the geography of her pleasure is far more diversified, more multiple in its differences, more complex, more subtle, than is commonly imagined."[19] Although I hesitate to make such sweeping generalizations about the nature of female sexuality, I do believe that, for at least some women, our sexual pleasure is not confined to a discrete physical or temporal point. It is not reducible to the "money shot" and it is not contained within a discrete bodily location. To the extent that feminist lesbian porn and feminist couples porn offer more richly contextualized representations of sexuality than mainstream porn, thereby offering representations that are more consistent with women's own experience of sexuality than mainstream porn, such representations may better meet our individual standards of what "feels right."

Discussion

Habits, including sexual habits, are developed over time, largely in response to personal experience. For example, as a young person fumbling around with a partner for the first time, we generally do not have a preference to lie on the left rather than the right side of the bed, or vice versa. As repetition begins to breed familiarity, however, we often acquire such preferences. To the extent that our experience with pornography is among the factors that shape our sexual desires and expectations, I am concerned that exposure to mainstream porn conditions many men to ignore – either inadvertently or with smug disregard – the subtlety and potentiality of women's sexuality, while a comparative lack of exposure to feminist porn simultaneously conditions women – either from ignorance or from shame – to do the same thing. The available range of feminist porn is rather limited, consisting primarily of lesbian porn and couples porn. I do not believe that women want pornography to center on a wedding any more rather than we want pornography to center, as it typically does, on other clearly delineated events such as penetration and ejaculation. I do believe, however, that many of us are looking for more richly contextualized representations of sexuality than pornography typically offers.[20]

NOTES

1 For examples, refer to Andrea Dworkin, *Pornography: Men Possessing Women* (London: Women's Press, 1981); Catharine A. MacKinnon, *Feminism Unmodified* (Cambridge, MA: Harvard University Press, 1987); and Andrea Dworkin and Catharine A. MacKinnon, *Pornography and Civil Rights* (Minneapolis: Organizing Against Pornography, 1988).

2 Nadine Strossen, "In Defense of Pornography," in James Elias et al. (eds.) *Porn 101: Eroticism, Pornography, and the First Amendment* (Amherst: Prometheus, 1999), p. 24.

3 Audre Lorde, "The Uses of the Erotic: The Erotic as Power," in Henry Abelove, Michele Barale, and David Halperin (eds.) *The Lesbian and Gay Studies Reader* (New York: Routledge, 1993), p. 339.

4 Ibid., p. 340.

5 Ibid.

6 Ibid., p. 341.

7 Ibid., p. 339.

8 Ibid., p. 340.

9 Ibid., p. 341.

10 Ibid., p. 340.

11 Stanislaw Lem, *Imaginary Magnitudes*, trans. Marc Heine (San Diego: Harcourt Brace Jovanovich, 1984), p. 17.

12 Amber Hollibaugh, "Desire for the Future: Radical Hope in Passion and Pleasure," in Carole S. Vance (ed.) *Pleasure and Danger: Exploring Female Sexuality* (Boston: Routledge, 1984), pp. 1–27.

13 Candida Royalle, "Porn in the USA," in Drucilla Cornell (ed.) *Feminism and Pornography* (Oxford: Oxford University Press, 2000), p. 541.

14 For examples, refer to Amber Hollibaugh, "Seducing Women into 'A Lifestyle of Vaginal Fisting': Lesbian Sex Gets *Virtually* Dangerous," and Becky Ross, "'It's Merely Designed for Sexual Arousal': Interrogating the Indefensibility of Lesbian Smut," both in Drucilla Cornell (ed.) *Feminism and Pornography* (Oxford: Oxford University Press, 2000).

15 For examples, refer to Drucilla Cornell, "Pornography's Temptation," and Candida Royalle, "Porn in the USA," both in Drucilla Cornell (ed.) *Feminism and Pornography* (Oxford: Oxford University Press, 2000). Also refer to Veronica Monet, "What is Feminist Porn?" in James Elias et al. (eds.) *Porn 101: Eroticism, Pornography, and the First Amendment* (Amherst: Prometheus, 1999).

16 I would like to acknowledge that kink.com, the parent site responsible for fuckingmachines.com, has adopted a values statement, as well as a set of explicit model rights and director rules, that is sensitive and responsive to the sorts of concerns raised by Dworkin, MacKinnon, and others regarding the potential victimization of women within the porn industry. I would also like to acknowledge that, insofar as it aims to "demystify and celebrate alternative sexualities by providing the most ethical and authentic kinky adult entertainment," as expressed by its official tagline, kink.com offers a genuine alternative to mainstream pornography. My personal distaste for fuck machine porn should not be misconstrued as an attempt to censor or censure kink.com or any other safe and ethical producers of fuck machine porn.

17 Luce Irigaray, *The Sex Which is Not One*, trans. Catherine Porter (Ithaca: Cornell University Press, 1985).

18 Ibid., p. 28.

19 Ibid.

20 I am very grateful for helpful comments received on an earlier draft of this essay presented for the University of Idaho and Washington State University Philosophy Colloquium, April 2006. I am also grateful for discussions with and feedback from Gary Krug.

CHAPTER 11

BUMPER STICKERS AND BOOBS

Why the Free Speech Argument for Porn Fails

Pornography is free speech applied to the sexual realm. Freedom of speech is the ally of those who seek change: it is the enemy of those who seek to maintain control. Pornography, along with all other forms of sexual heresy, such as homosexuality, should have the same legal protection as political heresy.

(Wendy McElroy)[1]

"I'm shocked, I tell you, shocked!"

You have picked up this book and no doubt have been titillated and maybe shocked by some of what is written herein. The title of my essay has the same goal as the cover of a porn magazine: titillate, shock, and hopefully get you to keep looking. I title this essay "Bumper Stickers and Boobs" to titillate. I subtitle it "Why the Free Speech Argument for Porn Fails" to shock many free speech advocates and get everyone thinking. I will expose myself early. I hope to convince you that whatever else porn is, it is not free speech just applied to the sexual realm. There may be reasons not to censor porn, but violating freedom of speech is not one of them.

"But wait a minute!" you say. "If pornography is expression and America (at least) is founded on freedom of expression, then shouldn't there be a freedom to distribute, look at, and salivate over good porn?" Wendy McElroy says, "Pornography, along with all other forms of heresy, such as homosexuality, should have the same legal protection as political heresy." If McElroy is right, the only difference between porn and political heresy is the message expressed.

Philosophers like things in the nice neat package of an argument. So let us render McElroy's statement into an argument. We can call it the free speech argument for porn. It goes like this:

1. The right to express one's religious and political views no matter how heretical should be protected from censorship.
2. Looking at, making, and publishing pornography are forms of sexual expression.
3. Sexual expression, no matter how heretical, should be protected the same as political and religious expression.
4. The right to express one's sexual views no matter how heretical should be protected from censorship.
5. Looking at, making, and publishing pornography, no matter how heretical, should be protected from censorship.

Invoking the term "freedom of expression" or "right to free speech" has a way of stopping arguments. Appeal to a right to freedom of expression and you have just played the trump card. If sexual expression is included in the right to expression, then there is a strong reason to leave it alone. When you apply the term "right" to the ambiguous term "expression" it does cause some rather ludicrous law enforcement. Two adults have sex in a motel and one gets paid by the other and it is called prostitution and someone goes to jail. If both get paid for making a film, however, it is called expression and no one goes to jail. That seems . . . silly. Both are forms of sexual expression. If premise three is correct, sexual expression no matter how heretical to others, should be protected the same as any other kind of expression.

I am going to try to convince you the free speech argument for porn is seriously flawed because premise three is seriously flawed. In order to do that, I am going to appeal to your intuitions. I am going to try to convince you that people do not treat porn as just another form of expression like political and religious expression, and that is a good thing, too. I am also going to try to persuade you that if we did treat porn like any other heresy, there would still be a major difference between expressing a political opinion and using porn to express a sexual opinion.

BUMPER STICKERS AND BOOBS   141

The Preacher and the Porn Star

There is a debate that goes on over and over again in modern society. It usually takes place on some late night talk show like Jerry Springer or Howard Stern. Some porn star and some preacher sit in a studio. The topic (of course) is porn. The preacher wants to ban it. The porn star wants to celebrate it. When the subject of censorship comes up, the porn star howls that showing her boobs on film is sexual speech (this point might even be occasioned by said porn star bearing her chest, which is blurred out for the folks back home). She argues that she is proud to display her expression just as the preacher proudly displays his own expression with the "Get sanctified or get French Fried" bumper sticker.

The preacher usually defends his bumper sticker slogans as religious speech or political speech protected by his (and everyone's) right to freedom of expression, but denies the display of girls on film should be protected in the same way. The porn star counters that if we allow bumper stickers we should allow sexual expression. And on it goes until commercial or someone throws a chair.

The problem is that both the preacher and porn star are wrong. The good reverend is wrong that showing boobs is not expression. The porn star is also wrong. Her boobs and his bumper sticker are not the same when it comes to freedom of speech. Before being all philosophical, let us take a case from history to illustrate this point.

Picnic Sex and the Prudes

In 1971 Robert Paul Cohen expressed his disapproval of the mandatory draft by writing "Fuck the Draft" on his jacket. When he walked into a California courthouse, he was arrested. The Supreme Court ruled that Cohen's right to free speech was violated. Cohen had a right to express his disapproval of the Vietnam War in no uncertain terms. In essence, Cohen's jacket became his bumper sticker expression. We tend to think if something is free expression, it is like a bumper sticker or Cohen's jacket. You should be able to put it on a bumper sticker and express yourself all over the East Coast.

Now I am going to do something philosophers love to do. I am going to take this case and wrench it out of its context to make a point. Suppose instead of writing "Fuck the Draft" on his jacket, another guy – we will call him Schmoen – had instead hired a prostitute to wear a banner designating her (or him) "The Draft" and Schmoen proceeds to express his disapproval of the war by having sex in a public space in order to express the same sentiment as Cohen's jacket actually did. The question is, should Schmoen's performance be protected the same as Cohen's jacket? Notice, I did not ask if they were both expression. They are both expressive. The question is whether they should be treated the same.

Before you answer, let me take this one step further. Suppose Schmoen did not have an angry anti-war message, but instead wanted to extol the joys of sexual liberation. He thinks that Americans, especially religious conservatives, are prudes and should lighten up about sex. He places a sign next to his little copulation vignette that expresses the sentiment that sex should not be taboo. It says, "You picnic and I'll do this."

All of these are expressions in one way or another. The intent is to express some opinion in all three cases, and they are not too fanciful. People have bumper stickers that express their feelings on war, rights, political candidates, etc. Masking sentiments with innuendo (e.g., "Buck Fush" or "First Hillary, then Monica, now Us!") only serves to draw attention to the real idea.

People also make and look at porn as a form of expression. Larry Flynt has made a career satirizing political figures with porn-related imagery. Obviously, a lot of porn has no "grand protest." Most porn falls into the category of pure porn. This "porn purely for porn's sake" is analogous to Schmoen's attempt to convince us all to drop our sexual hang-ups by enjoying his picnic sex. In fact, if there is one thing the porn industry wants to make clear, it is just what Wendy McElroy has stated: "Porn is free speech applied to the sexual realm."

But if porn is free speech about sex like preaching is free speech about religion and campaigning is free speech about politics, then why do most of us intuitively want to treat Schmoen's protest of prudery via "picnic sex" differently than political speech or religious speech? Enough questions – time for some philosophical analysis.

"Don't look, Ethel!"

Most of us would not treat the bumper sticker and the public sex the same. In fact, most of us would treat them very differently. We would allow Cohen to walk anywhere he pleased with his jacket saying "Fuck" anything he wanted to. We might bar him from walking the halls of the elementary school (if for no other reason than to keep the kids from making their own jackets), but on the street he is fine.

But when it comes to sexual speech acts, most of us would not. In fact, we would want Schmoen out of the sight of passersby. We would probably make him do his protest in a private venue open to the public with a warning sign in red letters. Some people would want the warning sign to be roughly the size of a 1979 Buick and ID checked at the door. The fact is that we treat sexual speech much differently than we do political or religious speech. In other words, we do not treat boobs like bumper stickers and we do not treat bumper stickers like boobs. But I owe you a reason why.

Tease Me, Whip Me, Persuade Me

The intuitive answer is that looking at a bumper sticker is different from looking at some Tom, Dick, or Schmoen in the park trying to convince you to stop being a prude. Intuitively, why do most people think bumper stickers are more important than boobs when it comes to free speech? The reason is that most people think of bumper stickers as an attempt to persuade others to believe something, whereas boobs are well, just titillating. Perhaps persuasion is more important than mere expressive acts.

This is exactly what a philosopher has argued recently. George Sher says that we ought to treat persuasion as distinct and as more valuable than mere expression. The reason is that we tend to be able to evaluate clearly someone's *opinion* when it's expressed verbally. However, expressive *actions* are more ambiguous.[2]

Now someone might object that if the concern is about ambiguity, Schmoen can add a sign to make clear what he wants to express. Whatever you think of Sher's argument, one thing seems to emerge from all of this intuiting. The value of Schmoen's expression is not so much that he can vent about American prudes (he could do that without being stark naked), but that he can try to convince those who do not agree with him and to do that he must be able to confront some people who (he thinks) are prudes.

The heart of this intuition is that freedom of expression is not just about expression. Rather, it is expression to convince others. That is in fact what political and religious expression is designed to do. From the church that passes out Bibles to the congressman who passes out bumper stickers, religious and political expression persuades. Most porn does not persuade anyone to any particular opinion. It is made, bought, and consumed for a lot of reasons (masturbation, instruction, etc.), but persuasion is not usually one of those reasons. Even those who read *Playboy* "for the articles" are looking for keen political commentary and satire *along with* their porn.

Biting the Bullet

But you say, "Suppose I don't share the intuition of most people. What if I think what's good for the politician is good for the porn star? If we protect one, we should protect the other regardless of how it persuades." This is a good point. My argument so far has relied on a lot of assumptions about what most people would think about boobs and bumper stickers. It is far from conclusive that most people share the intuition that porn should not be treated the same as public religious or political expression. My argument could very well be wrong even if most people do have that intuition. If there is one thing philosophers know it is this: just because most people believe something does not make it true – not by a long shot.

What if we bite the bullet and say Schmoen's expression is no different from unwanted political or religious expression? Some porn defenders do just that. Nadine Strossen, president of the American Civil Liberties Union, in her *Defending Pornography*, says that pornography should be as free as political speech even if it does force us to look at images and actions we find not fit for public display.[3] "Biting the bullet" is a euphemism for an unpleasant activity that philosophers have to do all the time. It means that sometimes philosophers have to swallow an implication of their argument that they do not want to, in order to keep the argument consistent. If porn is free speech applied to sex then we should treat it like bumper sticker speech. But in order to do that, we would have to allow it to be as public as bumper stickers or billboards, as Strossen suggests. Before we bite this bullet let us stop and examine it.

Suppose you are in the audience for the late night show. Let us say also that you are not there *just in case* the porn star decides to bare all. You are really there for scintillating moral discussion. Now the porn star (we shall call her Pamela) wants to convince you that what she does and those who watch her do it are not doing anything wrong. To illustrate her point and to shock you out of your prudery, she bares her boobs. What has she just done? She has tried to convince you that looking at boobs is okay by making you look at boobs. Now if you had bought her argument that porn is good, then you could have subsequently bought her DVD. However, Pamela's persuasive method is to make you do what she wants in order to convince you that watching her do it is okay. This seems more than just persuasion. This starts to sound like coercion.

Porn star Pam is right. Porn is expression. It may even be used as a kind of persuasion. But not all persuasion is the same. Let's compare Pamela topless on TV with the preacher's religious speech. Suppose you are driving down the interstate and you see a billboard rented out by the preacher you saw on the show last night. It says "Going to church is good for your soul" and there is an appropriate religious picture. Maybe it is more offensive:"Get sanctified at our church or get French fried in hell." Now you are not opposed to religion per se but the billboard makes you annoyed. It might be offensive to suggest that a lot of people will be burnt to a crisp in hell.

But there is a kind of distance between you and the conclusion of the argument, isn't there? Sure you are exposed to some offensive sight, but you haven't engaged in any act against your will. If, for instance, instead of a billboard, the prudish preacher started a revival on your front lawn and you had no choice but attend, you still would not be "going to church." You would be captive at a church service. The same would be true if, in order to convince you to buy into a political agenda, you were handed a sign saying "Vote for President Schmoen" and carried on the shoulders of a crowd against your will, you could be confused with the crowd but you would not be said to be "campaigning for Schmoen."

The point is that when Pamela shows her boobs she's not just exposing you to an offensive sight, she, in effect, causes you to engage in an act – looking at her boobs. You are not just considering an offensive message. You are engaging in looking at a sexually suggestive performance – one you didn't seek out. You may or may not be sexually aroused by this act, but even amateur porn performed by unattractive people is still porn. However, when someone says something offensive without your consent, there is still a distance between their speech and your actions. Religious speakers cannot make you pray by praying in front of you. Neither can politicians make you political by exposing you to their rhetoric.

The idea of showing naked people having sex on a billboard would ostensibly have only one kind sexual message. It would be something like

"Sex is good" or "Looking at pictures of naked people, especially ones having sex, is good." However, such displays attempt to convince a person that looking at pictures of naked people having sex is good by making interstate drivers look at naked people having sex.

In philosophical terms, public displays of porn would persuade without consent because they do not just express, they make the audience do something they may or may not want to do. This is the one good reason for all those warning signs in red letters. The signs make it clear, "If you walk in here, you want to look at naked people and people having sex." However, political and religious expression persuade without making the audience do anything. In fact, it is impossible to make someone engage in religious acts or political acts without their consent.

The upshot of these examples is that to treat porn as the same as any political or religious heresy would end up being very *illiberal*. Public displays of porn, unlike public displays of political opinion, coerce others by causing them to engage in the act of looking at pornography. This bullet is hard to swallow indeed. But if we do not bite this bullet then we are left with the conclusion that we should not treat boobs the same as bumper stickers.

Hard Cases

But some might object that if you buy this argument, there could be some other bullets to swallow and they may be far worse. Two such objections come to mind. First, if porn is not protected, what about offensive art? Second, what if porn is expressive of some other opinion? Just because pure porn is not persuasive does not mean it cannot convey some other message than "It is good to look at porn." Let us look at these one at a time.

Hard case 1: The gallery downtown vs. the "downtown" gallery

What makes art a hard case for my argument? The difficulty is found in the pun. The gallery downtown displays works of art. It says so right on the sign outside. Websites have galleries, too. "Downtown" is a euphemism often used for oral sex. There are plenty of "Downtown galleries" on the web with page after page of oral sex. The problem is where to draw the line between the arts on display in the gallery downtown from the galleries on the web. This is a tough call for anyone to make, but – make no mistake – laws are designed to stop us from having to make these tough calls. That is after all the nature of law – to take the moral judgment out of the hands of individuals in favor of legislation based on moral principles. But it has been notoriously hard to draw this line. When does literature become obscene? As one of those stuffy Supreme Court justices, Harlan, said of Cohen's "Fuck the Draft" slogan, "One man's vulgarity is another man's lyric."[4]

To make this a little more concrete, consider a case recently at my own Bowling Green State University. A sculpture by the renowned James Parlin was removed from an exhibition at a satellite campus because the sculpture depicted an adult male receiving oral sex from an underage teen. The work bore the ponderous title: "The Middle School Teacher Makes a Decision He Will Live to Regret," which implies that the artist may not necessarily be trying to glorify this act of pedophilia. The powers that be at the university told the gallery director to pull the sculpture. The gallery director refused to censor one work and shut down the exhibition in protest.

Was anyone's freedom of expression violated? I don't think so. The university did not want negative publicity for the gallery since it shared a building with a children's theatre. James Parlin was not arrested for making the sculpture. Freedom of expression allows one to persuade, as Parlin wanted to do, but it does not imply that the artist has a right to any particular audience.

The same holds for the galleries on the net. They probably are not art, but suppose they are art? Does this entitle them to public display on a par with political or religious speech? It does not seem so.

I do agree with Nadine Strossen about one thing, however. If we shielded everyone from every offense, we would have a world of warning signs. Galleries and museums have tons of nude art that might force some people to look at something they do not want to see. Do we hang red lettered signs 20 feet from Michelangelo's "David" or the Venus de Milo? The problem with obscenity is that it is subjective. It certainly is not defined by the presence of nudity. If we say persuasion is what counts, not expression, then a lot of the arts are going to be at the mercy of any half-wit who wants to paint fig leaves on classic works of art.

But do we really have to play the obscenity game? Justice Potter Stewart said that he could not draw the line between art and hardcore porn but he knew it when he saw it.[5] I am not as confident as Stewart and anyone should be nervous about the state drawing that line for them. The convoluted mechanizations of constitutional interpretations aside, one does not have to draw that fine a line to accept that porn is not sexual speech though it is expression.

That most people do not emerge from the Metropolitan Museum exhibition of Rodin shocked and befuddled by all the porn is proof that museum-goers know that they can expect some displays of nudity, just as those who punch "sex galleries" into Google know what they are getting into and do not confuse it with the displays at the Met. If, however, lots of people start getting shocked by the Met's sculpture, then it might be prudent to warn, but doing so would not be censorship. The point is that warning labels are a matter of judgment often best left to the museum in question, not the state.

Hard case 2: "Is that supposed to be the vice president in a thong?"

I have argued that porn is an expression but not on a par with religious and political speech. But what if the porn is expressing some political opinion? This is a hard case because porn as a form of political satire could be said to be the medium for a political opinion designed to persuade others. The most prolific purveyor of porn as political statement is Larry Flynt. Flynt's political satire famously raised the hackles of conservative minister Jerry Falwell. Recently, Flynt has upped the ante by producing a porn piece using look-a-likes for Sarah Palin and Hillary Clinton, among others. Artist Jonathan Yeo also expressed a political sentiment with porn when he made a collage portrait of George W. Bush out of porn magazines.

As Sher says, it may be a difficult question just what we are supposed to be persuaded to believe by Flynt's satirical porn or Yeo's collage. Flynt's speeches and articles defending porn are far more clear and compelling than the bad acting in his movies. But whatever the exact content of these messages, this is one bullet I am willing to bite. Porn as political satire is something more than just pure porn. There may still be issues with consent. If Flynt pushed for public displays of his *Who's Nailin Paylin?* he might be forcing others to look at porn to convince them of his political message and this seems illiberal, but it is no worse than parades or protests which force others to deal with loud noises, offensive language, or displays of violent imagery as the medium to persuade others of some opinion.

If Porn Isn't Free Speech, What Is It?

So if you have stayed with me, maybe you are convinced that the free speech argument for porn just does not hold up. Does this mean that the gates are wide open for censorship? Not by a long shot. Just because porn is not free speech applied to the sexual realm does not mean we can sharpen our censor pens or start fining the publishers of *Penthouse*. This is because we protect all sorts of expressive acts that are not speech.

There are several other arguments for why porn should be tolerated. Privacy, individuality, and autonomy might make arguments against state censorship just as well or better than freedom of speech without confusing bumper stickers and boobs. How these arguments hold up will depend on the premises of the arguments and the criticisms against them. If the argument in this essay holds up, however, it means that porn advocates must abandon the notion that censoring porn is like censoring political or religious speech. In the end, the porn star, the preacher, and the prude would have to change their arguments. But that can be a good thing for everyone.

NOTES

1 Wendy McElroy. *XXX : A Woman's Right to Pornography* (New York: St. Martin's Press, 1995), p. 141.
2 George Sher, "Freedom of Expression in the Non-Neutral State," in George Klosko and Steven Wall (eds.) *Perfectionism and Neutrality: Essays in Liberal Theory* (Lanham: Rowman and Littlefield, 2003), pp. 219–30.
3 Nadine Strossen, *Defending Pornography: Free Speech, Sex, and the Fight for Women's Rights* (New York: Scribner, 1995), pp. 69–71.
4 *Cohen v. California* 403 US 15 (1971).
5 *Jacobellis v. Ohio* 378 US 184 (1964).

PART V

THE ART OF DIRTY

Porn and Aesthetic Value

CHAPTER 12

THE "FINE ART" OF PORNOGRAPHY?

The Conflict Between Artistic Value and Pornographic Value

Can pornographic works have artistic value? Much pornography closely resembles art, at least in many superficial respects. Films, photographs, paintings, literary works – all of these can have artistic value. Of course, films, photographs, paintings, and novels can be pornographic, too. Is there any reason to believe that pornographic works cannot have artistic value?

We might get a better grasp of these issues by examining the kinds of attention that we pay to works of art and works of pornography. When attending to an object, whether it is an image, a text, or a piece of music, we can take an *artistic interest* in the work. Typically, when we do this, we will offer criticisms, interpretations, or judgments of the work; and the result of these activities seem to be fundamentally what we are concerned with when we attend to an object artistically. We can also take a *pornographic interest* in a work – our interest in the work is in the service of our own sexual arousal. That these two kinds of interest in a work are distinct should be immediately obvious – one need not be sexually aroused in order to appreciate the artistic value of a work, and one need not appreciate the artistic value of a work in order to be sexually aroused. But is it ever the case that one actually must be sexually aroused in order to appreciate the artistic value of a work?

Of course, I imagine that it is possible for someone to take a pornographic interest in a work at one time and take an artistic interest in the work at another time. A viewer could take an artistic interest in the texturing on Michelangelo's "David" at one time, and at another time simply take an interest in David. That is not very interesting. Think again of the initial question I asked – can pornographic works have artistic value? While some philosophers and art theorists have argued that they cannot,[1] other philosophers have argued that they can, but these "pro-pornographic-art" philosophers also seem to suggest that the artistic value of the work is somewhat independent of the work's pornographic content – that is, a work can have artistic value *despite* its having pornographic content.[2] I think that is probably true; however, I also find that to be a fairly weak argument. This claim is essentially the observation that one is able to take multiple kinds of interests in a work, which is not surprising. There are many kinds of interests and many kinds of values that one can attribute to a work – artistic, historical, financial, sentimental, and of course pornographic. Certainly, while these interests and values can sometimes be related, often they are not – a child's finger painting might be artistically poor but still have great sentimental value to the child's parents, or a work that currently demands a high financial value might turn out later to be historically unimportant.[3]

A stronger argument in defense of the "pro-pornographic-art" view would hold that a work has its artistic value *by virtue of* its having some pornographic content. This would be the claim that, in some instances at least, one discovers the artistic value of a work through taking a pornographic interest in that work – that it is a necessary condition for appreciating some work artistically that one take a pornographic interest in that work. That would be very interesting if true. Unfortunately, I think that it probably is not. The purpose of this essay is to explain why. To explain this, we will need to address the following questions: What does it mean to take a "pornographic interest" in a work? What does it mean to take an "artistic interest" in a work? And finally, is it ever the case that one discovers the artistic value of a work through taking a pornographic interest in that work? This last question is the philosophical "money shot" of this essay.

Two Caveats

Before I begin, two caveats. In this essay, most of the examples I discuss are taken from the visual arts. Despite this, the argument I am making is general enough, *mutatis mutandis*, that it would apply to all cases of pornography in whatever form they make take. The general question I am

ʍ   CHRISTOPHER BARTEL

asking is whether or not the aims of the production of pornography are consistent with the aims of the production of works of art. This general question could be applied equally well across all genres, styles, and forms of art, and in each instance the question is a pertinent one. Certainly, special problems may arise in the case of some art forms, problems that other art forms would avoid. Is pornographic literature necessarily artistically inferior as it seemingly must rely on clichéd or repetitive literary devices that limit the work's artistic scope?[4] Is it possible for pure music to be pornographic?[5] While these are certainly interesting questions, it is not my intention to address them here. Additionally, most of the examples I discuss are works that are typically intended for heterosexual males. However, this choice is not because I wish to promote any heteronormative conception of sexuality. Rather, this choice is motivated by a desire to write with some authenticity! The validity of the argument presented here is not dependent on my choice of examples; rather, my argument should be general enough to apply to all cases of pornography regardless of what sexual orientation that pornography assumes.

Second, I really do not think that my question – can pornographic works have artistic value? – has very much to do with whether or not pornographic works should count as *art*. My thinking is that whether pornography should be classified as art or not has little to do with the interests that these works serve for us or the values that we attribute to these works. Still, should works of pornography count as art? Seeking an answer to this question would be frustratingly complicated. We would first need to establish a satisfactory definition of *art*, which would be a particularly difficult task, and an examination of these problems would take us too far afield. Even if we had a satisfactory definition of art, we would then need to understand the reason to ever think that pornographic works might be restricted from being art. Is there some moral reason to think that pornography cannot be art? While some may be tempted to think so, this seems intuitively groundless to me. Is it necessarily true that all pornographic works are immoral? And if so, then why should an object's moral value have anything to do with its art-hood status? Some philosophers have argued that immoral works of art must be necessarily bad works of art,[6] but we should keep in mind that for something to be a "bad work of art" it must first of all *be* a work of art! For instance, in 1990 Rick Gibson constructed a piece of performance art that would become infamous. The work consisted of a 25-kilogram weight suspended above a rat, named Sniffy. Between the rat and the weight were two sheets of canvas. Gibson would take this contraption to a street corner where he would offer "art lessons" to any of the passersby. He would instruct his new-found art student to pull a lever that would drop the weight and crush Sniffy between the two sheets of canvas. Gibson never had a chance to complete the piece, however – an angry mob forced him to stop. He then returned the rat to the pet shop, where Sniffy was later sold off to be fed to a snake![7] Some would argue that Gibson's piece is not art by virtue of the fact that it is immoral. Without offering an argument for this here, it is my view that Gibson's performance is an immoral work of art – meaning that the piece both *is* a work of art and *immoral* for its use of animal cruelty. While this might be a rather extreme example, my thinking is that what makes something a "work of art" is quite different from what makes something "morally blameworthy"; that evaluative criteria like "being morally good" have little to do with an object's being a work of art; and that the concept of "immoral art" is *not* an oxymoron. So I would not think that an object's being "morally bad" should count against its being art, and that it matters not whether we are talking about Sniffy the rat or works of pornography.[8]

Alternatively, some argue that works of pornography cannot be art because they must rely on clichéd or repetitive artistic devices. It has been argued by some that pornography is too fantastical, or too predictable, or too sexually explicit to be art.[9] But again this seems to me a bad reason to restrict pornographic works from art. At best, these arguments could only serve to show that such clichéd, repetitive, fantastical, or predictable works are not very *good* works of art – but so what? It is not a necessary condition for something's being a work of art that it must be "good" (whether moral or aesthetic). So, in the end, should works of pornography count as art? I really do not care. The question that I wish to address in this essay is essentially about the interests and values we may attribute to objects. While an object's ontological category may affect the way in which it is valued, I am inclined to agree with Michael Rea that "pornography" is not itself a genuine ontological category.[10]

Distinguishing Interests and Values

One might think that the natural place to start is to examine what makes a work pornographic. The idea would be to determine what the necessary and sufficient conditions might be for a work to be considered pornographic; however, there appears to be no straightforward answer

CHRISTOPHER BARTEL

to this question. If we take all of the works that might be considered pornographic as a class of objects, then we would likely find that there is nothing that all objects making up this class have in common – nothing that is either necessary or sufficient for an object to be a member of the class of "objects that might be considered pornographic." Some pornographic works are not very explicit (e.g., the images in a *Playboy* magazine certainly depict nudity, but they are not terribly explicit), while other pornographic works do not even involve the depiction of nudity (e.g., Fragonard's painting *The Swing* may have been titillating to a contemporary viewer for its coded suggestion of illicit sexuality, but everyone in the painting has their clothes on). In the end, we should simply acknowledge that it would be complicated and rather tricky to define pornography, and even more tricky to explain away all of the seemingly idiosyncratic cases. Luckily, we do not need to define pornography in order to address my question. Rather, it would be sufficient for our purposes to determine what it means to take a pornographic interest in an object, whether that object is an innocent shoe catalog or a really hardcore, sexually explicit video.

A "pornographic interest" is a kind of attitude that a person can take towards a certain object. As stated previously, there are many kinds of interests we can take towards an object. Taking a pornographic interest means essentially two things: that the consumer identifies something in the content of the work that would normally excite his or her sexual interest, and that the consumer imaginatively engages with that feature of the work in a way that would normally result in his or her sexual arousal.[11] Of course, the kind of content that an individual finds sexually arousing will certainly differ from person to person, but despite this, instances of taking a pornographic interest always share this in common: that the individual focuses his or her attention on the arousing content in such a way that it would normally result in his or her being sexually aroused.

The necessity of the first condition of this definition – that one identify something in the content of the work that one would normally find sexually arousing – would appear obvious. If you are not into that sort of thing, then you are not going to take a pornographic interest in its depiction. It is the necessity of the second condition that needs some explaining. Imagine a case where someone identifies something in the content of a work they find to be sexually arousing, but they do not imaginatively engage with the object in the required way. Consider this example: I imagine that the editors of pornographic magazines choose which photographs to publish because they expect that one photograph will be more arousing to their consumers than another – that is to say, the editor identifies something in the content of the work that they expect would excite the sexual interest of the magazine's consumers. Despite this, a particular editor may not actually be aroused by a photograph in a particular instance, and even if he did recognize the photograph to be sexually arousing for him. Imagine that the editor is working on the layout of the magazine, like cropping the photograph to fit the page properly – it would be highly distracting for him to be sexually aroused at that moment! When an editor is attending to the design qualities of the image (the image's size, color, contrast, resolution, etc.), he need not at that moment take a pornographic interest in the image – that is, one might recognize that the image contains some content that one would normally find sexually arousing, but one is not at that moment imaginatively engaging with the image in order to be sexually aroused. Rather, the editor is just trying to get his job done. Without imaginatively engaging with a work in a way that would result in one's sexual arousal, one is simply stuck in the mode of attention that the magazine editor is in: the content is identified as containing something that would be arousing in an almost detached, academic way. So, to take a properly pornographic interest in a work, the "imaginative engagement" condition must be necessary.

What does it mean to "imaginatively engage with an object in the required way"? As a general claim, I would think this means to imagine oneself in some way participating in a sexually fulfilling action with the depicted subject. Of course, this would differ from person to person depending entirely on what the individual happens to find "sexually fulfilling." If an individual is aroused by Michelangelo's "David," then I would expect his or her arousal to partly be the product of his or her imagining participating in some sexual act with the person that the sculpture depicts. Again, I should point out that the idea of "pornographic interest" that I have described is an entirely subjective, psychological state. The exact details of what one finds sexually arousing or sexually fulfilling are entirely down to individual sexual preferences. That being said, my general claim would still hold – that to take a pornographic interest in something is for a consumer to identify something in the content of the work that would normally excite his or her sexual interest and to imaginatively engage with that feature of the work in a way that would normally result in his or her sexual arousal.

If this is what it means to take a pornographic interest in a work, then what does it mean to take an "artistic interest" in a work? This concept may be somewhat more controversial, mainly because the range of objects that one can take an artistic interest in would appear to be far more

𝔥 CHRISTOPHER BARTEL

diverse than the range of objects that one can take a pornographic interest in, and one would wonder whether there is one distinct kind of interest that could be described as *the* artistic interest. The worry is that there may be many interests that one can take in works of art that may all with justification be described as an artistic interest. This is a much deeper problem, which I unfortunately do not have the space to address here. Still, if the definition of artistic interest that I will provide is not exhaustive of the phenomenon, it still remains to be seen whether my definition of artistic interest is compatible or not with pornographic interest.

A common understanding of artistic interest holds that this is not simply the interest that one takes in the content of a work. Rather, when one takes an artistic interest in an object, one is fundamentally concerned with the formal qualities of the work. If the work happens to contain some recognizable content – that is, if the work is not wholly abstract – then one's artistic interest may include the way in which the content is represented through that particular medium. In this case, one's interest strikes a balance between form and content. Specifically, what one takes an interest in is the manner in which the artist has rendered their chosen content given the constraints of their medium and technique. One does not take an interest solely in *what* is depicted, but rather one takes an interest in the *manner* of depiction. As Jerrold Levinson says:

> An image that has an artistic interest, dimension, or intent is one that is not simply *seen through*, or *seen past*, leaving one, at least in imagination, face to face with the subject. Images with an artistic dimension are thus to some extent *opaque*, rather than *transparent*. In other words, with artistic images we are invited to dwell on features of the image itself, and not merely on what the image represents.[12]

When one takes no real interest in the formal qualities of an object, it is as if one simply looks through a transparent medium at the represented object, which would allow one a good vantage point to take a pornographic interest in the object.[13] Alternatively, when one lingers appreciatively on the formal qualities of the object, even if one is still in some sense mindful of the content of the work, then one is taking an artistic interest in the object. This distinction between *opaque* and *transparent* nicely captures the general idea of what I mean by "artistic interest," even if this distinction is rather difficult to apply in some cases. For instance, it is rather difficult to imagine how pornographic literature might be transparent in the way that Levinson describes.[14] Still, even in the case of pornographic literature, we might distinguish between the interest we take in the author's use of metaphor, allusion, or alliteration, on the one hand, that is, a *literary interest*, and the interest we take in the scene or actions that the author describes, on the other hand.

Employing this distinction between a pornographic interest and an artistic interest, we may offer an analogous distinction between *pornographic value* and *artistic value*. Essentially, to take an interest in an object in a certain way is to value that object in a certain way. So, if you take a pornographic interest in an object, you place some pornographic value on that object; and if you take an artistic interest in an object, you place some artistic value on that object. An object is "valued as pornography" insofar as it is the sort of object that would reward a pornographic interest. If taking a pornographic interest in a work is to identify something in the content of that work that one would normally find sexually arousing and to imaginatively engage with that feature of the work in a way that would normally result in one's sexual arousal, then a work has some pornographic value if it is conducive to this sort of interest. Some objects will be more rewarding as pornography than others. Likewise, an object is "valued as art" insofar as it is the sort of object that would reward an artistic interest. Of course, we should notice that, as these notions of value are inherently tied to a psychological state of taking a particular kind of interest in an object, then which objects have pornographic value and which have artistic value would be relative to the subject – thus, pornography really is in the eye of the beholder![15]

Of course, these are not the only values that we can place on an object – as stated previously, objects can serve many interests and can hold many different kinds of value. For instance, if I have a historical interest in an object, then I place some historical value on that object. Pornographic value is merely one value among many, and one that may sit alongside and be weighed against other values that we may attribute to a work. Furthermore, the degrees of value that we ascribe to an object may differ greatly, depending on what kind of value we are talking about. It is not the case that objects having a high value in one regard must also have a high value in its other regards; or, just because an object rewards one kind of interest does not mean that it must reward any other kind of interest. For instance, think about the early musical compositions written by Mozart when he was a young child. Artistically, these works might not be very good – we might place very low *artistic value* on Mozart's childhood compositions – but still, these works hold a high *historical value*.

ᛘ   CHRISTOPHER BARTEL

With this distinction in place, we can think about the pornographic value of a work in relation to the artistic value of that work.

Relations Between the Pornographic and the Artistic

I take it to be uncontroversial that a single work can be valued in many different ways or excite many different kinds of interest in a consumer. It seems intuitively obvious to me that a person may use a single object to serve different interests at different times, and as one's concern for the object shifts between these different kinds of interests, one may attend to distinct qualities of the object that serve these interests (though in some cases it may be true that one's different interests in an object are actually directed towards the same qualities). To take an artistic interest in the paintings of Elvgren, for example, is to appreciate the way in which the artist handles his medium in the representation of his chosen subject. Alternatively, to take a pornographic interest in the paintings of Elvgren is simply to find something in the content of his paintings that one finds sexually arousing, which in this case would be ladies in various stages of undress, and to imaginatively engage with that feature of the work in a way that would result in one's sexual arousal – imagining oneself helping those ladies in getting undressed! Elvgren's paintings would be valued as art to the extent that his paintings reward an artistic interest, and Elvgren's paintings would be valued as pornography to the extent that his paintings reward a pornographic interest.

While I think it is obvious that a single object can satisfy many different kinds of interest and could be valued in many different ways, what I am uncertain of is how these kinds of interests and values might be related. Is it ever the case that valuing a work artistically necessarily requires one to take a pornographic interest in that work? Is it ever true that one *cannot* appreciate the artistic value of a work *without* taking a pornographic interest in that work? I believe that this is false – to value a work artistically never requires one to take a pornographic interest in that work. Indeed, I would go further and say that taking a pornographic interest in a work is incompatible with one's taking an artistic interest in that work. The reason is because taking a pornographic interest in a work requires the consumer to look past the medium of the work and fix one's attention solely on the work's content, while taking an artistic interest in a work requires the consumer to attend explicitly

to the medium of the work. Certainly, a consumer could shift her attention between her pornographic interest and her artistic interest in the
work seemingly at will. My point, however, is that a work does not
excite her artistic interest *by virtue of* its exciting her pornographic
interest – what makes the object good art is not what makes the object
good porn.

We should remember the distinction between transparent viewing
and opaque viewing: to view something "transparently" is to look
through the object in such a way that one pays little attention to the
medium through which one is looking; to view something "opaquely" is
to linger on the particular formal qualities of the medium in an appre-
ciative way. Now, to take a pornographic interest in a work is to identify
something in the content of the work that one would normally find sexually arousing and to actually imaginatively engage with that feature of
the work's content in a way that would normally result in one's sexual
arousal. To take a pornographic interest in a work is to treat the medium
of the work as if it were transparent, that is, to treat the medium of representation as if it is just a vehicle for representation. One need not
artistically appreciate the formal qualities of the medium in order to
take a pornographic interest in a work – certainly, one can, but the point
is that taking an artistic appreciation in those formal qualities is not
necessary in order to take a pornographic interest in a work. Alternatively,
to take an artistic interest in a work is to appreciatively linger on the
formal qualities of the work's medium – that is, to view the medium of
the work opaquely. And here is the problem: one takes a pornographic
interest in the content alone, not in the balance between content and
form. To a pornographic interest, the medium is transparent – one sees
past the formal qualities of the object to behold and imaginatively
engage with the content of the work itself – and an artistic interest is
opaque. One will never find the artistic value in an object that one
regards transparently because one must regard the object opaquely to
appreciate its artistic value.

Incidentally, I wonder if the reverse kind of scenario is ever true – does
one ever appreciate the pornographic value of an object through taking
an artistic interest in that work? This would be a case where one's pornographic interest in a work is somehow satisfied by paying attention to the
formal qualities of a work, where one finds sexual arousal in attending to
those qualities of the work that are normally associated with one's artistic interest. A possible case might be bondage photographs. Someone
who is sexually aroused by bondage might pay special attention to the

stillness of a photographic image. Perhaps paying attention to the stillness of the photographic image actually heightens the consumer's sense
of anxiety and suspense, or the sense of being "bound" by the photographic image aids in the consumer's sexual arousal. If this is what one
is sexually aroused by, then this might be a case where taking an artistic
interest in a formal quality of a work serves the double-duty of also contributing to the consumer's sexual arousal. However, one point should
be made clear about this "double-duty." If the case I have described
above is correct, then what is happening may simply be that the same
formal feature is involved in the consumer's artistic interest as well as in
her pornographic interest. But this is not to say that the consumer must
take an artistic interest in the object in order to take a pornographic
interest in that object. Rather, it just happens to be the case that the stillness of the photograph – a formal feature of the object that the consumer
takes an artistic interest in – also serves the consumer's sexual interest.
Basically, this consumer would appear to have a "formal fetish"[16] for
photographic stillness. I see no reason to doubt this possibility; however
idiosyncratic this fetish may be, the possibility of this sort of case is really
an empirical question.

How would we explain this case? The possibility of formal fetishes
does not conflict with the argument of this essay. Rather, this just simply
illustrates a point that I made earlier – that there are many interests that
a consumer may take in an object; and while these distinct interests may
be served by attending to distinct qualities of the object, in some cases
the various interests that a consumer may have are actually directed
towards the same quality. The case of bondage photographs may simply
be one of those cases – the stillness of the photograph serves both a pornographic interest and an artistic interest. However, importantly, this
does not yet prove that one appreciates the pornographic value of an
object through taking an artistic interest in the photograph. To prove this,
we would need to establish that the consumer's artistic interest is a necessary condition of their pornographic interest, and that has not been
established by this case.

So, can pornographic works have artistic value? Yes, an object could
satisfy both an artistic interest and a pornographic interest. But is it ever
the case that one artistically values a work *by virtue of* one's taking a pornographic interest in that work? No, because an artistic interest requires
one to take an interest in the formal qualities of the work, and a pornographic interest ignores these qualities in order to attend to the content
of the work solely.[17]

NOTES

1 See, for instance, Jerrold Levinson, "Erotic Art," in Edward Craig (ed.) *The Routledge Encyclopedia of Philosophy* (New York: Routledge, 1999), pp. 406–9, and "Erotic Art and Pornographic Pictures," *Philosophy and Literature* 29, 1 (2005): 228–40; Joel Feinberg, *Offense to Others* (New York: Oxford University Press, 1985); and George Steiner, "Night Words: High Pornography and Human Privacy," in Douglas Hughes (ed.) *Perspectives on Pornography* (New York: St. Martin's Press, 1970), pp. 96–108.

2 Specifically, I have in mind Matthew Kieran, "Pornographic Art," *Philosophy and Literature* 25 (2001): 31–45. See also Levinson, "Erotic Art and Pornographic Pictures," for his response to Kieran's argument.

3 An example that springs to mind is Damien Hirst's sculpture *For the Love of God*, produced in 2007, which is a platinum cast of a human skull encrusted with 8,601 diamonds. This sculpture may be worth quite a lot of money today, but this alone does not make it artistically valuable or even historically important. Personally, I like much of Hirst's work; however, I wonder whether *For the Love of God* will really stand the test of time.

4 See, for instance, Steiner, "Night Words."

5 By "pure music" here I simply mean music that has no lyrics – instrumental music. Certainly, some pure music might be associated with pornography, but this association does not make the music pornographic. For pure music to be pornographic I would think that the music itself would need to be sexually arousing. Whether this is possible or not may really be an empirical question.

6 See, for instance, Mary Devereaux, "Beauty and Evil: Leni Riefenstahl's *Triumph of the Will*" and Berys Gaut, "The Ethical Criticism of Art," both in Jerrold Levinson (ed.) *Aesthetics and Ethics* (New York: Cambridge University Press, 1998).

7 I am unaware of any philosophers who have directly discussed the moral problems associated with Gibson's piece, but Thomas Heyd offers an interesting discussion of this work with regard to the artistic status of performance art in an essay titled "Understanding Performance Art: Art Beyond Art," *British Journal of Aesthetics* 31 (2001): 68–73.

8 A more plausible suggestion in my view is that the immorality of Gibson's piece necessarily renders his work *artistically* flawed. This is a claim that would be supported by Gaut's theory of ethicism in "The Ethical Criticism of Art." While I think this claim has some plausibility, I also have my worries. Would we think the same about pornography? If some pornography is immoral, then is that pornography necessarily artistically flawed? I hesitate to accept this because, as the argument of my essay shows, an object can serve many interests for a consumer. Moral interests and artistic interests seem to me distinct kinds of interests, as are pornographic interests and artistic interests. However, my hesitation is due to the observation that one's aesthetic response sometimes is

CHRISTOPHER BARTEL

dependent upon one's moral sensibilities. Think of dirty jokes: to appreciate their humor, it seems that one must recognize that the joke is dirty – that is, one must be aware of the ethical implications of the joke in order to appreciate its risqué humor. This suggests that moral sensibilities sometimes do play a role in our aesthetic responses. Unfortunately, I do not have the space to pursue this thought here and must leave it aside.

9   Steiner, "Night Words," argues that pornography is necessarily repetitive because the pornographic imagination is limited to what one finds sexually pleasurable, which he thinks must be rather limited. As he says, "In most erotic writing, as in man's wet dreams, the imagination turns, time and time again, inside the bounded circle of what the body can experience. The actions of the mind when we masturbate are not a dance; they are a treadmill" (101). See also Feinberg, *Offense to Others*, ch. 11.

10 Michael Rea, "What is Pornography?" *Nous* 35 (2001): 118–45. Rea makes a similar point regarding the category *work of art* in his essay "Constitution and Kind Membership," *Philosophical Studies* 97 (2000): 169–93. While I am tempted to agree with this too, I also think that the category *work of art* is relevant to evaluation and appreciation in a way that the category *pornography* is not. The category *work of art* is useful to evaluation even if this is not a genuine ontological kind.

11 I say "normally" here in order to avoid cases where defeating conditions arise – like being impotent, or being otherwise distracted, or whatever. We should of course also recognize that what is "normal" about one's sexual arousal will differ from person to person.

12 Levinson, "Erotic Art and Pornographic Pictures," p. 232.

13 For the idea of photographic "transparency," See Kendall Walton, "Transparent Pictures: On the Nature of Photographic Realism," *Critical Inquiry* 11 (1984): 246–77. For discussion of the "transparency thesis" and the aesthetic value of photography, see Roger Scruton, "Photography and Representation," *Aesthetic Understanding* (London: Methuen, 1983) and Dominic Lopes, "The Aesthetics of Photographic Transparency," *Mind* 112 (2003): 433–48.

14 It is worth noting that Levinson regards photography as "the prime medium for pornography, that which has displaced all other such media in that connection. For photography is the transparent medium *par excellence*, that is, the medium that comes closest to simply presenting the requisite object – typically, a woman or a man or combinations thereof – directly, as material for sexual fantasy and gratification" ("Erotic Art and Pornographic Pictures," p. 232). To my knowledge, Levinson has not commented on the idea of pornographic literature.

15 Again, it is for this reason that I do not think of *pornography* as a substantial ontological category.

16 Thanks to Dave Monroe for this phrase.

17 My thanks go to Jennifer Courtney-Bartel and Dave Monroe for the many helpful suggestions that they each made on earlier versions of this essay.

CHAPTER 13

AN UNHOLY TRINITY

The Beautiful, the Romantic, and the Vulgar

This study examines the differences between fine art, erotica, and pornography in the visual arts. Of paramount importance is the issue of drawing parameters that would allow one to recognize the difference between erotic presentations from pornographic presentations. Furthermore, and as a compliment to aforesaid distinction, I want to address the aesthetic attitude and the role it may play in estimates of pornography. Ultimately, the focus will be to underscore the central place of aesthetic distance for declaring a work as erotic or pornographic.

Erotica and Pornography: From the Romantic to the Vulgar

We use the word "erotica" to refer to any phenomenon that provokes sexual desires relating to sexual love. In this regard I raise two questions. First, in what way is erotica distinct from pornography? And secondly, does erotic art meet the criteria required for fine art? The second question, to be discussed later, relates to the conditions needed for the development of the aesthetic attitude of the observer as a prerequisite for aesthetic experience. I intend to examine whether or not the works of visual art falling under the category of erotica satisfy the demands of fine art insofar as fine art enables the viewer to have a disinterested interest in the art object;

simply put, that means having an interest solely in the contemplation of the object free from any other interests or motives one might have.

In such instances the viewer has intrinsic interest in the art object for its own sake. So when asking if erotic art meets the standards of evaluating a work as fine art, and the answer is no, then I maintain there are problems characterizing erotica as fine art. But if the answer is yes then erotic art may well indeed come within the domain of fine art.

These issues are not unrelated to visual presentations of pornography. Just the same, the promiscuously public men and women of the world appear to be confused over the difference between erotica and pornography. In practice these forms of production are often confused, perhaps because of the overlapping sexual content in both kinds of presentations. I believe this confusion is due more to a focus on moral issues, with little or no interest regarding aesthetic considerations about fine art as distinct from related visual presentations.

Historically, the term "pornography" has been used to refer to the activities of prostitutes, including the various media (pictures and literature) that are meant to arouse sexual feelings and desires. Thus, the definitions of erotica and pornography are similar in that both relate to the stimulation of sexual desires. Nevertheless, there is at least one outstanding difference that we can take as a point of departure for this essay. The products of erotica are related to romantic love whereas pornographic works exclude love, romantic or otherwise, in the effort to arouse the basest forms of lust by the sexual activities of would-be porn stars.[1]

I would now like to focus on how one might go about drawing a sharper division between erotica and pornography. Theses remarks are restricted to visual presentations as examples of either erotica or pornography. While the common use of the word "erotica" may be a point of departure for this inquiry, it does nothing to unpack basic differences between it and pornography.

My view asserts a fundamental difference between erotica and pornography. Erotica may share aesthetic qualities possessed by works of fine art but not pornography. I suggest that the ideal of what ought to be considered erotica as something much different from the rules constituting pornography. Undoubtedly, I will admit that in practice there will be instances where the division between the two is not as obvious as I recommend, and the same might be said for the differences between erotica and fine art.

We may start by highlighting the salient features of erotica. Erotica encourages the *provocation* of sexual love. To say that erotica is provocative means that the object is capable of *inciting* some emotion in the viewer as it is drawn toward the object: the viewer's emotion is aroused to the level of excitement. In no way is he or she detached from the experience of the object. This follows Arthur Berndtson's insight that in the erotic aspect of art, "eros begins with the pleasure of admiration, which here is directed toward the sexual being of another: the pleasure contracts into desire for union with that being; the desire represents itself as moving toward a dark ecstasy, a passage beyond clear areas of the self, pleasure, and consciousness."[2] In Berndtson's expressionists aesthetic, the attentive audience is stimulated in a particular way that involves, *inter alia*, the "desire for union with that being." Clearly, the appeal of erotica in the visual arts is not the same as that of pornography. Erotica stimulates *affection* for the erotic object. In most cases the object depicted is a person or persons, though it may be a non-human object as well, or the person(s) depicted may be involved with erotic objects. By saying erotica stimulates affection we are bringing attention to the *empathetic relation* the artist evokes between the aesthetic perceiver and the erotic depiction. Additionally, the arousal of sexual desire is not one of an autoerotic kind; the perceiver is not self-absorbed by his or her own sexuality, but is in fact interested in the object for its own expression of aesthetic qualities of grace, harmony, and balance. The erotic presentation *reveals its sexual character through aesthetic qualities.* The affection has an aesthetic quality due to the attention of the perceiver to enjoy a degree of disinterest in the art object; thus his or her concern is not vulgar sexual lust. Again, there is a residue of *detachment* between the aroused observer and the expression provided by the erotic object, thus some aesthetic distance is sustained by the perceiver and the object. The affection is not purely sexual simply because part of the reason for the attraction to the erotic object is its success in expressing aesthetic qualities of the object. For example, the aesthetic qualities are prefigured in the artist's intention to express the emotion embodied in the object engaged by the aesthetic perceiver. The aesthetic features of balance, grace, unity in diversity and harmony are generated by the artist and her technique to impress the observer with beauty expressed in an *ambient sexual milieu.* The permeation of sexuality within the work is secondary to the artistic expression of the object.

Given these remarks about erotica and its relation to sexual arousal we are now in a position to sharpen the contrast to pornography. I suggest that there are several key differences between the two. Starting again with the common uses of the terms cited above, erotica involves erotic love as an integrated feature of sexuality, but the same cannot be said for pornography. Pornography tends to emphasize pure sexuality in the raw, so to speak; it appeals is to the common and vulgar nature of humanity. The view I hold is opposed to that held by Feinberg. He writes:

> A painting of a copulating couple that satisfied the relevant standards for good painting would *ipso facto* be a work of pictorial art; it might be done in exquisitely harmonizing color, with properly balanced composition, subtlety of line, successful lighting effects, and depicted figures of memorably graceful posture and facial expressiveness. Such a painting might also be designed to stimulate the genitals of the observer. Insofar as it also achieved that goal it would be a work of pornography.[3]

In contrast to this passage, one could argue that when we take into account the aesthetic observer it may not be the case that the work can be fine art and pornographic at the same time. This is because Feinberg's appeal to genital arousal prevents the observer from having a disinterested interest in the object for its own intrinsic worth. His example may, in principle, be an instance of fine art or pornography, but not both. If it is a case of fine art then it holds the potential to be viewed with disinterest, but pornography, not bearing aesthetic properties, forfeits the opportunity for aesthetic contemplation. The above passage highlights the aim of the artist at the expense of the disposition held by selective attention of the observer.

Let us take into account another consideration. Consider pornography being more closely related to fetishism than it is to erotica. The fetish/pornography connection may help clear up the misunderstanding, and thus the conflation, of erotica with pornography. First, note that fetishism has a sordid history largely because of religious disapproval of using *non-natural* means to achieve sexual gratification. Fetishism does imply the deliberate use of some artificial means to stimulate sexual desire. There are too many fetish objects and the playing out of fetish roles for me to list. Among fetish objects would be shoes, boots, masks, costumes, feathers, whips, and chains, not to mention an assortment of foods, lubricants, aphrodisiacs, etc. Porn movies, magazines, and other visual material often, though not always, use these props as a means to do the same things as Viagra does, namely, excite the genital organs in the quest for carnal pleasure. Whether or not the porn artisan employs fetish objects, the goal is the arousal of heightened sensuality. Pornography serves a utilitarian role, thus the product serves as a means to the pleasure of the customer. The sexual stimulus plan for pornography need not involve any residue of loving affection, erotic or otherwise. Certainly, an art object can be pornographic without the use of fetish objects or role playing that is also part of the fetish repertoire; more underbrush has to be cleared away to discern the boundaries between erotica and pornography. For instance, a nude photo or painting may be erotic or pornographic – or perhaps neither. I would argue that if it meets the conditions I have stated for erotic art then it is best classified as erotica and not pornography. But what qualifies as a pornographic object? The idea presented here suggests that pornography appeals to the baser forms of sexual attraction, so what if the nude photograph intentionally and deliberately attracts the viewer's attention to an explicit display of the sexual organs that is *out of proportion and balance* with the nude body perceived as a gestalt? Or, what if proportionality and grace are disrupted through exaggeration of one aspect of the object to the neglect of other features of the nude? On the view here advocated one would be inclined to judge that such a photo is pornographic and not erotic; fetish instruments and roles need not be part of the sexual stimulus plan. However, the nude so depicted is far different than the erotic art.

This again takes us back to the origin of pornography as related to prostitutes and their commercial activities. Attraction to the pornographic object has nothing to do with any sort of empathetic relation with the object. What affects and attracts the viewer is of a purely sexual nature denuded of any authentic care for the subject of the presentation. One could make the same point involving the relation he or she has with a prostitute; the relation has nothing to do with authentic care for the person as a being worthy of moral respect, nor need it involve love, if by that term we mean interest in the interest of another, or of unconditional openness to the other. It lacks concern for the interest, goals, ideals, or respect for the other. More to the point, the prostitute is a *commodity* intended to satisfy the interest of the buyer, and the buyer, in turn, returns coins for flesh. Outside of that, there is no care involving the prostitute for his or her own sake.

One other point may be made to separate erotica from pornography. Earlier, I maintained that the pornographic object explicitly draws the viewer's attention to the distorted feature of the object. Whether or not erotica qualifies for fine art is a question considered at the end of this inquiry, but it should be clear that pornography is distinct from erotica and fine art for the same reasons. The visual presentation of the object does not have the properties of proportion, theme and variation, and gradation of color, nor does it display unity in diversity. In fact, part of what makes it pornography is just the opposite of these traits. Stephen Pepper, for instance, might well argue that pornographic depictions cause sensory and attentive fatigue. The pornographic object is purposely out of harmonic balance, it does not display unity within diversity; moreover, the features one is drawn to end in repetition and, as Pepper argues, to fatigue in the long run.[4] It is for this reason that the viewer of pornographic material is attracted to the object. Some features are exaggerated out of proportion for the purpose of fixating the viewer's attention on one character or feature of the work to the neglect of other aspects of the presentation. Thus the viewer can feed off of his or her own vulgar desire for self-indulgence in the exaggerated feature of the work. In this case we lose focus on the gestalt and on the "distance" between the perceiver and the object in works of erotica. Pornography then becomes a vehicle of selfish absorption. This being the case we can further add that disinterestedness in no way plays into the observer/object relation in pornography.

The concept of disinterestedness introduced here is an essential trait of the aesthetic experience. It allows the work of art, its expression of embodied emotion, to be communicated by the artist – at least in rare cases – to the disinterested aesthetic percipient. As I have characterized pornography, such disinterestedness plays no part whatsoever in the viewer. In fact the viewer comes closer to being a *voyeur*; one who seeks sexual gratification by watching the sexual activities of others from an undisclosed hiding place. The voyeur cannot be entirely disinterested because she must guard her private vantage point; fear of being discovered and objectified would strip away her subjectivity. Moreover, the porn object cannot be viewed with disinterest since the would-be aesthetic properties are intentionally violated for the purposes of genital arousal.

Up to now I have endeavored to highlight basic differences between pornography and erotica. And where I have argued that pornography, at least as I have characterized it, ought not be placed in the category of fine art, there still remains works of erotica that I find more ambiguous and problematic when trying to classify them as fine art or not. Part of this ambiguity is due to the fact that erotica, as I have characterized it, seems to share some of the traits that go along with fine art. At the same time, the above account of erotica raises questions that may be central to whether or not it is to be classified as fine art. Thus the following questions: How far can disinterestedness be operative to the viewer of erotic material? To what degree does the sexual arousal of erotic art compromise the distance of the viewer, therefore conflating the boundary between erotica and pornography?

Aesthetic Contemplation: The Romantic and the Beautiful

The answer to these questions rests with the attitude in which erotica is or is not deemed to be fine art, still keeping in mind the demarcation between pornography and erotica.

Remember that erotic works of art involve sexual arousal at the core of their disclosure to the perceiver. So if disinterestedness is essential to the aesthetic attitude, is it possible for the viewer to be disinterested in his/her perception of erotic works? In the case of erotica it would appear that the viewer is not excited in the same way that one who views porn is; on the other hand, there is more involved in erotica than simply the display of aesthetic qualities like proportion, balance, and unity in diversity. Keeping with this thought, we may recall Pepper's analysis of aesthetic design and say that the exposure to pornography may lead to fatigue on the part of the perceiver, yet this need not be true of the viewer in his/her relation to the erotic work as long as the artist has expressed the qualities identified with fine art.

Having said this, however, it would appear to be problematic as to whether or not erotica meets the requirement of disinterestedness necessary for a genuine aesthetic experience. While the concept of aesthetic contemplation certainly deserves an essay of its own, one may briefly characterize the aesthetic attitude as it has come down to us from two noteworthy figures: Arthur Schopenhauer and Edward Bullough.

Schopenhauer writes:

> If one . . . surrenders the whole power of his spirit to the intuition, sinks into the intuition, and lets his entire consciousness be filled by the peaceful contemplation of the directly present natural object, such as a landscape, a tree, a rock, or a building, that is, forgets his individuality, his will, and remains only as pure subject, as a clear mirror of the object; so that it is as though the object alone were there, without anyone that perceives it, and he can no longer separate the person that intuits from the intuition, but both have become one, since the entire consciousness is filled and occupied by a single intuitive image; if in such degree the object has passed out of all relation to something outside itself, and the subject out of all relation to the will: then, what is so known is no longer the individual thing as such, . . . thereby the person engaged in the intuition is no longer an individual: for the individual has lost himself in such intuition.[5]

This passage reflects the interconnection of Schopenhauer's metaphysics, which is founded on a blind striving *Will*, with his account of aesthetic disinterest. For our aim, it is not necessary to discuss the metaphysical ideas associated with his theory of the aesthetic attitude. I do however believe that regardless of his thought about reality it is possible to extract his notion of aesthetic distance. One can choose to accept or reject the metaphysics that goes along with it and still discern what is said regarding the attitude of the perceiver in the aesthetic contemplation. The dissolution of the ego's desire is a prerequisite for the highest level of aesthetic attention. Edward Bullough labeled this attitude "psychical distance," in that the perceiver, in this attitude, concentrates "direct attention to the features 'objectively' constituting the phenomenon."[6] Berndtson's analysis brings together the core idea of these two accounts. He avers that two traits are prevalent in aesthetic contemplation: (1) "intrinsic interest," because the perceiver has interest in the art object for its own sake without concern for any pragmatic or other value, and (2) "disinterest," because the perceiver is detached from his own interest while being absorbed in the art object. Part of what it means to be disinterested is that the viewer is not *uninterested*, but that the sole concentration is directed objectively to the work of art for its own sake. (Notice that this is the opposite in cases of pornography, where the viewer is self-absorbed in the exaggerated disclosure of the pornographic material.) In works of erotica – as I have characterized it – part of the problem is that the perceiver will not be capable of the disinterested attitude and have intrinsic interest, since erotica has to do with the arousal of sexual feelings in the perceiver. She or he is not completely detached from the erotic work since erotica draws one to the object for romantic intentions. This is true even though we have admitted that in the erotic work the artist has succeeded in impregnating the erotic object such that it is endowed with the aesthetic qualities that are also expressed in works of fine art.

For the perceiver to be disinterested he/she must assume a contemplative attitude that permits attention to the object *for its own sake*. Obviously, this is not always the case; one can imagine a person never having an aesthetic experience in their entire life. And I also acknowledge that there may be other reasons why one attends to a work of art other than for pure aesthetic appreciation. For example, one may consider the utility of a work or one may even be so distracted by their own interests that having a disinterested attitude is not possible. I certainly cannot assume a disinterested attitude when I'm currently worried about paying bills or distracted by a noisy neighbor. But things are much different in works of erotica, since erotic works *provoke* rather than *express* sexual feelings in the observer; in erotica the observer is called to action.

As I suggested earlier the difference between provoking and expressing is crucial to the theme I want to convey. Provocation by the art object greatly diminishes the possibility of disinterested distance by the perceiver because it stimulates in him or her some type of action for union with the object. Artistic expression, on the other hand, means the intent of the artist is embodied in the object; moreover, the emotive content expressed can be made present to the disinterested aesthetic observer without the perceiver being motivated to act in some way toward the object. What Bullough called "psychical distance" between the perceiver and the art object cannot be achieved in works of erotica because the viewer is incited to attend to the erotic object. That attention differs from the pure contemplation of the work. One might say that ulterior motives are involved in the relation between the perceiver and the erotic object. Again, it seems that Feinberg misses the point about distance concerning *both* pornography and erotica when he claims, "Not only erotically realistic art but also artful pornography *can* satisfy the criterion of interest. . . . Distance is preserved in erotic pictorial art through the use of artificial stylized images."[7] Here Feinberg does acknowledge the criterion of distance. But because erotica minimally involves some degree of sexual arousal, the object is reflected back to the interests of the observer rather that to the interest of the object for its own sake. Another way of saying this is that the provocation of the erotic object, due to its sexual nature, subverts the possibility of attending to the object for its own sake. I maintain that if it did not do this then it would not succeed in being a work of erotica.

We have then another reason for distinguishing erotica from fine art. The aesthetic attitude endures in the work of fine art, but the same cannot be said for works of erotica. However – and I think this point is crucial – if the above characterizations of erotic art and fine art are correct, the difference between the two is a difference of degree, not of kind. Erotica in the visual media are indeed art, though it may not have the capacity for psychical distance that works of fine art possess.

One is apt to criticize my view in the following way: "Look who's conflating the issue now. On the one hand, you argue that the aesthetic attitude is an essential feature for the appreciation of fine art and we can't have that with erotic art. Then you flip flop and say that there may be some overlap between fine art and erotica, thus maybe erotica can, *in some instances*, fulfill the demands of fine art."

Am I unable to distinguish dusk from dawn? Perhaps, but there may be good reasons why I cannot. Fine art and erotica, I confess, do share aesthetic qualities. Both are objects of art appreciation. But my focus has

𝄞 LAWRENCE HOWE

been on the attitude of the aesthetic observer, more so than on the art object, and even less on the intent of the artist. I propose to look at fine art and erotica as limiting concepts, or if you will, as ideals that may or may not be achieved. Sometimes there may be clear-cut cases where, on my criteria, it is possible to distinguish one from the other, but not *all the time*. This is likely because psychical distance has much to do with the psychological attitude or mindset of the aesthetic observer. Perhaps an example will allow me to demonstrate my inability to definitively draw a line between fine art and erotica in some cases. As an illustration one may take Degas' *Nude Study*. This piece is exquisite and graceful, evoking as it does a complex of emotions that may split the psyche between the embodied form of pure art and the joyful lust of erotic pleasure. I view this as a paradigm case indicative of the murky line between fine art and erotica. Why? Because I have intuited it, at different times over the years, as erotica sometimes and as fine art at other times. What makes this confused evaluation possible? We may well be reminded that the aesthetic distance takes a psychic effort on the part of the perceiver to achieve. According to this paradigm case, *Nude Study* is erotic one time and at other times the disinterested contemplation of line, shape, color, harmony, and balance delivers my attention to the domain of fine art.

One may now draw a sharper and more definitive contrast between pornography and erotica. The difference between the two is not just a difference of degree, but rather a difference of kind. Of course pornography, like erotica and fine art, may appeal to various tastes. But when it comes to aesthetic considerations alone it would appear that pornography can in no way – unlike erotica – be mistaken for fine art because it does not allow an aesthetic attitude to be taken with respect to the object. The pornographic object attracts the vulgar and common themes of brute sexuality. If the aim of pornography is sexual arousal this can be achieved in a variety of ways without involving aesthetic properties as part and parcel of the perceptual attitude; it renders no capacity for psychical distance. Further, even if we reject the possibility of psychical distance as a conceptual myth – and some aestheticians do – it still would not follow that pornography could be reckoned among the fine arts, owing to the fact that pornographic works do not embody aesthetic features disclosed in fine art. I hold that fine art has the potential to yield an aesthetic experience for the perceiver – on the condition that one possesses the necessary disinterest without thought of other motives. When attending to pornographic works, there is no interest in the work for its own sake. The interest one has in pornography is motivated by sexual interest that has more to do with the viewer than with the object. In this case the object has instrumental value and is a means to an end, the end being vulgar satisfaction and base sexual arousal.

The distinction endorsed above between erotica and pornography may seem obvious, though it has been my intention to show that there are clear boundaries between the two so that one is less likely to confuse one with the other. Part of my argument for drawing this distinction hinges on the notion of psychical distance between the viewer and the object. Because the works of erotica infuse aesthetic qualities into the object there is a degree in which one may consider the work for its own sake, but this is not entirely true since sexual arousal plays a role, thus compromising the psychical distance between viewer and object. Pornography, however, falls under a different set of categories in which it is to be characterized as a work of a significantly different kind than erotica or fine art. Largely because the interest the viewer has in the object is not, and cannot be, disinterested; the motivation is to channel the erotic stimulation of the viewer back upon him or her self. It would appear then to serve a purely pragmatic function.

Erotica, as I have characterized it, serves more than a narcissistic interest; it may approach works of fine art if the viewer is able to intuit the work on the basis of its aesthetic expression alone. If so, then it bears a much closer relation to fine art than it does to pornography.

What this essay amounts to is an attempt to categorize erotica and pornography in contrast to norms of fine art. We will admit that more issues emerge about fine art than are answered here. Be that as it may, the parameters I have suggested, and the reasons given for drawing them, demonstrate fundamental differences between two types of work that are often fused together: the allurement of erotica and the vulgarity of pornography.

NOTES

1　For an example of an erotic object, as opposed to a pornographic one, consider the scene of a Tahitian woman swimming nude in a lagoon or the film of Marilyn Monroe singing happy birthday to President Kennedy.

2　A. Berndtson, *Art, Expression and Beauty* (Austin: Holt, Rinehart and Winston, 1969), p. 267.

3　J. Feinberg, "Obscenity, Pornography, and the Arts: Sorting Things Out," in B. Leiser (ed.) *Values in Conflict: Life, Liberty, and the Rules of Law* (New York:

Macmillan, 1981). Reprinted in R. Trevas, A. Zucker, and D. Borchert (eds.) *Philosophy of Sex and Love* (Upper Saddle River: Prentice-Hall, 1997), p. 291.

4   S. Pepper, "Principles of Aesthetic Design," *Principles of Art Appreciation* (New York, Harcourt, 1949).
5   A. Schopenhauer, *The World as Will and Representation*, *vol.* 1, trans. E. F. Payne (New York: Dover, 1966), p. 231.
6   E. Bullough, "'Psychical Distance' as a Factor in Art and an Aesthetic Principle," *British Journal of Society* 5 (June 1912): 88–9.
7   See Feinberg, "Obscenity, Pornography, and the Arts," p. 295.

CHAPTER 14

THE PROBLEM WITH THE PROBLEM WITH PORNOGRAPHY

The Problem with the Problem

There is a problem in assuming there is a problem with pornographic images and objects. Not because they are not problematic, but because that problem itself is very difficult to articulate. It rests on the assumption that we ought to treat pornography as very different from other aesthetic objects (literature, films, paintings, etc.) because pornography necessarily involves immoral practices. Accepted artistic objects are judged aesthetically separate from any considerations of immoral practice in their production or immoral ideas in their expression, and immoral practices or decisions on the part of artists, such as Gauguin's treatment of his family, are very often excused because of the value of the object itself. But this is not so with pornographic objects. Art can be immoral and the artist who exploits others is censured or punished, but art need not involve these practices. An accepted intuition about pornography is that one cannot make or participate in pornography (including consuming it) without being party to some wrong. However, what this immorality might be is more difficult to discern.

So, we must first identify something about pornographic objects which is different from other aesthetic objects and, second, be able to ensure a consensus of agreement that this thing deserves an attitude of disapproval.

It is no good me, the individual David Rose, stating that pornography is obscene for me personally and ought, therefore, to be banned because I might also object to use of capers in cooking, but that would be just my opinion and no one is obliged to agree even if they respect my right to express it. Let us also, initially, distinguish between two levels of moral judgment. If you steal or kill (in most cases), then you will be punished by the state and subject to its laws. Moral wrongness of this sort requires legal sanction. If you are unfaithful to your wife, the state will not intervene, but you will probably be subject to the disapproval of friends and family. If the wrongness of pornography is of the first form, then pornographic images should be subject to law and censure. If its wrongness is of the second sort, then the images and their use will be subject to public condemnation.

In this chapter, I hope to show that it is impossible to identify anything about pornography which can ground the specific disapproval of pornographic objects, much less legal sanction, and that there is no real motive for treating pornography as different in kind from other aesthetic objects. Oddly, though, treating pornography as an aesthetic object does not admonish its producers and consumers of social commitments and obligations and actually allows us to engage with it in a less simplistic and moralistic manner.

What is Pornography?

There is, of course, a very serious problem with defining what is and what is not pornography. Many definitions have been proposed: the production of sexual material for the purpose of exchange; artistic material with little, if any, aesthetic value; material that represents persons as mere sexual objects; material that represents institutional inequality between the sexes; and material produced with the aim of aiding sexual gratification. Most of this analytical work is, though, unnecessary for the present chapter, simply because for once I can proceed with a paradigm example of pornography in order to begin the discussion. Definitional work is important when we have already agreed that a practice is immoral. So, for example, we all know that killing is wrong, but there are gray areas: self-defense, abortion, euthanasia, and war. So, the vague term "killing" is replaced by "taking an innocent human life" and then we avoid irritating counterexamples by adding "without good reason." Then the argument moves to discussions of these other concepts: "life" (in abortion), "innocents" (in war and abortion), "good reasons" (in self-defense and euthanasia). However, there is no such controversy over cases where a man walks into the high street of a town and shoots dead a passerby, be it for pleasure, whim, or money. What the man has done is uncontroversially wrong.

The difference between the case of killing and the case of pornography is that killing is, in most cases, immoral and all we need to do is to decide whether such and such an action is a case of killing or not. However, we do not intuitively agree that pornography is wrong. Here, all we need to discuss is a paradigmatic example of pornography in order to see whether it can rationally be judged immoral.

Imagine a professionally produced and marketed seven minute scene downloaded from youporn.com, or some other similar site, which involves explicit scenes of fellatio, cunnilingus, and penetrative sex. There is no plot or characterization and it has very little, if any, aesthetic value: the camera work is poor and the mise-en-scène is hackneyed. Furthermore, there is no evidence of what we would normally understand to be violence, the presence of which would make the moral discussion more complicated. Violence, at least as we normally use the word, is normally wrong and does not have to be present in pornographic material (although there is obviously a very intimate relationship which we do not have time to discuss, unfortunately).

I believe anyone would be hard pressed to deny that this is an example of a pornographic object. In the case of killing above, the wrongness of the act was not an issue; here, however, the very issue is whether or not this object is immoral or necessarily involves immoral practices. If there is anything necessarily wrong with pornography, then such a scene ought to express, embody, or communicate that wrongness. Thus, we can avoid the problem with definition because if we can show that this paradigmatic case of pornography is wrong, we can later worry about defining porn in order to deal with the gray areas. If we cannot, then morally, the definitional work would be a waste of time (but may not be for other discourses).

The Wrongness of Pornography

Standard characterizations of the wrongness of pornography could be reduced to four major objections: it is obscene; it involves coercion and exploitation of the participants; it specifically harms women; or, it harms society as a whole. Let us consider these reasons one by one.

DAVID ROSE

Avoiding the difficulties with the term "obscenity" is very easy by reducing it to the term "offense." Obscene images cause offense. Offense is, of course, justified (or excused) in art if the object in question expresses some sort of aesthetic value. So, Medem's *Lucía y el Sexo* definitely has aesthetic worth, whereas *Debbie Does Dallas* does not. Bataille's *Story of the Eye* and de Sade's *The One Hundred and Twenty Days of Sodom* would be controversial.[1]

Obscenity can pre-reflectively center on concern whether the object in question is a simulation of an act or a record of a real act. There seems to be an intuitive need to distinguish between "real" and "simulated" acts since it apparently tracks the distinction between soft and hardcore pornography. More significantly, it has some moral bite because snuff movies are immoral because the killing constituent of them is real and not simulated. Snuff movies are a matter of legal sanction because the "actors" actually die rather than pretend to die. But, as we have seen, killing is wrong and sex is not. We sanction people for killing but not for having sex. (Laws may still prohibit certain sexual practices such as sodomy, but they are rarely enforced.) However, we do sanction sex in public places because it is obscene and so there might be more to this than we first thought.

But such a claim is puzzling. It is often difficult to judge whether the actors did or did not actually have sex: *Last Tango in Paris* and *Caos Calmo* are examples which jump to mind.[2] Most softcore films are equally problematic – all of which is incidental to our paradigmatic example. It is obviously a case of actual rather than simulated sex and so is a prime candidate for moral disapproval. One may believe it is obscene because it revels in its veracity; we see penetration and the cum shot in close-up in order to, arguably, *prove* that the sex being observed is real.

However, actors in mainstream cinema kiss. They actually kiss and do not pretend to kiss. In softcore films they kiss, lick, bite nipples, and so on. There is no simulation of these actions. What changes is that certain practices are deemed offensive when they are not simulated: actual penetration, the tongue on the vagina, the penis in the mouth, and so on. So, it is not the distinction between simulation and reality which matters but what actions are being filmed.

Of course, some might say that "One can kiss, but not mean it, whereas one cannot have sex and not mean it." But on what basis can they hold such a claim? Both are simple, physical actions that involve emotional connotations. Those connotations will differ from person to person, from historical age to age, and, more importantly, from culture to culture.

So, is our seven minute scene obscene because it reproduces an action which is not publicly acceptable?

The word "obscene," though, does not track any identifiable quality of the object in the same way that the word "salty" tracks a quality of the sea. Rather, "obscene" describes the way in which a viewer is affected. Something is obscene if it kindles in the spectator an attitude of distaste, disgust, or revulsion. Such responses are therefore dependent on persons and their attitudes. Attitudes cannot supply the foundation for a consensus; they will inevitably change with age, place, and time. Obscene may be defined for a specific culture, but even within that culture history will change such attitudes. Given such variables, attitudes cannot form the basis of moral judgments and, much less, legal sanction. However, we shall reconsider the cultural aspect below.

Moving away from the obscene may be more fruitful. Bearing in mind the example of snuff movies, we can see that such films cannot be made without participating in immoral actions. Perhaps pornography is similar. When we say snuff movies are immoral, what we mean is that the actors would not – if they were not coerced or manipulated or simply not irrational – have agreed to act in the film. We might want to say that the intimacy of sex is such that no actor – unless they are coerced, manipulated or irrational – would consent to perform actual sex for others' media consumption. That moves us on from considerations of obscenity to a consideration of victims.

The Victims of Pornography

Let us take as a starting point that there can be no moral wrongdoing unless one can identify a victim. There can be no wrongdoing, whether moral or legal, unless there is someone who has been wronged. Offense is sometimes included as a form of harm and the offended could then be identified as the victim, but the same problem with relativism and subjectivism will arise: who should we count as the arbiter of proper harm? We should understand harm broadly to include physical and mental harm and violations of rights. Exploitation is a wrong because it violates the individual agent's right to liberty; I would not have acted in this film had it not been for the presence of another agent who coerces me to do as I do. If he or she had not been present, I would have done otherwise.

DAVID ROSE

Pornography is often cited as a case of exploitation of the women who are coerced into performing. Often, little is said of the male actors. Exploitation is a wrong. I cannot take your wallet from you by threatening you with a gun because I violate your liberty. Had I not possessed the gun, you would not have given me your wallet. I exercise unjustified power over you because of my possession of a gun. A producer may exercise power over an actor because the former possesses money. The offer of money cannot be coercion, though. Neither can the combination of money and some sort of distorted web-celebrity, as sites such as moneytalks.com (if real!) seem to operate whereby members of the public are offered money to perform sexual acts for webcasts. Otherwise, that would rule out any person's working for another or exchanging goods with another, practices that we implicitly consent to day in, day out. It can, of course, be exploitation when the actor is in extreme poverty and the producer knows this, or when they need the money because they suffer from some chemical addiction that requires funds to satisfy and have no other way to procure the funds. Similarly, if the actors have been brought from their own country on false pretences and their passports have been confiscated, or they are forced to perform by the simple threat of violence, then such circumstances are immoral.

However, none of these conditions need necessarily be the case in the making of a pornographic film or image. There are many examples of exhibitionist amateur porn where no form of economic motivation is involved. But that is not so with our paradigmatic example. It is a professionally produced film. Given that, there is no reason to suppose in the example that the actors were not paid a fair wage for their time and performance and that they prefer to earn their money doing this than earn an equal amount of money in an office or teaching. Exploitation is wrong and it is the subject of legal sanction. If exploitation occurs in the production of pornography, it ought to be punished as it ought to be if it occurs in the picking of cockles or the manufacture of clothes. But the crime here is exploitation and not making pornography. The actual industry or product made is incidental to the moral wrongness.

Interestingly, if the ideal of a victim is upheld, then it seems that pornographic literature is not the subject of moral judgment at all because it does not involve any actors at all. Both the novels *Emanuelle* and *The Story of O* should rightly be considered pornographic and *Lady's Chatterley's Lover* was famously, of course, once described this way.[3] Verbal pornography involves an author and a reader and no one else. One might want to bite the bullet and say there is a difference between verbal and aural-visual pornography, but then the problem of animated porn would raise new questions. However, there is a further participant: the consumer. Can the consumer be considered a victim?

To be unprejudiced, let us term the watchers, readers, and observers of pornography as "enthusiasts." Can the enthusiast be a victim in the participation in pornographic practices? Well, children are excluded from the consumption of pornographic objects, whether aural, verbal, or visual, because it harms them in some way. In most countries, consumption of pornographic objects will be legally prohibited to a certain age group, usually those below eighteen. What if it were the case that the nature of pornography was such that even the most adult or rational among us is somehow harmed by viewing or reading it?

Like offense, it is very difficult to imagine how a legal or moral consensus could be reached on this point – at least within a constitutional democracy and not a theocratic state – because we are allowing certain people to decide what is best for others, and this contradicts our commonly held belief in personal autonomy. However, there is, in some very broad sense, a truth in the claim that experiencing pornography is harmful. Not, though, in a simple, measurable way and we shall return to this point below. Prior to this, there is a more obvious contender for the description of victim who is harmed by both aural-visual and verbal pornographic objects.

The feminist critique of pornography claims that women alone are wronged in the production and consumption of pornography. Some align this with exploitation, but that is not gender specific and has been discussed above. Women are specifically harmed because we live in a patriarchal society where equality is not yet institutionalized and that is wrong. So, females in our society ought to be equal and the present state of inequality is reinforced and maintained by the institution of pornography. (Much like the recitation of Irish jokes is thought to be harmless but, in fact, determines subconsciously how the majority in the UK perceive the Irish.) Pornography creates victims of the females in a society since they are denied equality as a consequence of its existence. There are two aspects to this critique: (1) pornography harms individual women; (2) pornography necessarily degrades women as a group.

It might be claimed that pornography harms individual women because it encourages their maltreatment at the hands of males, most extremely in a causal relationship with instances of rape, and more subtlety in ways such as harassment and objectification of particular females. Yet, the empirical claims of the influence that pornography has on the behavior of its enthusiasts, causal or otherwise, are controversial and contestable at best. What one report asserts, another denies and how one interprets the data is often very much from the perspective of prejudice. The concepts and definitions used in such empirical studies seem to support the desired conclusions from the beginning and no empirical study will ever be able to resolve the issue of pornography's relationship to behavior in a way which is final and inveterate.

The more subtle claim is that women as a group may well be maltreated by males due to the latter's consumption of pornography. The particular man may see women first and foremost as sexual objects, as inferior to him, as wanting him and, as such, his perception of women has been distorted by his use of pornography. The supposed relationship of equality between the two sexes has been distorted. In the paradigmatic example, there is no real difference between what the man is doing and what the woman is doing. They are reciprocally having sex. Nevertheless, it is very natural to use the active grammatical forms for male actions and the passive forms for female actions and that reflects the disparity; pornography maintains the unjustified inequality of contemporary society. He is penetrating, she is being penetrated. He puts his cock in her mouth, she takes it in her mouth and so on. Pornography reinforces these ways of seeing the scene; it represents women in hierarchical relationships with men.

There is, though, nothing specific to pornography about the representation of women and many rap and hip-hop music videos are far more demeaning because they objectify women and celebrate hierarchical relationships; 50 Cent's "P.I.M.P." being a prime example.[4] But they too could be the subject of moral judgment akin to the moral judgment of pornographic objects and very often are. One might want to counterassert the countless female producers and directors who are now taking control of large parts of the pornographic industry and state that it is possible that pornography could be a way to address and abolish the unjustified, cultural inequality between the sexes. One could make a pornographic film which empowered women and *Baise-moi* seems to attempt this, whether it was successful or not.[5]

But the real problem with the egalitarian critique is that any hierarchical power relationship which is unjustified and rests solely on power is as injurious to men as it is to women; the dominator will have a distorted self-understanding because he is uncertain that his supposed understanding of a relationship will be reciprocated. The woman may play the role of the lover, but she may have no sincere interest in the man as a person. Without a reciprocal, honest relationship he is unable to know how she perceives him and, hence, how he really exists for others. The representations of social relationships at the heart of pornography allow neither men nor women (or other sexualities, races, and so on) to appreciate or partake in practices and relationships that would be beneficial to their own development and self-understanding. So, again, this is not a problem unique to women.

Does it make sense, then, to talk of our culture being a victim of pornography? Let us make a summary of the inconclusive comments above because they all embody some truth about pornography, but unfortunately only a partial one. If any wrongness can be perceived in pornographic objects, it must arise from these considerations. Certain practices, as determined by a particular culture, are considered taboo and not for accessible, public consumption. These practices are open to change and the production of certain films, literature, or images will open a space between the public understanding of what is taboo and what has generally, up to that historical point, been taken to be taboo. Hence, public kissing is *now* acceptable, but public intercourse is not. Public understanding is dependent on a particular culture which is malleable and undergoing change. These practices exclude certain groups (such as children) who are unable to understand them because of a lack of concepts or experience that will have the consequence of distorting their own experience of the practice. Some contemporary pornography is such that enthusiasts are prone to objectify social relationships in a distorted rather than a healthy way. Pornography is a representation of what is taboo but, even if not necessarily so, is arguably a contingent and historical representation of inequality between the sexes. Its wrongness, then, lies in its representing relationships between males and females which distort equitable relationships and maintain and support institutions of inequality.

Children, for example, are not allowed to consume violent material in the media because such images need to be clearly categorized as either fiction or fact. Mass media represent, almost universally, violence as desirable, as a resolution, and rarely represent the real consequences of actual violence. A child who is unable, due to a lack of experience and knowledge, to distinguish between the representation of violence and the reality of violence may develop undesirable behavior. If children were allowed undiluted access to these images they may well procure certain undesirable moral attitudes: that might is right, that power is desirable, that violence is a solution, and so on. Only the subtlety of "adult" drama, film, and literature can do justice to the complexity of violence and its relationship to our society. Similarly, adults who lack the requisite social and emotional intelligence may view pornography and form attitudes concerning social relationships that are undesirable: the lack of consequences of emotional entanglement, the superficiality of emotional exchanges, the over-determination of sex as a constituent part of a healthy relationship, the necessity of a sexual dimension in all relationships, and so on. These attitudes do not just relate to male-female relationships, but also to black-white, hetro-gay and gay-gay relationships. Unfortunately, as many Shakespeares, Tolstoys, and Dostoevskys as there are for the Seagals, Willises, and Schwarzeneggers of this world, there is very little adult pornography to compensate for the amount of the childish, immature sort. And that is the greatest wrong at the heart of pornography.[6]

Culture is "harmed" or "wronged" because the taboo must function in accordance with the central principles of a society. A rational, axiomatic principle of our society is equality and the vast majority of pornography is incoherent with this principle. Note that this deviates from the feminist critique in saying that not just a specific group of society but all society and all human relationships will be harmed by the unrestricted production, exchange, and consumption of pornography. However, this is again no different from other aesthetic objects – film, television, music, literature, and so on – which supply some of the ways, concepts, and forms of social relationships through which individuals can form a self-understanding.

A Different Tack

The various moral objections to pornography are not wholly false. They do all grasp something of the wrongness of specific examples of pornography and so encapsulate an aspect of the truth. But they also over-extend their own objection into a definitional criterion of pornography: obscenity draws the line between the publicly acceptable and the taboo, but assumes that the "obscene" is somehow fixed and not cultural; the charge of exploitation concerns the freedom of people to participate in things they would or would not do, but rests on an assumption that there are limits to what we are free to do which are, once again, fixed. Feminists see all pornography as the expression of female subordination; if it is not, it is not pornography. Finally, pornography is assumed to harm culture because it distorts our own self-understanding, but no space is made for pornography that could help or aid our own self-understanding which it, like other aesthetic objects, could do. The problem is that we view pornography in isolation from other aesthetic objects, as though it is a "pretend" or a "disingenuous" artistic object.

Pornography should not be treated as different in kind from other aesthetic objects, but should also be subject to the same moral judgment. Is the work conservative or progressive? Does it encourage the violation of rational, social relationships? Furthermore, the judgment ought to be an aesthetic one, e.g., "this is a poor example of the pornographic genre because it misrepresents human reality." One obvious illustration is the anonymous nature of most pornographic films, from the characterless (and faceless) actors to the current trend for glory hole porn. The message is obvious: sex is isolated from communication, interaction, and intimacy and is best when it is between available strangers with no consequences or involvement. Such considerations should never lead to legal sanction, but they are adequate grounds for moral approbation or condemnation in the same way the genre of "blaxploitation" films deserves moral condemnation. Morally it makes no sense to isolate the discourse of pornography from other spheres of art because the moral considerations are the same, but it does make sense to criticize and engage pornographic material as one would with all other aesthetic objects. We should not just brush it under the carpet and, by that, I mean *either* ignore its existence *or* haphazardly categorize it in simplistic moral terms.

Pornography's relationship to culture is complex, but also necessary. A society will always identify taboo in order to regulate the norm and an experience of taboo should reinforce our understanding of the norm. The question is whether or not a particular social taboo is consistent with certain moral concepts important to that culture: equality, liberty, individual welfare, and so on. It is not a question of whether pornography should or should not be banned, restricted, or heavily regulated, nor a question of whether it is or is not moral, but a question of a dialogue between what is and what is not acceptable. If such a dialogue is not carried out – and pornography itself is one way to engage in this conversation – then specific cultural attitudes may well violate or obstruct agreed and public norms of right and moral conduct. Moral concepts and categories arise from our self-understanding and this is, in so many ways, ultimately related with a culture's representation of itself. It is not a question of whether pornography is moral or immoral, but whether it identifies the correct taboos and norms of social relationships and represents an easy way for us to understand ourselves in relation to others. Art regulates culturally appropriate behavior by engaging with both actions of supreme wilfulness and eccentricity, but also with the public expectations of individuals. It oscillates between these two extremes to develop culturally appropriate behavior and limits of behavior while overthrowing taboos which, as Hamlet would have had it, are "out of joint." Contemporarily, due to its almost exclusively capitalistic nature, the pornographic industry is more interested in making money than valuable art, as are so many domains of cultural production.

But, then, there is no specific, isolated moral problem with pornography, but only with art and art's relationship to culture. And the problem may well then be with the material reality of art's production; that is, capitalism. But that is another, much longer, story.

NOTES

1 George Bataille, *The Story of the Eye,* trans. J. Neugroschal (London: Penguin, 1977); Jim Clark (dir.) *Debbie Does Dallas* (School Day Films, 1978); de Sade. *The One Hundred and Twenty Days of Sodom and Other Writings*, trans. A. Wainhouse and R. Seaver (London: Arrow Books, 1990); Julio Medem (dir.) *Lucía y el Sexo* (Alicia Produce, 2001).

2 Bernardo Bertolucci (dir.) *Last Tango in Paris* (MGM, 1973); Grimaldi, Antonio (dir.) *Caos Calmo* (*Quiet Chaos*) (Fandango, 2008).

3 Emmanuelle Arsan, *The Best of Emmanuelle*, trans. L. Blair and A. Hollo (Bungay: Chaucer Press, 1980); Pauline Réage, *The Story of O* (London: Corgi, 1972); D. H. Lawrence, *Lady Chatterley's Lover* (London: Penguin, 1997).

4 50 Cent. "P.I.M.P., Snoop Dogg Remix," *Get Rich or Die Tryin'* (Interscope Records, 2005).

5 Virginie Despentes and Coralie Despentes (dirs.) *Baise-moi.* (Canal+, 2000).

6 Although certain films may well fulfill this role, for example *Lucía y el Sexo* and J.-J. Beineix (dir.) *Betty Blue: 37°2 le matin* (Gaumont, 1986).

PART VI

PORN AND TECHNOLOGY

CHAPTER 15

SOMETHING FOR EVERYONE

Busty Latin Anal Nurses in Leather and Glasses

Technological advances have changed our lives in ways too numerous to count. From transportation and communication to entertainment and cooking, we use devices today that were unheard of just three decades ago. Technological advances have been both master and servant to the changing "needs" of the public. While many advances improve our lives in ways that are unquestionable, others create convenience or extravagance. Far from being "needs," the latter developments create new markets and thrive on a society ready to consume whatever is new. The question remains whether technology is driving our desires or being driven by them. Did we really want 400 cable channels, heated cup holders, and microwave popcorn, or do we crave it now because such things are available to us?

Perhaps nowhere have these changes become as acute as in the world of pornography. At virtually any point on the entertainment technology curve one can easily find pornography at the cusp. Eager to take advantage of any method that will allow them to improve and personalize their material, pornographers have ventured bravely if sometimes blindly into whatever new frontier lies ahead. Technical advances have given pornographers the ability to deliver their product directly to the end user, cutting out what were once the primary forms of delivery for their merchandise, the adult theatre and retail store, and has had far-reaching ramifications not only for the adult entertainment industry, but also for the end user. Newly developed modes of content delivery have continually reshaped the porn industry by allowing it to cater material to an ever-narrowing audience in a cost effective manner. This fact, however, has also enabled modern pornography to develop in much more specific and fetish oriented ways. So the question begs to be asked: Is modern pornography driven by the narrow niche fetishes of its new audience, or is it driving them into uncharted territories simply by showing the audience that such "wonders" exist?

The 1970s: Adult Film Theatres

Even though magazines and pulp paperbacks were the preferred form of pornography throughout the 1950s and 1960s, the audience craved moving pictures. Though "stag films" existed in the early days, they lacked a delivery system enabling them to thrive. Often shot in 16mm, these films were difficult to obtain and could only be viewed by those who owned the proper projection equipment. A better system for delivering adult films was needed and the most obvious answer was to mirror mainstream Hollywood and use adult movie theatres to reach the audience.

Despite being the best mode of delivery for pornographers at that time, adult theatres were few and far between in the 1970s. They were primarily located in large urban areas, and local zoning ordinances often forced them to be tucked away in less than desirable neighborhoods. The crowds who regularly attended such theatres were notorious as well. The stereotype of the single male clad in a trench coat to conceal his masturbatory activity was so pervasive that it lives on today. Fans in search of harder-edged porn (in contrast to the cable-friendly, couples marketed, "softcore" movies) are still commonly referred to as "raincoaters." As if long drives to questionable neighborhoods and unsavory audience members were not enough, adult theatres were not popular with politicians, who often sought to shut them down. Pornography was seen as immoral, undesirable, and a magnet for other criminal behavior. To further diminish the adult theatre as a quality outlet for adult product, frequent raids by law enforcement for anything from prostitution sweeps to drug searches kept all but the most ardent fan away.

The year 1973 changed all that. It ushered in a Golden Age in adult films with *Behind the Green Door* and *Deep Throat*. Both films had relatively high production values. Both also helped usher in the "porn star," with leading ladies Marilyn Chambers and Linda Lovelace. More importantly, however, both films were massive cross-over success. Though only shown on a few hundred screens nationwide, *Deep Throat* and *Behind the Green Door* became overnight sensations. These films were the first to find an audience beyond the typical adult theatre patron and generated mainstream buzz that led to a brief period of "porno chic." Porn had, to some extent, gone mainstream. Suddenly, "normal" people and even some high-profile celebrities were seen attending adult films. Although this was a step forward for the pornography industry as a whole, most moviegoers still faced limited and less than optimal access to even the most popular adult films.

In many markets, the lack of outlets for adult material effectively limited audiences to a single choice. Since the primary delivery system was limited by distance and often suppressed by legal entanglements, it was difficult for theatre owners to offer much of a choice to their patrons. Theatres would run a popular adult film for weeks or months at a time. *Deep Throat*, for example, ran continuously for sixteen years at the Aladdin Theatre in Portland, Oregon, beginning in 1975. Its run at the Aladdin ended only when the theatre closed its doors in 1991. Though few theatre owners went that far, the medium inherently limited the viewers' choice to a few select titles, titles that the theatre owner would have considered as having the broadest appeal.

Because of this, adult theatres amounted to a quite limited distribution system for pornography. This limitation also affected the creative possibilities of the product. With perhaps a thousand possible outlets, the few adult films made in the early 1970s needed to appeal to the broadest possible audience in order to maximize profits. While mainstream Hollywood produced films in a variety of genres, such as comedies, horror films, action/adventure films, and family features, the adult film industry had to hit its entire target audience with every shot. There was little freedom for sexual exploration given that each film, in order to be a financial success, would have to fit with rather broad sexual interests. In some ways, of course, all explicit sex on film was new and exciting to the mainstream audience, but having to target a broad audience meant that most (if not all) adult films conformed to a rather standardized form of sexual intercourse. Although anal intercourse, oral sex, lesbian sex, and a smattering of S&M were sometimes involved, most adult films offered little in the way of variety. They were intentionally vanilla, trading on the novelty of explicit sex while avoiding any fetish that might limit their appeal. Of course, there was no need to appeal to specific fetishes or appeal to niche-oriented audiences. They were, after all, the only game in town.

The 1980s: Home Video/VHS

Adult theatres remained the predominant delivery source for adult movies until the 1980s. The new decade ushered in the advent and subsequent saturation of VCRs, and adult films were suddenly available to a new audience. Viewers no longer had to risk questionable neighborhoods or risk being seen sneaking into adult theatres only to watch pornography surrounded by strangers. The full length feature film that was once available only in the theatre could now be transferred to video tape and thus be viewed in the privacy of the home. The level of awkwardness and potential danger was dramatically reduced. Fans in search of erotic thrills merely had to slip behind the swinging saloon doors or through the beaded curtains at the "adult" section of their local video store.

With home video recorders replacing adult theatres as the primary delivery method for adult films, a few thousand viewing outlets suddenly ballooned into several million. The audience was no longer locked into specific show times or titles selected by theatre owners. They were free to view movies at home at any time of the day. Renting a VHS tape generally cost only a fraction of what a ticket at the theatre did, so fans were able to afford to see multiple titles during a given week. While theatre owners were limited by time and could often show only one title per week, video store owners could stock hundreds or even thousands of adult titles. With increased distribution possibilities for this larger audience came an increased demand for more product. Spurred on by the increased privacy that now accompanied the viewing of pornography, porn fans were freer to seek out new and more experimental sexual themes. Studios raced to keep up with demand and began to experiment with new formats and more specific titles. Producers still had to appeal to a relatively broad audience, but the medium and marketplace allowed them to target audiences more specifically than ever before.

Throughout the 1980s the home video explosion pushed pornography in new directions. Home use of VCRs had been virtually unheard of at the start of the 1980s, but rose quickly. By 1985, VCRs had already penetrated 10.5 percent of television households in the US.[1] As the number

ᴧ

ofVCRs in America rose from under 2 million early in the decade to over 62 million (roughly two-thirds of American households) by the end of the 1980s, the need for new adult product increased dramatically. And with an increased audience came a product that could, and often did, appeal to a wider variety of sexually explicit themes.

Though the audience grew and a broader range of sexual themes were touched upon, 1980s video porn still followed certain, albeit rather loose, templates. VHS pornography bore many similarities to its 1970s predecessor. Most still followed scripts and basic plot formulas remained unchanged. Pornographers tried to sprinkle sexual variations into their product, but did so cautiously to make their product as broadly appealing as possible. A typical example of this came in the form of the "mandatory lesbian scene." At some point in virtually every video feature came a scene with two or more women together. Conventional wisdom was that most members of the audience had an interest in seeing some form of lesbian exploration in each film. While this practice would later be called into question when pornography became more specialized, it remained in place throughout most of the 1980s. Exploration into other sexual variations would become more popular as porn expanded throughout the decade.

Anal sex was always a leading contender. A frequent area of exploration in early adult films, anal sex became a full-time focus in the new video-dominated pornographic landscape of the 1980s. No longer just a flavor in the sexual stew, anal sex became the main course. Titles like *Caught From Behind* and *Between the Cheeks* took the existing formula for adult films and greatly narrowed its focus.[2] Though plot and character development were always secondary (if not tertiary) concerns in adult films, VHS pornography began to abandon them altogether. These traditional elements were replaced by specific sex acts that became the foci of many video releases. Individual titles now focused on anal sex, lesbian sex, oral sex, and other broadly categorized fetishes as producers expanded the scope of adult movies and began to specialize. If these new genre-specific features of the late 1980s seemed narrowly focused, this was nothing compared to the massive changes that lay on the horizon.

The splintering of the adult movie industry during the late 1980s would accelerate in the 1990s. The video tidal wave all but washed away celluloid pornography and drowned the adult theatres. Home video viewing and adult "arcades" replaced them as the viewing medium of choice. Viewing adult movies at home or in X-rated video arcades was simpler, cheaper, and offered greater discretion. These delivery methods gave rise to new kinds of adult movies. "Gonzo" and "Wall to Wall" pornography would dominate 1990s adult cinema.

Part of what drove these changes was the fact that, as video cameras became smaller, lighter, and cheaper, pornographers were able to shoot product that was unthinkable just a few years earlier. The use of hand-held cameras enabled directors of gonzo porn to become characters in their own movies. They became sexual proxies for their audience, sharing their fetishes, failures, and fantasies with viewers watching at home. These projects had strong voyeuristic qualities and allowed the viewer to see sex from angles unheard of in the days of stationary cameras and full film crews. The movies also tended to focus on either specific sex acts or, more commonly, specific body parts. Easier to shoot and less expensive to produce, the new medium of video allowed pornographers to seek out smaller audiences looking for specific elements that had been missing or underrepresented in prior pornographic efforts.

Audiences craving large breasts no longer had to sit through an entire film to see one well endowed starlet. Entire movies and complete lines of product were now dedicated to busty vixens of every shade. Frustrated admirers for firm derrieres were no longer forced to watch in utter horror as the camera skipped over the object of their desire. There were now entire series devoted to long, loving camera shots of women from angles that were previously either impossible (as heavy cameras were not made for such anatomical exploration) and impractical (for every one butt lover in the audience, producers still risked alienating ten customers who could care less) to capture. From *The Adventures of Buttman* to *Breast Worx* gonzo porn had taken the focus away from mere fantasy stories involving sex and placed it on more narrowly appealing fetishes.[3]

The 1990s: DVD

Expansion into fetish-oriented product experienced exponential growth in the 1990s as the adult industry shifted from VHS to DVD as the favored delivery format. The extended storage capacity offered by DVDs, and an ever-increasing catalog of existing movies which could be converted to the new format, gave rise to a new pornographic phenomenon: the compilation. Companies had long taken scenes from different, older movies and packaged them together as new product. It was, after all, pure profit to resell something that had already recouped its costs. VHS, however, was a limited format in this regard. A single, 140-minute tape could be filled with close to seven hours of material (the theoretical limit for the format), but only by using a very low transfer speed, resulting in a poor quality product. The advent of DVD removed this barrier. Now producers could pack four to six hours of higher-quality pornography onto a single DVD and they did so with increasing regularity, as the new format gained acceptance. Compilations also allowed pornographers the freedom to choose from vast libraries exactly the type of scene they wanted to market. It suddenly became easy to offer six hours of a particular actress, a particular type of actress (e.g., hair color, body type, ethnicity, etc.), particular sex act, or even a specific fetish.

Full movies featuring five scenes of anal or lesbian sex could be chopped up and included as pieces in compilations featuring anal sex with brunette women or lesbian sex featuring naturally busty women. Entire lines could now be dedicated not just to anal sex, but to more specific (anal-sex-related) themes such as "gaping" (a term used to describe a close up shot of a distended female anus, left open after anal penetration) or "anal cream pies" (anal intercourse ending in internal ejaculation with a subsequent shot of the semen being intentionally expelled) or even something more exotic like "felching" (semen that is expelled from the anus and into a partner's mouth).

DVD's ability to allow a viewer to skip directly to specific scenes or even exact points within a scene further broke down the traditional adult movie. Fans no longer had to sit through dialogue if they did not want to. They could jump directly to the sex or even to the climax if the intercourse was too pedestrian. If there was an actress they found unappealing, a single click of a button could skip over her scene. When they found a position they particularly liked, they could easily move to view it with no waiting for a tape to forward to the appropriate cue. And of course if they wanted to time their masturbatory climax to match that of a male porn star, they could easily do so with just the remote. Adult movies had truly become nothing more than collections of scenes and even more to the point, short special interest clips within those scenes.

Specific body types had also long been focused upon. Magazines featuring busty women had been around from the very beginning of porn, and some of the porn's Golden Age favorites gained their legendary status as a result of their ample chests. Similarly, women of specific ethnic backgrounds were featured in magazines and even some early adult films. As DVD became the dominant format and individual scenes overtook full feature movies, genres begat subgenres and every possible combination of ethnic mix, body type, and sex act was there to be hand-picked from local store shelves. The idea that a filmmaker had to appeal to the broadest possible audience was gone. In its place, the target audience could now consist of just a few hundred customers willing to pay money for four hours of "Big Booty White Girls," "Barely Legal Asians," or "Anal Lesbians." If these subgenres seemed specific at the time, they were nothing compared to what was to come.

The Oh-Oh Age of the Internet

Pornography on the Internet has existed for nearly as a long as the Internet itself. Long before companies made it a priority to market their products, old and new, on the web, fans used the new technology to share their collections, discuss their favorite starlets, and explore beyond the boundaries of the local smut emporium. The rapid spread of high speed Internet over the past decade has opened even more doors for pornographers. With the ability to deliver higher definition video directly to the end user, came a world of new possibilities. Users were now free to seek out exactly what they wanted and pay for individual scenes rather than for entire movies. Producers could skip expensive duplication and shipping charges and focus leveraging even narrower target audiences. Companies still making DVDs were quick to figure out that customers would use a pay per minute model for video on demand, allowing them to skip over anything they did not want and only pay for the sort of scenes they were interested in.

Web-based delivery models caught on early, and pornographers began to customize their content to meet very specific needs. While early gonzo movies could feature girls with large derrieres, the world of Video on Demand minutes, niche websites and customization required a more delicate parsing of content. Websites now promised big booties in every possible shade. Like Caucasian women with large butts? You can watch "Big White Asses." If you prefer darker complexioned backsides, give "Big Black Asses" a try. If Latinas are more your speed, "Big Latin Asses" can be found. If that is not specific enough, liquid can be brought in to give the gigantic glutes sheen, giving us "Big Wet Asses." If even that won't do, then the wet asses can get an ethnic breakdown treatment as well. One need only add "White," "Black," "Latin," or "Asian" to "Wet" and "Asses" and you open up another rainbow of sexual possibilities.

Advances in technology have advanced pornography, turning the once-limited world of adult films into a vast empire capable of reaching into nearly every home in the civilized world. The once narrow "adult film" industry has blossomed into a customer-driven industry. Once dominated by films shown on a limited number of screens to the broadest possible audience, pornography now uses the vast array of inexpensive delivery modes to produce material directed to more specific tastes. This has both expanded the audience for pornographic material while simultaneously narrowing the focus of the individual work. The standard adult movie of the 1970s with five to ten sex scenes, a scripted story, and basic cinematic elements has been replaced. No more sticky floored theatres in seedy neighborhoods showing generic films filled with porn clichés. They have been replaced, first by a similar product available in local video stores offering greater privacy and a wider selection. But even this would pale to the changes offered by later technology. First came a DVD driven model with five to six sex scenes, few recurring performers, no scripts, and minimal production values. With movies now split into interchangeable scenes, it was easy to take the next step and market each scene individually. Websites and DVD lines have been refined to cover every possible body part. Ethnicity and corresponding stereotypes have become sufficient central themes for countless lines. Even specific sex acts have been split off, categorized and turned in fetishes of their own. Gone is the Golden Age of adult films, and even video tapes seem ancient by today's standards. In their place is a high definition world of desktop delivery debauchery in every flavor dreamed up by the human psyche. Websites, scenes, and video clips can be tailored to virtually any fetish.

Driven by technological advances, pornography has evolved from full length films shown in theatres to neatly packaged scenes designed to please the most specific sexual taste directly to the home of the end user. Technology has undoubtedly changed the future of pornography. The question remains, however, as to whether these changes have been for the better or for the worse? In a word, both.

Modern pornography is both superior and inferior to that seen just three decades ago. Better, cheaper, and smaller cameras have improved picture quality immensely. Grainy films have been replaced by slick HD porn. Handheld cameras allow pornographers to get in close to the action and show the audience every possible detail of any act. These technological improvements bring with them their own set of issues. High definition video leaves little to the imagination. Brightly lit scenes and ultra-sharp pictures show the audience every blemish, bruise, and wrinkle.

With cameras only inches away from their subjects, today's porn performers are unable to hide from the harsh reality provided by HD porn. As a result, a layer of fantasy has been removed from pornography, revealing a reality that is a little less ideal.

Pornographers today can make feature films that are technically far superior to anything possible in the Golden Age of porn. Better cameras, lighting, and editing make it entirely possible to create an erotic art form only dreamed about in the days of *Deep Throat*. Instead of taking this path, most pornographers have chosen to produce neatly packaged scenes where themes and specific fetishes are far more important than anything resembling "art" or even filmmaking. Scripts, when used at all, are often written for single scenes to set the stage with a line or two of dialogue rather than tell a complete story.

While some would mourn the loss of porn as an art form, few would argue that modern pornography is a better product. Gone are the days when a consumer had limited choices and had to wait through an entire movie in hopes of seeing whatever specific body type or sexual activity they were most interested in. Websites abound featuring performers of every race, color, and sexual orientation engaged in sexual acts ranging from the basic to the most exotic. Video on Demand websites even allow the porn consumer to only pay for the exact material they want. The result is a product that can be exactly what the end user wants it to be.

Modern pornography is also delivered to the end user in the privacy of his own home. He does not even have to rent or buy VHS tapes or DVDs that must be hidden from disapproving spouses or curious children. Porn can be viewed on a computer and deleted after viewing. It is both discreet and disposable, offering a convenience that simply was not possible before the rise of the Internet.

Yet, such convenience is not without a downside. In generations past, curious children had to go to great lengths to uncover dad's "secret porn stash." Such efforts were often rewarded with ample bosoms and a fleeting glimpse of pubic hair provided by a *Playboy* magazine. The prevalence of Internet porn has put the whole world of sexuality, both healthy and deviant, literally at the fingertips of millions of children. How easy is it for a child to reach hardcore pornography? Painfully so. Starting with a popular search engine and the word "boobs," it takes three clicks of a mouse to go from giggling curiosity to full length hardcore porn available free of charge with no age verification. Few would argue that such easy exposure comes without negative ramifications. Arguments about how best to curtail such access could fill volumes and the full affect of widespread access to pornography will not be known for decades.

Ironically, many standard porn clichés have survived and remain firmly entrenched in the landscape. The lucky pizza delivery boy, naughty schoolgirl, and overexposed plumber still manage to thrive in modern pornography. They now serve as central themes in DVD lines devoted completely to their unique qualities. Instead of being clumsily written into a feature film, the saucy secretary or bubbly babysitter now star over and over on websites designed to give consumers the sexual fantasy scenario time and again.

As a direct result of massive technological changes, modern pornography is produced by a fractured industry delivering specific material to a much larger, but more narrowly focused, audience. The end user now enjoys privacy as he or she downloads or streams only the material that appeals to their unique sexual interests. Pornography has both driven and been driven by the niche fetish desires of this new, massive, and increasingly particular audience.

NOTES

1 Julia Dubrow, *Social and Cultural Aspects of VCR Use* (Hillsdale: Lawrence Erlbaum Associates, 1990).
2 Hal Freeman (dir.) *Caught From Behind* (Hollywood Video, 1982); Gregory Dark (dir.) *Betweeen the Cheeks* (VCA, 1985).
3 John Stagliano (dir.) *Adventures of Buttman* (Evil Angel, 1989); Bobby Hollander (dir.) *Breast Worx* (LBO, 1991).

CHAPTER 16

SEX, LIES, AND VIRTUAL REALITY

 Science fiction writers and futurists describe a technological "tipping point" we are hurtling toward as a global society. They call this tipping point "the singularity," though they characterize this transformative event differently. One vision of the singularity is when artificial intelligence will surpass human intellect. Another singularity is when computers gain self-consciousness.

The singularity I portend is social: when technology achieves virtual realities that are qualitatively indistinguishable from our real world. While benefits of such computer-generated environments are numerous, such unbounded simulacra will present potential dangers: particularly, virtual pornography.

A technological garden of earthly delights looms on the horizon as virtual reality technology increases yearly. What will the effects be upon romantic relationships when men can have discreet, recreational sex with coquettish supermodels at a few clicks of a mouse, or when wives can have ongoing virtual relationships with handsome hunks who show them the romance and care their husbands do not?

Easy accessibility to virtual pornography threatens to rip apart the social fabric that binds human beings together. I term this tipping point the "pornographic singularity." The pornographic singularity may arrive within our lifetimes, and with it, far-reaching consequences that will erode the foundations of our society.

In this essay, I explore probable effects of this singularity upon future individuals, families, and society. I extrapolate from current examples of low to medium grades of virtuality – including *Second Life*, simulated-reality video games, and Internet pornography generally. I also consider the proliferation of online sexual fetish cultures – furries, amputee "devotees," bestiality, incestuous age-play, and so forth – and will discuss the negative impacts of such desires, unbounded in the virtual world.

The warning signs of the approaching pornographic singularity beg our attention. This essay, however, should not be misinterpreted as a puritanical screed against pornography, recreational sex, or moderate sexual deviance. And though our discussion may include some religious allusions, any metaphors are for stylistic purposes only. I bear no religious moral commitments, and I take no exception with recreational sex, fetishes, and pornography consumption being compatible with living a good life.

I will argue, however, that virtual forms of pornographic sex may threaten a healthy psyche and prevent individuals from achieving a good life. Moreover, the coming pornographic singularity will exacerbate a host of current social problems that derive from pornography, exploding their prevalence and degree.

Virtual Reality: Immersive Pornography

Pornography may be as old as *Homo sapiens*. In May 2009, archeologists in Germany found the earliest pornography on historical record: a 35,000-years-old ivory figurine of a woman, its sexual characteristics exaggerated.[1] The only thing that has changed through the centuries is the advancing media of our sexual depictions; from etchings, drawings, photography, video, and ultimately to virtual reality.

Virtual reality is the endpoint of pornography's journey. By "virtual reality" I mean a computer-generated "dream," qualitatively indistinguishable from the actual world (like the virtual world Neo experiences in the movie *The Matrix*).[2] Future virtual realities will optimize four aspects of pornography:

- *veridicality*, a life-like experience, qualitatively identical to the actual world;
- *immersion*, in which the user will be an integral part of the pornography, rather than be separate from it;

- *interactivity*, where the user's own decisions and actions will determine the course of events;
- *unboundedness*, meaning that any pornography will be available, no matter how peculiar, bizarre, or paraphilic.

Though virtual reality technology is not yet sufficiently immersive or veridical, this virtual Promised Land will be reached, according to several estimates, in a few decades. Already in 2003, Sony patented the goal of a non-invasive introduction of ultrasonic waves into a user's brain in order to stimulate all five senses: in essence, tailoring vivid "dreams" into subjects' consciousness.

The best window into the future is current virtual worlds such as *Second Life*. Second Life provides computer-generated environments populated by avatars: animated characters, which are controlled by over an estimated 230,000 computer users around the world. *Second Life* offers only a medium-grade virtual reality, as it lacks total immersion and veridicality.

The virtual realities of the near future will shore up such deficits, offering veridical, immersive experiences that fully engage all five senses. This will provide users with limitless real-life-like possibilities, including virtual sex. Virtual sex could even surpass real sex in offering "hyperreal" pornography, which may ultimately render real sex as inferior.

Welcome to the Hyperreal World

Fashion magazine covers of airbrushed women represent the hyperreal; even the models themselves do not measure up to what appears on the glossy pages.[3] In this way, postmodern cultural theorist Jean Baudrillard defines the hyperreal as "The simulation of something which never really existed."[4] The airbrushed models represent unreachable ideals, by which real women henceforth are judged as inferior.

Like "computer-enhanced" images of models on magazine covers, human representations in virtual environments are also hyperreal: depictions of what never has and never will exist in reality. Females, for instance, tend to be cartoonish exaggerations of male desires: enormous sag-less breasts, vanishingly small waists, long curvaceous legs, round buttocks, luminous eyes, flawless skin, perfect hair, and pouty lips. These hyper-beauties of the virtual world defy the laws of gravity, as Mattel's

Barbie has long defied the realistic proportions of any living woman. Barbie, too, is hyperreal.

"Pornbots" are the sexual Barbies of the future – virtual reality prostitutes run by artificial intelligence (not that they will need much intelligence). Virtual reality will peddle the hyperreal via pornographic simulacra: programmed pornbots as sexual partners and sexual behavior that replaces reality, which in their wake may make "the real" deficient in comparison.

In "The Porn Myth," Naomi Wolf explains the damaging hyperreality of pornography in our present age: "For the first time in human history, the images' power and allure have supplanted that of real naked women. Today, real naked women are just bad porn."[5] The hyperreality of pornography creates an unattainable standard; everything real pales in comparison.

Sociologist Harry Brod explains this devaluation of real sex from his personal experience with pornography:

> There have been too many times where I have guiltily resorted to impersonal fantasy because the genuine love I felt for the woman wasn't enough to convert feelings into performance. And in those sorry, secret moments, I have resented my lifelong indoctrination into the aesthetic of the centerfold.[6]

In this way, the hyperreal in current pornography tends not to over-sexualize men toward women in real life; rather, it seems to deaden men's desire for real women and real sex.

The danger of the hyperreal ideal will increase as pornography becomes immersive, interactive, and veridical in the virtual world. When there is no longer any carnally gratifying advantage to sex with a real woman as opposed to sex with a virtual woman, males may no longer expect their current or potential girlfriends to look or sexually perform like porn stars; instead, they may find no desire to have real romantic relationships in the first place.

The Future Obsolescence of Real Women

Already, women must compete with pornography. Breast implants offer women one option. Such surgical enhancements signify a "Barbiefication" of real women; women conforming to the hyperreal male fantasy.

Naomi Wolf reports that college-aged women complain that they cannot compete with the hyperreality introduced by pornography:

For how can a real woman – with pores and her own breasts and even sexual needs of her own (let alone with speech that goes beyond "More, more, you big stud!") – possibly compete with a cybervision of perfection, downloadable and extinguishable at will, who comes, so to speak, utterly submissive and tailored to the consumer's least specification?[7]

Virtual reality will throw wide open the doors of Barbiefication, since users can embody whatever "physical" form they want in virtual environments. As such, women will be incentivized to embody avatars that are the virtual sex-dolls of the hyperreal male sex fantasy. Even a committed real-life couple may be tempted to make "improvements" to their self-styled avatars when engaging in virtual sex online: the man might want a larger penis and a bit more musculature; the woman might want larger breasts and flawless skin. This indulgence in hypersex online may make real sex deficient for this couple, when they seek intimacy off-line.

The Barbiefication of women extends from appearance to action. And when real women have to compete with the female pornbots of the future, there may be little choice for women but to play into the male fantasies of hypersex, stammering the "More, more you big stud!" that male porn consumers have progressively come to value.

The arrival of virtual fantasy may betray a crass reality: that a major advantage real women have over current pornography is the real experience that they provide to men. A man can try to sate his sexual desires through various forms of pornography, but current porn pales in comparison to real sex. A hand is not a vagina, and even sophisticated sex toys for men are dim shadows of the immersive, multidimensional experience that real sex affords. Virtual sex will erase this "advantage." It will offer qualitatively identical (or even "superior") sex. In its wake, real sex may become obsolete, conditioning males to view real women as just "bad porn."

Hyper-Romance is Porn Too

Men and women desire not just sex, but romantic companionship as well. Virtual reality proffers simulacra of such companionship, which may not be healthy for users. A significant portion of virtual romantic companionship can be termed "hyper-romance": romance idealized and dramatized beyond the real. Like hypersex, hyper-romance should be considered a type of pornography, though predominantly emotional rather than physical.

⋔   MATTHEW BROPHY

The romance and drama of virtual environments beckon the closet romantics of the world, where the mousy librarian can become a princess courted by a storybook prince in a virtual kingdom of their own making. A woman can find her needs – for care, romance, validation, intimacy, and sex – supposedly satisfied via hyper-romances in the virtual environment, by other virtual world residents.

Hyper-romances in virtual reality are like romance movies on theatre screens and they promise similar detrimental effects to real-life relationships. Experts at Heriot Watt University blame romantic comedies for promoting unrealistic expectations when it comes to relationships.[8] They found that consumers of rom-coms (e.g., *You've Got Mail*, 1998; *Notting Hill*, 1999; *Runaway Bride*, 1999; *The Wedding Planner*, 2001; *Maid in Manhattan*, 2002, and so forth) are more likely to believe that sex should be perfect. They are more likely to believe that a romantic partner should know what they need without having to communicate it, to idealize love as thrilling and predestined, and to expect trust and committed love as immediate rather than achieved through time and hard work.

Hyper-romance places unattainable expectations on males, rendering real males as "deficient" in failing to live up to hyper-romantic standards. Women who find their current real-life relationships dissatisfying may seek emotional and physical gratification in these idealized virtual relationships. Already, women have left their husbands – and sometimes their children – to seek romantic satisfaction in real life with men they have begun idealized relationships with online. They wake to realize that these new men are just as flawed in reality as the dissatisfying husbands they left.

Yet with hypersex and hyper-romance, one need never wake up to reality. The immersive virtual world is without boundaries, duration, or limitation; it is a vivid dream without an end. We may worry, however, that hypesex and hyper-romance will ultimately corrupt the users, satisfying their desires while thwarting their needs.

Down the Rabbit Hole: Sexual Deviancy
Flourishes in Unbounded Realities

The dominance of hypersex and hyper-romance in virtual worlds may cause its share of social problems, both for its users and for real-life relationships. Perhaps more disturbing, however, are the strange fruits of deviant sex, low-hanging and abundant, in virtual gardens. Users might indulge in these forbidden fruits, only to find themselves hooked on the taste.

Virtual environments proffer various sexual deviancies to users, which they might never otherwise encounter. In turn, such unbounded environments tend to normalize such deviances to users, and progressively condition users toward deviancy, while alienating them from their "normal" sexual desires. In real life, for instance, individuals deemed "furries" dress up in elaborate animal costumes to engage with each other socially and sexually. In real life, one would not typically run into a "furry," but *Second Life* teems with them; furries comprise an estimated 6 percent of its populace. One might worry that users who embody animal-human hybrid avatars in a virtual world, or have sex with such furries, are delving into a deviance that may diminish their drive for normal sex in real life. One might also fear that there may be indeed a slippery slope between having sex with a furry and pure bestiality, as furries vary greatly in their human-to-animal proportions. According to one article, sex with animals is increasingly popular in *Second Life*.[9]

Yet perhaps bestiality is compatible with psychological health and a good life, as philosopher Peter Singer suggests.[10] This could be true of a range of sexual deviancies. While "sexual deviance" tends to carry a negative normative connotation, the term itself is merely a statistical notion. Homosexuality, for instance, was once considered by the DSM – the standard handbook in psychology – to be a disorder, since it was a statistical deviancy.[11] Yet I hope we could all recognize that sexual attraction to the same sex, for any statistical deviancy, is compatible with a good human life. I leave it to the reader to determine by her own lights which deviancies are compatible with a good life, and which are contrary. My only contention is that those contrary deviancies will be propagated and normalized by the pornographic singularity.

Beyond bestiality, *Second Life* proffers an assortment of additional paraphilias: rape play, amputee sex, snuff sex (where one avatar is "killed" during the sex act), infantilism, sexual devouring (called "vore"), necrophilia, fecophilia, and anything else conceivable by the deviant imagination.

Age play is one sexual deviancy rampant in *Second Life*. It refers to the virtual sexual intercourse that occurs between an avatar-adult and an avatar-child, both users of variable age and background, who not only trespass into pedophilia, but oftentimes incest as well, where the avatar-adult plays a parent, and the avatar-child plays the son or daughter. There is a spot in *Second Life* nicknamed "molestation grove," where child-avatars wander around looking for a "mommy" or "daddy" adult-avatar to sexually

MATTHEW BROPHY

abuse them. Some adult users purchase child "skins" – child-avatars to embody – in order to prostitute their child-avatar to pedophilic adults, willing to pay. *Second Life* has moved to restrict such age role-play, with very limited results. Needless to say, enforcing regulations in a vast expanse of virtual environments proves very difficult, if not a practical impossibility.

Beyond the virtual world of *Second Life*, some video games offer virtual environments where deviant sex is promoted. *Rapelay* is a 2006 Japanese video game, where the initial goal for the gamer is to stalk and rape a girl in a subway station bathroom, afterwards snapping pictures of her semen-covered body with his cell phone. Ultimately, the player is to stalk and rape a mother and her two young daughters, who are described as "virgin schoolgirls" – "tears glistening in the young girl's eyes" as one is sexually assaulted. Finally, the gamer needs to turn all three women into his sex slaves. If one of them gets pregnant, the player has to force her to have an abortion, lest the player's character die and lose the game. What's worse is the "gang-rape" mode, in which one player can join with other players via the Internet to stalk and rape these women as a group.

Rapelay is one of many computer games that involve violent sex, a second game being *Battle Raper*, produced by the same company, which involves fighting female non-player-characters, and raping them upon winning. Such games offer an example of the boundless sexual fantasies by which computer users can gratify themselves in virtual environments.

Conditioned to be Sexually Deviant

The sexual deviancies described above are easy to dismiss as the pitiable fetishes of abnormal individuals. Virtual reality, however, is poised to increase sexual deviancy dramatically, normalizing it and proliferating it. The ubiquity, accessibility, and anonymity of deviant sex opportunities tend to normalize these activities; they are no longer shocking, they seem no longer deviant. Normalization is furthered when a user is surrounded by cyber-peers or "normal" people who are known to engage in deviant role-playing.

In real life, the normalization of deviant sex has negative effects on relationships. Consider a study about the "rape myth," the myth that most women actually enjoy having sex forced upon them. The study determined that depicting and promoting this myth as true tended to reduce inhibitions against using violence during sex, and altered attitudes in male and female respondents. They begin to view rape no longer as a sexual deviation but normal sexual behavior. Males who believed this myth were more likely to act out these fantasies. Even the acknowledgment itself of the rape myth as a viable sexual possibility had negative effects on both females and males, especially those in intimate relationships.[12] The Internet abounds with rape-related pornographic content. Some websites, such as www.rape-tube.com, cater to this particular fetish, while other general porn sites offer users a pornographic box of chocolates: rape-themed videos intermixed among an eclectic assortment of other types of porn.

Hard boundaries between the sexual and the deviant rarely exist both on the internet and in virtual worlds. In *Second Life*, deviant sexual stimuli abound and pervade the environment. The avatars you see in virtual bars in *Second Life* – anthros, dominatrices, child prostitutes – peddle their sexual deviancies, seeking sexual partners. And why shouldn't a user try it? It is safe, it is anonymous, and a user may be curious. No one gets hurt, right?

Sexual deviance does hurt the user, research suggests, and individuals are far more susceptible to it than they realize. Sexual deviancy insinuates itself into an individual's psychology through voluntary or involuntary exposure. Usually, sexual deviance grows through inadvertent or accidental conditioning.[13] That means that an individual's vulnerability to developing deviant sexual appetites largely depends on the stimuli to which they are exposed. Consider a classic study by Rachman and Hodgson (1968), who successfully conditioned their male subjects, after repeatedly viewing women's knee-length boots in association with sexually arousing pictures of nude women, to become sexually aroused when viewing a picture of a woman's boot by itself.[14] This demonstration of the strong susceptibility of males toward sexual conditioning suggests that sexual deviance can be instilled by mere repeated exposure.

Exposure to forbidden fruits in virtual Edens proves dangerous, as any minor indulgence can lead to a (empirically verified) slippery slope. A six-week study suggests that repeated exposure to hardcore non-violent adult pornography negatively influences individuals' attitudes, contributing to an increased callousness toward women, an appetite for more deviant, bizarre, or violent types of pornography (a phenomenon called "escalation"), devaluation of monogamy and diminishing assurance that marriage would last, and the view that promiscuity was a normal and natural sexual behavior.[15]

As stated above, indulging in deviant sex fantasies *escalates* and supplants previous "normal" sexual fantasies. Psychologist R. J. McGuire explains the increase in desire for deviant sex in men: "As a man repeatedly masturbates to a vivid sexual fantasy as his exclusive outlet, the pleasurable experiences endow the deviant fantasy with increasing erotic value. The orgasm experienced then provides the critical reinforcing event for the conditioning of the fantasy preceding or accompanying the act."[16] Furthermore, this conditioning toward deviance cannot easily be reversed, even by the enormous guilt that the user may come to feel about their deviant attachments.

A shift in users' preferences toward deviant sex in the virtual world may ultimately cause users to undermine real-life relationships. Consider the case of Lisa Best of the UK. She woke up late one night to discover her husband, John Best, at his laptop.[17] On the screen, her husband was simulating gay sex with a male-avatar in a bondage-dungeon environment. John's *Second Life* avatar was named Troy Hammerthall; the virtual environment was called the "Bondage Ranch." Lisa Best told reporters that she felt sick to her stomach, and is now divorcing her husband. John Best denied having any gay or sadomasochistic tendencies, protesting that he was just "messing about." Perhaps he was, at first. But his wife traces her husband's progressive addiction to *Second Life* as the reason for their degenerating marriage, now destroyed. But perhaps sexual deviancy and infidelity is merely a symptom rather than cause of a degenerating marriage. While this is one possibility, I suspect that in many cases, sexual deviancy and internet infidelity represent both a symptom and a cause.

Indulging in Forbidden Fruits Online

Infidelity statistics show that, in the United States from 1998 to 2008, wives who cheated on their husbands rocketed from 14 percent to 50 percent, more than tripling.[18] Husbands who cheat on their wives more than doubled to 60 percent in 2008, from 24 percent in 1998.[19] What happened in those ten years? The Internet happened. It started pervading our culture in the mid-to-late 1990s. The Internet provided unprecedented accessibility, anonymity, and communicability.

Marital fidelity is not necessarily a conscious moral choice by spouses. Fidelity is in part due to the circumstances that facilitate extramarital affairs. In real life, an extramarital affair tends to be rare happenstance: the right two people, the right mood, the right place, the right time. A married person resists temptation not just on the basis of moral rectitude, but also from fear of being caught by their spouse, suspected by neighbors, and shamed by their community, as well as varied sexual anxieties such as fear of sexually transmitted diseases, pregnancy, or sexual dysfunction. Cheating in a virtual reality eliminates all of these obstacles.

How many otherwise faithful husbands would stray if a sexy and willing lingerie model lived next door, beckoning them on a daily basis? In the virtual worlds of the near future, temptation would be nearer than right next door, and even more private and discreet, only accessible to the mind of the user and a remote computer server. Such affairs might occur between users and pornbots, or between users and avatars. Either way, we may suspect the effects would be the same: the erosion of intimate relationships on a large scale.

Already, with mere low-grade virtual sex, the erosion of relationships is evident. Even loving and sexually active marriages are vulnerable to the temptations of simulated sex on the Internet. "Sex on the Net is just so seductive and it's so easy to stumble upon it, people who are vulnerable can get hooked before they know it," reports physician Dr. Jennifer Scheider, who conducted a survey of 94 couples affected by cybersex addiction.[20] All of the couples experienced "broken relationships" with partners with cybersex addictions. Commonly, these partners reported feeling "betrayed, devalued, deceived, ignored, and abandoned and unable to compete with a fantasy."[21]

Consider a 2008 case that comes from the UK. Amy Taylor divorced her husband, David Pollard.[22] A private detective she had hired determined that David was having sex with another woman, a female-avatar in *Second Life*. Taylor's husband, however, was only unfaithful in *Second Life*; he was never unfaithful to her in real life. Nevertheless, she felt he had betrayed the intimacy of their relationship, a response typical of the couples described in the study above.

Once again, consider the staggering occurrence of extramarital affairs in 2008, skyrocketing since the advent of the Internet in the past decade. Now introduce veridical virtual worlds – profuse with opportunities of sex and romance, and absent of the dangers of cheating. We can imagine these statistics would explode upward even further.

As our society sails toward the future, a new virtual world approaches on the horizon. As we near its shores, the sirens' call of hypersex and hyper-romance will beckon louder toward its temptations. If we give in to such seductions in the virtual world, it may make us realize tragically that what we want is exactly what we need not to have.

User Malfunction: Virtue Theory for a Virtual World

The Garden of Earthly Delights is a famous 1503 oil-on-wood painting by Hieronymus Bosch.[23] It traces the decadent devolution of humankind from the Garden of Eden in the first panel, to a deviant orgy of nude figures – incorporating fantastical animals and oversized fruit – on the next panel. The last panel portrays a hellscape: human beings tormented and damned. Art historians interpret this triptych as a warning of the path of temptation and its ultimate destination.

This religious painting provides an archetype, which figuratively expresses the real dangers of human beings indulging in unbounded desires. While residents in virtual reality perhaps need not fear religious damnation, we all need to fear the negative effects of unbounded desires upon the human person and the community which they comprise.

Virtual worlds where "anything goes" will allow human beings to realistically engage in any fantasies they have imagined, and many that they would not. Users can explore all manners of deviancy with safety and utter anonymity. Not only can such indulgences undermine romantic relationships, but they may harm the user himself. Users may find themselves unable to function well as human beings, and unable to flourish in their lives.

Traditional ethical theories would seem to condone, or even endorse, pornographic or deviant virtual sex. Utilitarianism might endorse maximizing pleasure, happiness, or user preferences while subjects are immersed in the virtual experience machine, Robert Nozick's thought-experiment made real.[24] Immanuel Kant's second formulation of the categorical imperative only prohibits a person using another human being as a mere means.[25] It says nothing against using pornbots, since a computer program has no intrinsic or unconditional value. Perhaps the users are using themselves as mere means – as sex objects from which to extract pleasure – but such condemnation seems weak when it would as readily condemn masturbation and casual sex in the real world.

Among the big three traditional ethical theories, virtue theory seems to stand alone in identifying why such pornographic and deviant sex might prove unethical. It is not unethical in being distasteful or objectionable to others, but because of the effect it may have on the subject himself. The user inhibits his own flourishing and functioning the further he departs into the hyperreal and deviant darkness. To be virtuous, a human being needs to have character traits in moderation. Yet the unbounded virtual world tempts with indulgences that may progressively encode vices into the user: lust, immoderation, avarice, cruelty, and so forth.

Intimacy is one primary need an individual must satisfy to function and flourish as a human being. Virtual sex threatens to undermine such intimacy via virtual cheating, hyperreal sex and romance, and sexual deviance. Virtual pornography consumers would malfunction, as they frustrate rather than cultivate real-life intimate connections.

Perhaps our current population can resist the temptations proffered by *Second Life* and other virtual environments. But what of the next generations, born into a society dominated by virtual worlds? By 2011 an estimated 53 percent of children 3–18 years of age will be using virtual worlds on a monthly basis, at the very least.[26] This percentage and usage are sure to dramatically increase as virtual reality comes to pervade our world in decades beyond.

Consider the possible damage that already has been done to children born into the Internet age, where pornography saturates cyberspace. Statistics indicate that 93.2 percent of boys, and 61.1 percent of girls, have seen Internet pornography before the age of 18.[27] Most exposure began between the ages of 14 and 17. A considerable percentage of children had, at least once, viewed images of paraphilic or criminal sexual activity, including sexual violence and child pornography. In 2007, the company behind *Second Life* was sued. The claimant alleged *Second Life* had been allowing minors "free access [where] users can mimick sexual acts, going as far as rape scenes, bondage, zoophilia and scatophilia."[28]

How many children in the "virtual age" will be exposed to sexual deviance before they are ready to cope? How will children resist virtual temptations before they can develop their autonomy? Even if we adults in the present age would have a fighting chance, these children of the future may not, delivered into an age pervaded by virtual worlds.

The Pornographic Singularity: A Bleak Prophecy

The purpose of this essay is not to denounce virtual reality or pornography, but to forewarn of the future effects their coupling will breed. A pornographic Pandora's Box will be opened by virtual technologies, releasing hypersex and hyper-romance, virtual cheating, and unbounded sexual deviancies. Such Freudian Ids run rampant will effect the corrosion of intimacy and social relationships. If so, what might be left? Users corrupted by desires, individuals bereft of committed relationships, a community without families, and a town square without neighbors.

We are headed toward a technological fall, where forbidden fruits will abound in virtual gardens. I cannot sufficiently convey the inexorable temptations promised by virtual advancements, nor statistically establish their far-reaching effects. After all, the future is not here yet, and by then it will have been too late for warning. For the present, I can only extrapolate based on current statistics regarding the dangers of pornography, coupled with the temptations promised by these eventual virtualities. This extrapolation provides sufficient reason to fear the future.

Like the prophecies of Cassandra in Greek mythology, warnings of the future often fail due to our "failure of imagination" in the present. But as technology outpaces civilization's ability to constructively adapt to it, we need to acknowledge that the downfall of civilization need not come from without, in the form of excessive carbon emissions, food shortage, or nuclear annihilation. Civilization's downfall may come from within; the tree of technology dangling before our mouths, fruits too abundant to ignore, too tantalizing to resist.

NOTES

1   G. Mudur, "'Porn' Art in Ivory, 35,000 Years Old," *Telegraph*, Calcutta (May 2009).
2   Larry and Andy Wachowski (dirs.) *The Matrix* (Warner, 1999).
3   See Dove's award-winning television ad campaign and commercial, "Evolution." Available online at www.youtube.com/watch?v=iYhCn0jf46U.
4   Jean Baudrillard, *Simulacra and Simulation*, trans. Sheila Faria Glaser (Ann Arbor: University of Michigan Press, 1994).
5   Naomi Wolf, "The Porn Myth," *New York Magazine* (October 20, 2003).
6   Lynne Segal, "Sweet Sorrows, Painful Pleasures: Pornography and the Perils of Heterosexual Desire," in Lynne Segal and Mary McIntosh (eds.) *Sex Exposed: Sexuality and the Pornography Debate* (London: Virago, 2006).
7   Wolf, "The Porn Myth."
8   "Rom-coms 'spoil your love life,'" *BBC News* (December 16, 2008).
9   Kate Connolly, "Second Life in Virtual Child Sex Scandal," *Guardian* (May 2007).
10 Peter Singer, "Heavy Petting," *Nerve.com* (2001).
11 American Psychiatric Association, *Diagnostic and Statistical Manual of Mental Disorders*, 3rd edn. (Washington, DC: American Psychiatric Association, 1987).

12 Diana Russell, *Rape and Marriage* (Beverly Hills: Sage, 1982).

13 D. Zillmann and J. Bryant, "Shifting Preferences in Pornography Consumption," *Communications Research* 13, 4 (1986): 560–78. See also, R. J. McGuire, J. M. Carlisle, and B. G. Young, "Sexual Deviations as Conditioned Behavior: A Hypothesis," *Behavior Research Therapy* 2 (1965): 185–90.

14 S. Rachman and R. Hodgson, "Fetishes and Their Associated Behavior," *Sexuality and Disability* 20, 2 (1968): 135–47.

15 D. Zillman and J. Bryant, "Pornography's Impact on Sexual Satisfaction," *Journal of Applied Social Psychology* 18, 5 (1988): 438–53. See also, D. Zillman and J. Bryant, "Effects of Prolonged Consumption of Pornography on Family Values," *Journal of Family Issues* 9, 4 (1988): 518–44.

16 R. J. McGuire, J. M. Carlisle, and B. G. Young, "Sexual Deviations as Conditioned Behavior: A Hypothesis," *Behavior Research Therapy* 2 (1965): 185–90. See also F. M. Osanka and S. L. Johann, *Sourcebook on Pornography* (Lexington: Lexington Books, 1989).

17 Danny Shea, "Second Life Divorce: Woman Catches Husband in Virtual Gay Affair," *Huffington Post* (February 2009).

18 Lindsay Richardson, "Percentage of Married Couples Who Cheat," available online at www.catalogs.com/info/relationships/percentage-of-married-couples-who-cheat-on-each-ot.html (accessed August 14, 2009).

19 Ibid.

20 Jane Brody, "Cybersex Gives Birth to a Psychological Disorder," *New York Times on the Web* (May 2000).

21 Ibid.

22 Phillip Victor, "Virtual Affair Ends in Real-Life Divorce," *ABC News* (November 2008).

23 The painting is in the Museo del Prado in Madrid.

24 Robert Nozick, *Anarchy, State, and Utopia* (Basic Books: New York, 1974), pp. 42–5.

25 Immanuel Kant, *Groundwork of the Metaphysic of Morals (1785)*, trans. H. J. Paton (New York: Harper & Row, 1964).

26 Debra Aho, "Kids and Teens: Virtual Worlds Open New Universes," EMarketer (September 2007).

27 C. Sabina, J. Wolak, and D. Finkelhor, "The Nature and Dynamics of Internet Pornography Exposure for Youth," CyberPsychology and Behavior 11, 6 (December 2008): 691–3.

28 "French Watchdog Organization Targets Second Life," GamePolitics.com (June 2007).

PART VII

KINK
Alternative Porn and BDSM

CHAPTER 17

WHAT DO HETEROSEXUAL MEN GET OUT OF CONSUMING GIRL–GIRL PORNOGRAPHY?

"At the very least, curious"

The American feminist scholars Cindy Jenefsky and Diane Helene Miller preface their survey of seven years of what they term "girl–girl" pictorials from *Penthouse* with the observation that there is something "at the very least, curious" about the fact that heterosexual men frequently consume images of women having or pretending to have sex with one another.[1] After all, wouldn't such images threaten the image of dominant heterosexual masculinity that the magazine thrives off? I agree with Jenefsky and Miller's observation, but it is clear that their article is also curiously uninterested in whatever that thing might be. Their analysis, like many others by higher-profile second-wave feminist scholars such as Andrea Dworkin, seeks to make heterosexual men's consumption of girl–girl pornography depressingly explicable. In Jenefsky and Miller's case, they conclude by arguing that the role of girl–girl sex in *Penthouse* is to present a fantasy image of the sexually available lesbian, a woman whose "experimentation" reinforces the naturalness and superiority of heterosexuality. Presumably, what men are supposed to find attractive here is the idea that all women are eventually sexually available to men.

The aim of this chapter is to tell another story about the pleasures that heterosexual men experience when consuming girl–girl pornography. More specifically, I will argue that it is entirely possible to argue that what heterosexual men find most arousing about girl–girl pornography is the *absence* of male heterosexuality from the scene. In order to make this argument, I will critically interrogate Jenefsky and Miller's reading of girl–girl pictorials in *Penthouse*, which I take to be representative of a certain kind of second-wave feminist thought about the issue, and examine other ways that the issue can be thought through. I have chosen to focus on Jenefsky and Miller's analysis because their article is, in fact, clearer, more detailed, and better-structured than the disparate comments about girl–girl pornography in more famous feminist texts such as Andrea Dworkin's *Pornography*. Being so clear, it brings to light some of the problems with how second-wave feminist scholars have understood the question of what heterosexual men get out of consuming girl–girl pornography.

Don't get me wrong: I am not out to prove that Jenefsky and Miller are decisively "wrong" about girl–girl pornography. I owe thinkers such as Jenefsky and Miller a debt, as their work has influenced mine in ways too detailed to elaborate upon here. My aim, instead, is to think in other ways about what makes the phenomenon of girl–girl pornography so curious, hopefully in ways that maintain its curiousness. But, of course, curious things are rarely simple, and girl–girl pornography is not an exception.

What Do Jenefsky and Miller Say About Girl–Girl Pornography?

Jenefsky and Miller divide girl–girl pictorials in *Penthouse* into five categories spanning a spectrum of heterosexualization. At one end of the spectrum is the *ménage-à-trois*, two women and a man being sexual with one another. This is followed by the explicit staging of girl–girl sex for the sexual pleasure of one or more men not visible within the images, but included within the verbal narrative. Next on the spectrum is girl–girl sex with no males present within the narrative, but performed by heterosexually identified females. This is followed by girl–girl sex as an explicit *imitation* of heterosexuality, but with no clues as to whether or not the women involved consider themselves heterosexual

𝄞 CHAD PARKHILL

or lesbian. At the far end of the spectrum is the portrayal of girl–girl sex with no identified ties to heterosexuality.

As examples of the latter four categories, they read four narrative pictorials: "The Princess and the Clown," in which two actresses put on an erotic performance of girl–girl sex for their director, Carlo (who is not pictured in the photos); "Tales of the Morning After," in which two female roommates share stories about their heterosexual erotic adventures of the night before, get turned on, and have sex with each other; "The Wedding Game," in which two women, presented by the narrative text as "lovers," dress up as bride and groom and have sex; and "Lucy and Suki," in which an experienced Japanese woman (Suki) initiates a naïve Western woman (Lucy) in "the art of love." On the basis of these four pictorials, Jenefsky and Miller claim that *Penthouse* reduces lesbianism to a merely sexual identity, that pleasure within that sexual identity comes from penetration, and that the pictorials present penetration as a masculine prerogative. This, in turn, is supposed to support the notion that lesbian sex is somehow imitative of, or less "real" than, heterosexuality.

The structure of their argument allows Jenefsky and Miller to place the readings that best support their conclusion first, while relegating the two more problematic pictorials to the middle of the article. It is hard to argue with Jenefsky and Miller's readings of the "The Princess and the Clown" and "Tales of the Morning After." Both depict clearly heterosexual women having sex with each other either as an erotic performance for a man or as a convenient outlet in the absence of a man. However, their readings become more tenuous in the case of the last two pictorials. They understand the women in "The Wedding Game" to be heterosexual only because the narrative text does not explicitly identify them as lesbian. However, the narrative text explicitly calls them "lovers." Similarly, the fact that the women have sex while dressed as bride and groom is, at the very least, ambivalent. Jenefsky and Miller claim that this presents lesbian sex as derivative of heterosexual sex, thus reinforcing the idea that heterosexuality is "original" and "natural."

However, recent work by feminist philosopher Judith Butler (among others) emphasizes the destabilizing possibilities of gender imitation, presumably including the form of gender imitation performed by the "groom" in "The Wedding Game." Her article "Imitation and Gender Insubordination" argues that the performative nature of drag demonstrates the artificiality of *all* gender performances, rendering the question of "originality" and "derivation" moot. Jenefsky and Miller themselves quote part of "Imitation and Gender Insubordination" in their article: "if it were not for the notion of the homosexual *as* copy, there would be no construct of heterosexuality *as* origin."[2] Curiously, however, they neglect to quote a passage immediately following, in which Butler extends the argument and comes up with a decidedly different conclusion:

> On the contrary, *imitation* does not copy that which is prior, but produces and *inverts* the very terms of priority and derivativeness. . . . These are, quite literally, *inverted* inversions, ones which invert the order of imitated and imitation, and which, in the process, expose the fundamental dependency of "the origin" on that which it claims to produce as its secondary effect.[3]

Thus, contrary to Jefensky and Miller's analysis of the butch/femme couple in wedding drag in "The Wedding Game," it is by no means clear that the staging of a mock lesbian wedding followed by graphic girl–girl sex in *Penthouse* naturalizes heterosexuality. Indeed, as Butler's argument indicates, those very same activities in a different context – say, in a performance piece at an art gallery – could, in fact, be read as subverting the very structure of originality and derivation that Jenefsky and Miller's article relies upon to condemn the girl–girl pictorials in *Penthouse*. Clearly, there's more to what men get out of girl–girl pornography than this – unless we believe that the average pornography consumer is too thick to notice when his sexual identity is being challenged by a subversive gender performance.

What Do Jenefsky and Miller Assume About Men, Women, and Pornography?

In the introduction to this essay, I stated that it is not my intention here to prove decisively that Jenefsky and Miller are "wrong" about girl–girl pornography. Another way to put this is to say that Jenefsky and Miller's article operates within a certain tradition of thought with its own rules for determining whether or not a given statement is true, false, or can even be conceived of as either true or false. Within that tradition, Jenefsky and Miller's arguments are coherent and meet the rules for "truth." But in order to open up a space for a *different* understanding of what heterosexual men get from girl–girl pornography, we must examine the tradition that Jenefsky and Miller's article draws from, and sketch how its argument is limited by what this tradition takes for granted.

It is clear that Jenefsky and Miller position their article as a continuation of second-wave "anti-sex" feminist critiques of pornography. They approvingly cite Dworkin's work on pornography, neglecting to articulate some of the very many criticisms of her position made by other feminists. In fact, Jenefsky and Miller's description of the heterosexism in girl–girl pornography is entirely consonant with that of Dworkin, who summarizes a girl–girl photo in her book *Pornography* by stating: "The lesbian is colonialized [*sic*], reduced to a variant of woman-as-sex-object, used to demonstrate and prove that male power pervades and invades even the private sanctuary of women with each other."[4]

The position that anti-pornography feminists took was, in turn, a direct response to the sexual liberation movement, especially those legal theorists who sought to liberalize obscenity laws. Yet as much as these two camps engaged in prolonged intellectual and legal battles – exemplified by the fierce debates surrounding Dworkin and Catharine MacKinnon's proposed Antipornography Civil Rights Ordinance – their arguments share much in common. As Ian Hunter, David Saunders, and Dugald Williamson argue, both positions share a *negative* understanding of pornography, both in the sense of moral valence and in the sense that pornography is understood to be the byproduct of an unhealthy social pysche.[5] Thus the obscenity law reformer does not want to promote pornography, but rather to promote the healthy expression of sexuality through a literature of erotic realism, whose aesthetic superiority will soon render pornography as we know it obsolete. Similarly, the anti-pornography feminist construes pornography as both the expression of the misogynist erotics of the average heterosexual man *and* the means through which misogyny is transmitted to average heterosexual men. Thus her task is to lay the groundwork for a new form of non-misogynist heterosexual erotics through the censorship of pornography. In both cases pornography is construed as an aesthetic and ethical failure.

Jenefsky and Miller do not go so far as to call consumers of pornography "dirty old men," but they clearly do not consider *Penthouse*'s readers to be capable of critical reflection about their preferred one-handed reading. As I mentioned earlier, one can only cite Butler's work on drag to support the argument that two women having sex in wedding garb portrays heterosexuality as natural and lesbianism as derivative *if* one assumes that the readers of *Penthouse* are not intellectually developed enough to register real gender destabilization when they see it. Jenefksy and Miller thus entirely avoid the question of how *Penthouse*'s audience might respond to its message. This avoidance goes all the way down to grammar: *Penthouse*, we are told, "help[s] to reassert male sexual mastery, reinscribing heterosexual dominance more broadly."[6] In reply I would ask: to whom does *Penthouse* reassert male sexual mastery? Quite clearly it does not do so to Jenefsky and Miller themselves, otherwise they would not have been capable of publishing their feminist analysis of it. But if they have not been fooled by *Penthouse*'s attempts to use lesbianism to shore up heterosexuality, why do they not consider the possibility that *Penthouse*'s traditional target market might not buy it, either?

Since Jenefsky and Miller assume that the readers of *Penthouse* can only passively accept what the magazine tells them, they also assume that any action inside the photo shoots always signifies one thing: male dominance. Let me take as an example their discussion of the question of penetration. Having noticed that none of the women in these pictorials penetrates the other with fingers or a dildo, and that several shots focus on the "penetrable" vagina or anus, Jenefsky and Miller conclude that *Penthouse* constructs an understanding of penetration as a solely masculine prerogative. This is undoubtedly true. But it is also the case that if the pictorials that Jenefsky and Miller examine *were* to contain shots of women penetrating each other with, say, strap-on dildos or vibrators, they could nevertheless reach the same conclusion about what these acts of penetration ultimately mean.

For many lesbian separatist feminists such as Sheila Jeffreys, the use of dildos in lesbian sex is a reinscription of a patriarchal model of what sex constitutes; it reaffirms that for sex to take place, one partner has to penetrate, the other must be penetrated. Pro-dildo feminists have countered that there is a radical distinction between the *phallus* and the *penis*, and indeed there are several models of dildo that resemble ears of corn or the figure of the goddess instead of the anatomical penis. This defense of the dildo is not watertight, though, because the dildo has an indexical relationship to the anatomical penis; even as an ear of corn or a figure of the goddess, the dildo points to the absent penis. The homophobic mind can construe the very fact that such shapes are pleasurable to the female sexual anatomy as "proof" that vaginas are designed only for receiving penises, which would thus confirm, once again, the originality of heterosexuality and the inferiority of lesbianism as its replacement. We have seen that for Jenefsky and Miller anything that imitates heterosexuality in *Penthouse* casts lesbianism as derivative and inferior. Therefore, using the same axioms, it is entirely possible to argue that the deployment of dildos in girl–girl pictorials would constitute a form of heterosexism. Thus, penetration or no penetration, for Jenefsky and Miller the heterosexual male consumer of girl–girl pornography is *always* guilty of invading and "colonializing" a hitherto unsullied lesbian space.

Lesbian Utopias and Heterosexual Space Invaders

What we have examined so far points to a deeper question at the heart of the anxieties surrounding heterosexual men and girl–girl pornography. That is, how are we to understand the relationship between lesbians, understood as oppressed by a system of sexual and gender norms, and heterosexual men, understood as the beneficiaries of that system?

As Annamarie Jagose has made clear, in the past feminist theorists have found the project of conceptually distancing lesbianism from heterosexuality politically necessary.[7] They have articulated several theories that place lesbianism as an identity in one of several spaces *outside* that system of sexual and gender norms. Monique Wittig's claim that "Lesbians are not women"[8] is exemplary in this regard, for it works on two levels. It relies on an understanding that the term "woman" does not make sense unless that term is placed inside a social context of presumed heterosexuality. It also argues that the lesbian, as a woman who is not heterosexual, confounds that context's logic to the point that the lesbian really cannot be understood as a woman as such. The lesbian is therefore outside of that system.

Formulations of the lesbian such as Wittig's thus draw a distinction between the lesbian herself and the networks of patriarchal power that are understood to oppress her. They therefore partake in what the French historian and philosopher Michel Foucault has termed "the repressive hypothesis"[9] – the notion that in the realm of sexuality human beings experience power from the outside, in the form of prescriptions, regulations, and exclusions. Foucault takes pains in his *History of Sexuality* to spell out the fact that he does not deny the everyday reality of certain forms of oppression. Yet, in the Foucauldian schema, power is not merely something that one person uses against another person; instead, it is relational, existing between subjects and the institutions that govern them, and radically *productive*. Foucault's point is that power does not always repress; in fact, it *creates* new identities, especially sexual identities. Thus, although medical and psychiatric institutions of the late nineteenth century spent a great deal of time and effort attempting to understand and

cure the pathology known as "inversion" or "homo-sexuality," the proliferation of knowledge about this pathology allowed people who were
attracted to members of their own sex to understand that they were not
alone. They now had a name, were recognized as a unique subspecies of
the human race, and could therefore band together and work for political
change.

The consequences of this understanding of power are significant for
theorists of lesbianism, for if it is the case that power structures are not
merely oppressive but also enabling, then it logically follows that the
lesbian is a product of the very systems of patriarchy that theorists such
as Wittig believe she exceeds. Such an understanding of the complex and
enabling interrelations between lesbianism and the seemingly repressive
heterosexual norms that produce it cuts to the heart of the question of
heterosexual men consuming girl–girl pornography. For if it is the case
that lesbianism as an identity cannot be said to escape heterosexist power
systems, then we must ask why it is that so many people, gay and straight,
have such an emotional investment in declaring this to be the case. Such
an understanding produces an intriguing new possibility for understanding why heterosexual men consume girl–girl pornography: that instead of
seeking to invade and colonize a female-only space, the heterosexual
reader of *Penthouse* might seek instead to create an erotic illusion of a
pure female-only space by disavowing the links between lesbianism and
his own social world. If this is the case, then his pleasure is not one of
being present at the scene of girl–girl sex, but rather one of *being absent*.

A Crazy Little Thing Called *Jouissance*

The French psychoanalyst Jacques Lacan and his anglophone interpreters provide us with two important (and related) conceptual tools to
understand how this type of pleasure might work: "projective identification"[10] and *jouissance*. One way to introduce these terms is to think about
what happens when the average heterosexual man consumes pornography. A received psychoanalytic argument states that the heterosexual
male consumer of pornography identifies *with* the man (or men) in the
scene as the bearer-of-the-phallus. That is to say, the viewer imagines that
he *is* the man in the scene: his pleasure derives from imagining that the
women in the scene are having sex with him. (Consider here the fact that
men in pornography are frequently near-anonymous, often faceless.)

꒰ᴗ꒱   CHAD PARKHILL

The problem with such a model begins when we note that in order to identify with the male performer as *subject*, the male viewer of heterosexual pornography must, in fact, look at an actual penis. In porn, men can partake in the pleasures of curious examination of another man's penis, as long as a woman is present. The male performer is therefore just as much an object of the consumer's gaze as the woman (or women). This by no means renders the consumer homosexual, for heterosexual pornography remains obsessed with visually presenting female genitals as a means of exploring sexual difference. But just as the male performer is both subject and object for the consumer, so too is the female starlet (or starlets) both the object of the consumer's voyeuristic gaze but also a subject with which the male viewer can identify. In this form of projective identification, "the male viewer does not merge with the female on the screen . . . rather, he projects his own feminine traits of passivity and sexual urges onto the body of the woman as 'other.' Only then is the spectator free to desire the very qualities he himself has expelled."[11]

This idea of more complex mechanisms of identification challenges Jenefsky and Miller's argument. If it is not the case that the consumer of heterosexual pornography merely identifies with the male performer and objectifies the woman or women, then it cannot be the case that when the same consumer looks at images of two women having sex he objectifies the women and imagines himself outside the scene, ready to enter when necessary. Instead, the women would be both subjects and objects of the consumer's gaze. This profoundly ambivalent process of identification appears in the interviews conducted by David Loftus in *Watching Sex*. In this book, Loftus interviews over 100 self-professed consumers of pornography, including three who derive especial pleasure from girl–girl pornography. These men describe their pleasure in ways that suggest that they, on some level, identify with the women in girl–girl pornography.[12] Here, pleasure is not tied to colonizing women's spaces, but in the dissolution of heterosexual masculinity.

Francophone psychoanalysts and theorists distinguish between two types of sexual pleasure: *plaisir*, usually rendered in English as "pleasure," and *jouissance*, sometimes rendered as "bliss," but often left in the original French.[13] *Plaisir* is connected to ego-formation and contentment: it is that form of sexual pleasure that gives comfort and helps define the self as a self separate from others. *Jouissance*, on the other hand, is a more radical form of pleasure: it is a pleasure in which the integrated ego is destabilized, possibly shattered. Rather than being comforting, it is terrifying, an extreme experience. Naturally, this distinction is political in nature. *Plaisir* is understood as a conservative form of pleasure, whereas *jouissance* is understood as radical. Importantly, though, the distinction is gendered, with *jouissance* understood as a decidedly feminine form of pleasure. Indeed, Elaine Marks and Isabelle de Courtivron, in their collection *New French Feminisms*, claim that the word *jouissance* represents "that intense, rapturous pleasure that women know and men fear."[14] But if *jouissance* is the form of self-shattering pleasure that men fear and women know, it can at least be said that the consumer of girl–girl pornography wants to know what the women know. He has a libidinal investment in his own erasure; his pleasure is therefore a form of ego-dissolving *jouissance*.

Conclusion: The Ethics of Heterosexual *Jouissance*

Jouissance has at least one nasty side-effect: as a form of destabilizing pleasure, it cannot itself be made stable. In this way *jouissance* is similar to those logical puzzles that used to leave Socrates and his cohorts in bewilderment: can something be *by definition* destabilizing? Wouldn't that destabilization therefore extend to its own definition? For Roland Barthes, this means that it is impossible, in principle, to rigorously separate *jouissance* from *plasir*: "there will always be a margin of indistinction; the decision will not be the source of absolute classifications, the paradigm will falter, the meaning will be precarious, revocable, reversible, the discourse incomplete."[15] The paradoxical nature of *jouissance* means that it is impossible to make a habit of experiencing *jouissance*. For *jouissance* to become habitual it would have to be tamed, no longer threatening; that is to say, no longer *jouissance* as such. Instead, such a habitual *jouissance* would imperceptibly tip into *plaisir*. It would be a *false jouissance*, one that promises an extreme experience of self-dissolution but delivers mere sexual pleasure.

This, of course, is the situation of the heterosexual consumer of girl–girl pornography. As much as he may want to experience the unknowable pleasure that only a woman can experience – a woman, furthermore, in an elaborate erotic scenario devoid of men – he cannot escape his identity as a heterosexual man. For even if he takes pleasure in removing himself from the picture, after his moment of *jouissance* he will find himself a resolutely heterosexual man, engaging in one of the most heterosexual practices imaginable: masturbating to pornography.

Despite this, we can still argue that heterosexual men's responses to girl–girl pornography are not exhausted by Jenefsky and Miller's explanations. There is indeed something curious about heterosexual men consuming girl–girl pornography. Clearly, some men derive a great deal of pleasure from imagining themselves as the erotic conqueror of a pair of lesbians, ready to win them back to heterosexuality. On the other hand, it is equally clear that for some men what is most erotic about girl–girl pornography is their absence from the picture entirely. My point in this chapter has not been to adjudicate between the merits of these two claims, but to demonstrate that they are not mutually incompatible.

There is nothing, therefore, structurally progressive or retrograde about the consumption of girl–girl pornography. This entails that what is most ethically salient about girl–girl pornography has nothing to do with the genders of who is depicted and who watches. Even the most conscientiously non-objectifying, *jouissance*-chasing consumer of girl–girl pornography assumes that he has a right to access women's bodies, even if only representationally, for sexual pleasure. In this way, the ethical problems raised by girl–girl pornography are no different to those raised by garden-variety heterosexual pornography. Eventually, the male consumer of girl–girl pornography must realize that he has always been inside the scene that he has found so much pleasure in trying to escape.

NOTES

1   Cindy Jenefsky and Diane Helene Miller, "Phallic Intrusion: Girl–Girl Sex in *Penthouse*," *Women's Studies International Forum* 21, 4 (1998): 376. Throughout this essay I will retain a conceptual distinction between the terms "girl–girl" pornography (that is, images of women having sex with each other designed for consumption by heterosexual men) and "lesbianism," which will refer not to a type of pornography but to a social and sexual identity.
2   Butler, in Jenefsky and Miller, "Phallic Intrusion," p. 383.
3   Judith Butler, "Imitation and Gender Insubordination," in Sara Salih and Judith Butler (eds.) *The Judith Butler Reader* (Oxford: Blackwell, 2004), p. 129. Emphasis in original.
4   Andrea Dworkin, *Pornography: Men Possessing Women* (London: The Women's Press, 1981), p. 47.
5   Ian Hunter, David Saunders, and Dugald Williamson, *On Pornography: Literature, Sexuality and Obscenity Law* (New York: St. Martin's Press, 1993).
6   Jenefsky and Miller, "Phallic Intrusion," p. 383.
7   Annamarie Jagose, *Lesbian Utopics* (New York: Routledge, 1994).

8   Monique Wittig, *The Straight Mind and Other Essays* (Boston: Beacon Press, 1992), p. 32.

9   Michel Foucault, *The Will to Knowledge: The History of Sexuality, Volume One*, trans. Robert Hurley (London: Penguin, 1998), pp. 17–49.

10 I have taken this term from Dennis Giles, as cited by Linda Williams in *Hard Core: Power, Pleasure, and the "Frenzy of the Visible"* (Berkeley: University of California Press, 1989), p. 81.

11 Ibid., p. 82.

12 David Loftus, *Watching Sex: How Men Really Respond to Pornography* (New York: Thunder's Mouth, 2002), pp. 58–9.

13 For an overview, see Jane Gallop, "Beyond the *Jouissance* Principle," *Representations* 7 (1984): 110–15.

14 Cited in Gallop, "Beyond the *Jouissance* Principle," p. 114.

15 Roland Barthes, *The Pleassure of the Text*, trans. Richard Miller (New York: Hill and Wang, 1975), p. 4.

CHAPTER 18

HIT ME WITH YOUR BEST SHOT

The "Violent" Controversy Surrounding SM Porn

Aisha's Coming Out

Do you remember the first time that philosophy rocked your world?

For Aisha, it was during the heady excitement of freshman year. She had an ultra-cool prof. who introduced her to concepts like "hegemonic gender roles" and assigned women's liberation texts, from Mary Wollstonecraft's *A Vindication of the Rights of Woman* to Catharine MacKinnon's *Feminism Unmodified*. Later, Aisha joined the editorial board of Out*Rage*, a student-run journal that addressed female sexual subordination and strategies of resistance. The staff often worked into the night, hashing out their own experiences of oppression and connecting these traumatic personal incidents to patriarchal political structures. Aisha emerged from this cocoon of radical theory and consciousness-raising as an enlightened feminist in the mid-1990s. She understood that mainstream culture eroticized male dominance and female submission, resulting in the ubiquity of violence against women, from marital abuse to date rape to stranger danger in a dark alley.

Unfortunately, Aisha's body betrayed her politics during unexpected moments, particularly when cloistered in a movie theatre. Rape scenes in films left her riveted. When she saw *A Clockwork Orange*, excitement unexpectedly intruded on her rage and fear. In defense, she vehemently derided the filmmaker for his gratuitous exploitation of female victimization – surely not done for an artistic purpose, but instead to titillate with eroticized violence. The rush of arousal instigated by the rape scene in *Thelma and Louise* was more difficult to rationalize. Particularly when Aisha found herself more turned on by that moment of brutality than by the consensual sex scene with Brad Pitt. Even more shameful, she could not help getting hot and bothered after seeing a documentary that graphically displayed the horrors of the porn industry: a woman's nipples clamped tight, her legs pushed too far apart. Of course, the beauty of not having a penis is that your *hard on*, such as it is, can be discretely hidden away, and your flushed cheeks can be chalked up to indignation instead of arousal.

But this quarrel between feminism and flesh was disconcerting. The mind–body dualism – where intellect is elevated as human and spiritual, and corporeal impulses are disparaged as animal and base – was something Aisha had studied as an example of patriarchal philosophy and religion. Surely this was not the answer. Of course, Aisha was also familiar with the "myth of female masochism," perpetuated by early psychologists who claimed that women secretly yearned to capitulate to male domination.[1] She knew, however, that she had no desire to actually *be* violated. Yet the *representation* of sexual abuse continued to prompt an unwelcome tingling response. Aisha desperately sought an explanation, seeking answers in more feminist theory in the way that others might turn to the Bible for guidance.

It did not take long to discover a valid and exculpatory account for her treacherous excitement. According to feminist psychology, Aisha had internalized patriarchal prescriptions of sexuality as a result of relentless social conditioning. Apparently, she got wet at imagery of sexual abuse the way a Pavlovian dog salivates when it hears the bell. It was a learned response, not a natural one, so it could and should be unlearned. As Susan Brownmiller stated, "The rape fantasy exists in women as a man-made ice-berg. It can be destroyed – by feminism."[2] Aisha just had to persevere. Read more theory, join more support groups, and masturbate to images of healthy sexuality. And so she did. Until one day . . .

Aisha fell for Gabriel. Hard.

He was a roguish graduate student devoted to "sex positive" feminism and postmodern ideas about the ambiguity of meaning. Later, after the argument, Aisha and Gabriel talked about what had prompted him to present her with a copy of *Whiplash*, a Canadian magazine featuring sadomasochism (SM), fetishism, bondage, and discipline. SM porn had initially shocked the hell out of her system. They almost broke up over it.

"How *dare* you impose your perverse fantasy on me?" she sputtered, attempting to conceal a fervid arousal that seemed to leap out of her skin. "I thought you were progressive. I thought you cared about the issue of violence against women; I didn't think you got off on it!"

"It's not violence," Gabriel had protested. "It's role-playing." He captured her tiny wrists in one hand and bent down to kiss her. "Besides," he said arrogantly, before his lips closed the distance, "methinks thou dost protest too much." You can imagine how hot the sex was that night . . .

The Legal Controversy

Does SM porn signify insidious sexual violence or innocuous sexual variation? The answer to this question can have a determinative effect, not just on Aisha and Gabriel's love affair, but also on whether a court will find a sadomasochistic text to be obscene.

Defendants define SM as a "consensual exchange of power" that can involve fantasy, erotic pain, and/or restraint for the mutual pleasure of the players.[3] The argument here is that SM text is not a representation of violence per se, but rather a coded expression of the complementary sexual desires of dominance and submission. Adherents to this view, such as Gabriel, may define SM as role-playing in order to differentiate the theatrical nature of the sexual practice from genuine coercive exploitation. Furthermore, people who enjoy SM porn contend that consent is either expressed or implied in these representations. Some defendants have argued that sadomasochistic desire can be likened to or indeed is a type of sexual orientation, and that censorship of these materials will have a discriminatory impact on a sexual minority.

Critics and prosecutors have countered that if aggression, humiliation, hitting, bondage, and/or skin bruising or breaking is portrayed in a sexual context, it is self-evident that this conveys violence. For anti-SM advocates, demonstrations of consent do not neutralize the harm, but indeed can actually compound the dehumanizing nature of the text. Anti-SM feminists might further argue that this pathology – particularly when manifested in submissive-leaning women – is born out of a patriarchal monopoly on mainstream sexual representation. As Aisha had initially determined, those who fall prey to SM arousal are victims of a society that does not offer egalitarian images of sexuality. Finally, the critics have suggested that even if SM desires constitute a sexual orientation, it is still a dangerous pathology that is justifiably discouraged by the state through censorship of SM texts.

Understanding the Context

The critics of SM and its representations have a point. Violence against women exists and persists. Every woman knows this, whether from personal experience or third-party accounts from loved ones. This is what mobilized Aisha and her co-editors to expose the pervasiveness of the problem in the journal Out*Rage*.

Thanks to a courageous feminist movement, governments have been forced to take heed of the issue and form committees, create policies, and change laws, all in an effort to eradicate this atrocity. One particular area that has received an inordinate amount of attention is pornography, often seen as both a product and perpetrator of sexual violence. According to theories espoused by anti-porn feminists and social conservatives, the creation of pornography involves coercion and exploitation of female porn stars, and the consumption of pornography creates attitudinal changes in the male viewer, rendering women objects to be used and abused.[4] The USA, Canada, and the United Kingdom have enacted and repeatedly revised anti-obscenity legislation in attempts to counter such harms.

Although laws that prohibit sexual expression are nothing new, their justifications have changed over the years. Traditionally, judges rationalized that it was the state's duty to prevent the dissemination of sexual material on moral grounds. In the nineteenth-century case of *R. v. Hicklin*, an English court determined that society was entitled to censor material that "depraves and corrupts those whose minds are open to such immoral influences."[5] From this point forward, obscenity cases in the Common Law world were primarily concerned with protecting susceptible individuals from moral corruption.

In the twentieth century, certain jurisdictions sought to arrive at a more democratic definition of obscenity. Jurisprudence in the United States and Canada updated the test for obscenity by requiring decision makers to empathize with the "average" person. Under this approach, judges and juries applied contemporary community standards to determine if a work was "prurient," "indecent," "dirty," or "dangerous."

Most recently in the USA, Canada, and the United Kingdom, justifications for the prohibition of obscenity have shifted from morality preservation to harm prevention. This brings us to our current time period, in which certain types of pornography have been linked to sexual violence, and are thus justifiably censored on the grounds of women's safety and equality.

Of course, the question is how do we establish the causal connections required to justify criminal sanctions? How do we differentiate benign erotica from pornographic depictions that cause harm by detracting from women's equal status and increasing their vulnerability to sexual assault? The most common answer has been that sexual texts eroticizing hierarchy or depicting violence are literally prescriptive. Such an approach almost invariably categorizes SM porn as obscene, along with many other more mainstream varieties of pornography. The argument is that such texts create an association between misogynistic aggression and sexual arousal, inciting the male viewer to recreate the depicted pornographic scenarios in real life. This is what I call the "monkey see, monkey do" hypothesis. As for the porn actresses or models, their victim status is established through their participation in the making of such a text. If any disavow the victim label, they are dismissed as too damaged to even recognize their own subordination.

Violence

The social science evidence that links adult porn to violence is, to say the least, not convincing.[6] You do not have to be a criminologist, or to have meticulously combed through the data, to know this. Consider the fact that for at least ten years the Internet has made every possible variety of pornographic material, from fetish flicks to virtual snuff films, available for free with just a few keystrokes. Despite this, we have not seen a spike in reported sexual violence. In fact, studies have begun to show that sexual violence has been steadily decreasing even as porn becomes more readily available.[7] And yet the "monkey see, monkey do" hypothesis persists in law: porn watching is construed as mere foreplay that leads to a reenactment with non-consenting individuals. And while this premise *may* hold true for some viewers, it may also be true that any number of texts – commercials, horror movies, *CSI* episodes – also have similar deleterious effects on *some* people. So why is one criminalized, while the other is not?

In law, if a text has "artistic merit" – that is, if a judge decides that it appeals to one's intellect – then it is protected speech, even if one could present evidence linking the text to harm. If a judge decides that the text appeals solely to one's "base" sexual instincts, then it can either be denied the label of expression or be deemed illicit expression, regardless of proof of harm. This is why some movies depicting graphic sexual violence, like *Death Wish* or *Deliverance*, may be protected, while SM magazines like *Whiplash* may not – always depending, of course, on the whims of the particular judge or jury who happens to be evaluating the text.

Defenders of SM porn spend a lot of their time distinguishing SM from violence and rebutting the "monkey see, monkey do" hypothesis. They pull out social science evidence, they emphasize the interdependency of the dom/sub encounter, and they insist that mutual pleasure (not violence) is the end goal of all SM text. I agree with this. But for the rest of this essay, I want to try to spotlight the ways sadomasochist lovers and practitioners are vulnerable to violence, not from each other, but from society and from the state.

I contend that censorship of SM porn itself perpetrates violence on sadomasochists – both physical and psychological – but that this happens off-stage, outside of the boundaries of official legal discourse. And because of this, judges and anti-porn advocates are not concerned with, nor held accountable for, the consequences of such censorship. This infuriates me. I am tired of being on the defensive. It is time to launch a philosophical attack.

There are three kinds of overlapping violence I will address: physical violence, phenomenological violence, and epistemic violence. Each of these forms of violence represents an exercise of undue force by the state that culminates in undeserved and unwanted pain and degradation on the part of sadomasochists.

Physical Violence

Censorship does not simply keep naughty pictures out of the hands of vulnerable individuals. It sends people to prison. Prosecutors and police, often unable to catch or charge the people who actually commit violent acts, are quick to focus on bookstore owners, video store managers, and sometimes unwitting porn consumers, who have come into contact with texts containing hardcore sexual imagery. These "pornographers" are much easier to entrap than violent offenders.

Consider the American case of the *USA v. Guglielmi*.[8] The accused was convicted by jury of transporting obscene films through interstate commerce. This first-time offender was sentenced to 25 years in prison, a punishment usually reserved for the most extreme violence (murder or aggravated sexual assault) and/or for repeat offenders. To justify the sentence, the court found that the films were "violent" and "degrading" and would incite violent acts by some of their consumers. This claim was unsubstantiated. Indeed, it was later noted that most of the "customers" who had received the materials were in fact FBI agents. No evidence was introduced to indicate that the materials had incited anyone, either the undercover agents or genuine customers, to violence. After Guglielmi spent five years in prison, a Court of Appeal finally found that the sentence was overly punitive and remanded the case for reconsideration.

The notion of proportionality is an enshrined principle of justice. Your punishment should be proportional to the harm inflicted by your crime. In Guglielmi's case, the prosecution did not adduce evidence of direct harm, much less prove it beyond a reasonable doubt. Yet an overwhelmingly punitive sentence came to be imposed, signaling an abandonment of the principle of proportionality that is all too common in obscenity cases involving SM texts.

Regrettably, legal systems in Canada and the United Kingdom can also impose punishment in reliance on the "monkey see, monkey do" hypothesis. For example, the *Criminal Code of Canada* prohibits the making or distribution of obscene materials, with a punishment of up to two years in prison. Thus, for example, while Aisha and Gabriel would not be prosecuted for mere possession of *Whiplash*, the publisher that produced the magazine, and the bookstore owner who sold it, could be criminally convicted and sentenced to prison. England's legislation has an even broader reach, criminalizing simple possession of "extreme pornographic images."[9] If Aisha and Gabriel were caught reading *Whiplash* in England, they would be vulnerable to criminal prosecution and liable to a prison term of two years.

And what is the upshot of all this? State sanctioned violence against sadomasochists and those who cater to their unusual (or is it that unusual?) erotic tastes.

Prison is violence. Make no mistake. It is not a benign rehabilitative apparatus that simply incapacitates dangerous offenders and reprograms them for life on the outside. It perpetrates violence on the inmate, both psychological and physical. Autonomy and human identity are destroyed; one becomes a number. Every moment is tallied, controlled, and accounted for. Perhaps this is deserved if you have violated another's autonomy; for example, if you have assaulted an individual who now lives in fear because of post-traumatic stress. But when you have provided sexual texts for the pleasure of sexual minorities, or indeed if you are a member of a sexual minority who has found pleasure and affirmation in a text produced by consenting adults, this obliteration of your freedom, of your bodily control, is undue. It is excessive. It reflects a neurotic agenda of moral sexual conformity that masquerades as the state *doing something* to stop violence.

Prison also provides a venue for physical violence. Inmates are often victims of attacks, including sexual attacks, from other inmates or prison guards.[10] Again, some retributionists might argue that it is fair for an offender who has committed sexual assaults to now be vulnerable to similar violations in prison; an eye for an eye, a rape for a rape. But if you are incarcerated for multiple years for the "crime" of consuming or trafficking in sexual texts that have not been proven beyond a reasonable doubt to cause harm, and that have no complaining victims, the punishment is grossly unfair by Common Law standards of justice. In this case, justice is not blind, but rather suffers from a blind spot that overlooks a kinky person's right to be free from cruel or unusual punishment.

Phenomenological Violence

Phenomenology believes that inherent truths of human existence can be derived from our sensory interaction with the outside world. The philosopher credited with founding this school of thought, Edmond Husserl (1859–1938), advanced the idea of a "pure preconceptual experience," insisting that we must bracket preconceived notions of human nature, of reality, and of knowledge (including scientific knowledge) in order to access the genuine meaning of a lived experience. Later phenomenologist philosophers, like Maurice Merleau-Ponty, focused on the embodied nature of this lived experience, challenging the mind–body dualism of traditional philosophy and arguing that mental and corporeal processes are interpenetrative.

In view of this radical rethinking of the human condition, consider how Aisha initially fragmented her subjectivity by superimposing a preconceived and singular "truth" on her body's mutinous arousal to representations of violence. Her feelings *must* be the product of social conditioning and it *must* therefore be suppressed. From a phenomenological standpoint, Aisha should bracket her preconceived notions of healthy, progressive, or authentic sexuality. Instead, she should be attuned to her erotic impulses – not as simplistic corporeal truth that overrides her intellectual analysis, but rather as part of a holistic engagement with the sensations and narratives that turn her on.

By withholding judgment on her SM desires, Aisha might discover that repression is not the most effective form of resistance to patriarchal authority. To the contrary, she might decide that it is deeply transgressive for a woman to prioritize sexual pleasure for its own sake, and not for some speculative future goal such as "the better good of society" or even "the better good of womankind." Aisha might also find that SM's appropriation of hierarchal scripts within a contrived and consensual context provides an empowering and subversive way to confront her demons. A way to alchemize the pain of past sexual trauma, or the fear of its occurrence (what woman does not live with this fear?), into catharsis and courage.

But if Aisha were to fully embrace her sadomasochistic self, her SM activities might bring her to the attention of the authorities. This is what happened to a group of SM lovers in England who videotaped their sex parties for personal enjoyment and were criminally convicted in the *R. v. Brown* case.[11] During an unrelated investigation, police seized the tapes after searching private premises and were convinced they had discovered genuine "snuff" films. Millions of pounds were spent on an obscenity/murder investigation before the police realized that the footage had simply captured a group of gay men enjoying a consensual – albeit extreme – sexual experience. This did not deter the police from eventually charging the men with various assault-related offenses.[12] Their guilty conviction was upheld all the way through to the highest court in England. Punishments ranged from fines to prison terms that reached up to three years. As such, physical violence in the form of harassment, arrests, detentions, and imprisonments was perpetrated against these consensual lovers.

Much has been written about the injustice of the decisions and the sentences, particularly with respect to homophobia and sexual totalitarianism. These are very important critiques, but for purposes of this section, I want to highlight the phenomenological violence flowing from the police conduct and the House of Lords' decision.

While the videotape was not technically caught by anti-obscenity laws, as it had not been produced for commercial distribution, it was central to the case. In the face of this visual evidence, the authorities refused to accept the phenomenological reality of the accused men. While the dominant lovers were convicted of assault, the submissives were convicted of accessory to assault *upon their own bodies*. Criminalizing "assault" therefore has nothing to do with protecting the autonomy or bodily control of the "victim," rather it manifests as a way to impose an authoritarian view of proper sexual behavior. Indeed, when the submissive men insisted that the activities depicted in the video had been mutual and very much desired, the majority judges simply dismissed their testimony as "worthless."

This is what I call phenomenological violence. The embodied psychosexual experiences of the sadomasochist lovers are deemed "worthless." The pleasure and the agency of the submissive and dominant players become not just unacceptable, but unintelligible. And instead of allowing the "actors" in the private sex tapes to translate the meaning of the filmed events, the judges aggressively imposed an interpretation based on their own phenomenological reaction to the video footage. Over and over again, the judges employ rhetoric of antipathy to describe their assessment of the tapes. Words that were used include "disgust," "horror," "incomprehension," "bewilderment," "sadness," "revulsion," "repugnance," "moral objection," and "repulsively wrong." To hear practices that you find pleasurable, intuitive, appealing, sexy, respectful, and so very *right* described in this judicial language violates one's sense of subjectivity, of identity, of existence. It engenders self-hatred, shame, and repression.

My point here is not that the judges were inherently wrong to determine from their own subjective points of view that the depicted activities were objectionable. Instead, I want to emphasize that because of the judicial monopoly on the construction of reality, their definitive statements of the "truth" of SM violently enforce one version of the good (sex) life. This amounts to an incidence of interpretive force, culminating in both ontological as well as physical violence, inflicted in the absence of protesting victims or any other evidence that harm has resulted from these mutually satisfying sexual practices.

Epistemic Violence

That the SM lovers in the *Brown* case were considered incompetent to determine the significance of their own sexuality is perhaps not so surprising. Given pervasive mainstream cultural views that sadomasochists are "sick" or "perverse," their perspective is likely to be dismissed as a symptom of their pathology. However, as is demonstrated by the case of *Little Sisters v. Canada*, even the expert witnesses who do not identify as sadomasochists will be disregarded if they dare to challenge the judicial gaze on sexual minorities.[13]

At issue was the effective censorship imposed by Canadian customs inspectors, who were empowered to ban the importation of any materials determined to be "obscene" – a label disproportionately applied to SM texts destined for gay and lesbian or women's bookstores. For example, if *Whiplash* had been an American magazine on its way to the Toronto Women's Bookstore, there are good chances it would have been held at the border, deemed too dangerous for Canadians like Gabriel and Aisha to see. The applicants in the *Little Sisters* case argued, among other things, that such seizures amounted to a violation of their constitutional right to freedom of expression.

During the trial, the Little Sisters bookstore posited that the SM texts at issue had "artistic merit" and they should therefore not be found to be criminally obscene. It called expert witnesses from the fields of literary interpretation, semiotics, and queer culture who offered insights to assist the trial judge in understanding SM representation as a cultural, political, and artistic project.[14]

Among others, the court heard from Bart Testa, a well-known film and semiotics professor, Becki Ross, a notable sociologist who specialized in women's studies, and Nino Ricci, a prominent writer and professor of creative writing. These three experts testified that the reviewed SM texts could possess significant, but coded, artistic merit. It was further contended that people outside of the SM sexual subculture were likely to misunderstand the dynamics and the significance of the represented sexual activities.

The trial judge accepted that uninformed readers might misinterpret and misconstrue SM texts and that such texts could hold artistic value and could thus not presumptively be labeled obscene. On appeal, however, the Supreme Court of Canada played down the possibility that SM representation might hold artistic value. Ignoring the complex picture drawn by experts regarding the encoded meanings of SM, the court characterized a scene between a dominatrix and her "slave" – a classic SM erotic role-play – as "degrading" and "dehumanizing." The imagined submissive in the scenario was further labeled a "victim," with no regard to whether the text portrayed the activities as consensual and mutually pleasurable. Returning to the "monkey see, monkey do" hypothesis, the court found that SM representations were legitimately censored because of the harm that parliament *believed* might flow from their dissemination. Again, no evidence of harm was adduced to support the contention that the censored SM texts incited violence in their consumers.

This nullification of the expert knowledge produced within and about sexual subcultures is what I call epistemic violence. A fundamental question in philosophy has been the study of epistemology, that is, the ways knowledge can be produced, verified, or invalidated. More recent theorists, like Michel Foucault, have suggested that what counts as knowledge at any given time has more to do with power and historical circumstances than it does with ultimate and transcendent truth. This insight helps us to understand the Supreme Court of Canada's reading of an SM text in defiance of the witness testimony. The expert knowledge of the professors and writers, along with the personal knowledge of SM practitioners, was aggressively overridden by a judiciary that did not display any independent familiarity with or knowledge about the significance of the texts. What these judges did have was power. With a coercive state apparatus to enforce its judgment, the Supreme Court of Canada has the power to curtail the expressive rights of sadomasochists and impose its version of reality on their subculture.

A sadomasochist like Gabriel knows that his sexuality is respectful, enjoyable, and empowering, but this knowledge comes to be officially destroyed by a judiciary that decides his sexuality is inherently degrading, dehumanizing, and violent. This epistemic violence not only harms sadomasochists' freedom of expression and equality, but also harms their self-perception. It creates a fissure between what one knows and what one is told. Like phenomenological violence, this state-sanctioned epistemic violence stigmatizes sadomasochists and engenders shame and self-hatred in people whose "sex crime" is premised on mutual enjoyment and satisfaction.

Aisha's Crossing Over

Is there any sweeter pleasure, than the pleasure of giving into temptation?
Aisha flipped through the SM magazine in a haze of agitation and arousal. Her eyes hungrily consumed the images: a man hog-tied and gazing at the camera with vulnerable inviting eyes, a woman sporting a strap-on about to penetrate her prostrate lover. It was the first time she had seen representations of sexuality that turned her on without filling

her with dread, the way mainstream images of sexual violence had done. She later realized that her knee-jerk protest to Gabriel operated as a defense against her own rising excitement. What she found in this magazine was not just jack-off material, but recognition. Aisha realized that there were others who shared her complicated cravings. Through this magazine, Aisha began to understand her desires as an eroticization of the symbols of hierarchy, not an adoption of the weapons of patriarchy.

Throughout her life, Aisha had tried to convince herself that what felt so intuitive and attractive was evil and corruptive. Anti-porn feminism and dominant society had taught her to tone done her libidinous personality and avoid being a "pervert" or "slut." Finding affirmation in pornography was a welcome reprieve from this internalized conflict. It meant she could continue her critical analysis of oppressive relations without foreclosing the possibility that sexual feelings and practices could be a source of insight. Being attuned to her phenomenological reality could allow her to gain confidence in her own sexual truths. It could give her courage to resist the epistemic violence perpetrated by a society that constructs SM as both ludicrous and dangerous.

As for Gabriel, her initiator into SM sexual possibilities, he had read Aisha as a kindred spirit the moment they met. Given the ways both dominant society and anti-porn feminism have managed to drive perverts into silence, if not into self-loathing, it is heartening to know that people with a penchant for kink have an uncanny ability for finding one another.

Perhaps it is overstating it to claim that lust conquers all, but at the very least, it is a powerful force to be reckoned with.

NOTES

1   For an exploration of the origins of this myth, see Paula J. Caplan, *The Myth of Women's Masochism* (Toronto: University of Toronto Press, 1993).
2   Susan Brownmiller, *Against Our Will: Men, Women and Rape* (New York: Simon and Schuster, 1975), p. 359.
3   Patrick Califia, *Sensuous Magic: A Guide for Adventurous Couples* (New York: Richard Kasak Books, 1993), p. 150. See also Darren Langdridge and Meg Barker (eds.) *Safe, Sane and Consensual: Contemporary Perspectives on Sadomasochism* (New York: Palgrave Macmillan, 2007).
4   Anti-porn theorists usually pay scant attention to gay or lesbian pornography, despite the fact that gay and lesbian pornography gets disproportionately labeled obscene in criminal prosecutions. To the extent that same-sex pornography

is addressed, it is generally seen as mirroring or aping the exploitive hetero-sexual paradigm of dominance and submission which perpetuates sex inequality and misogyny. A notable example of this school of thought is Christopher Kendall's book, *Gay Male Pornography: An Issue of Sex Discrimination* (Vancouver: University of British Columbia Press, 2004).

5   *R. v. Hicklin*, LR 3 QB 360 (1868).

6   For an excellent overview of the social science literature from the 1980s, see Dany Lacombe, *Blue Politics: Pornography and the Law in the Age of Feminism* (Toronto: University of Toronto Press, 1994). See also W. A. Fisher and G. Grenier, "Violent Pornography, Antiwoman Thoughts, and Antiwoman Acts: In Search of Reliable Effects," *Journal of Sex Research* 31 (1994): 23–38.

7   See Anthony D'Amato, "Porn Up, Rape Down," *Social Science Research Network*, 6/23/06 (2007). The anti-porn response to such studies argues that rape and sexual assault statistics are unreliable, as the crime is extremely under-reported. However, this fact was surely true before the advent of the Internet. Thus, while the number of reported rapes do not accurately reflect the actual number of rapes, there is no reason to think that the relative rate of reporting would be going down.

8   The facts for this case were taken from the following judgments: *US v. Guglielmi* 819 F.2d 451 (4th Cir. 1987), *US v. Guglielmi* 731 F. Supp. 1273 (WDNC 1990), and *US v. Guglielmi* 929 F.2d 1001 (4th Cir. 1991).

9   Criminal Justice and Immigration Act 2008, Part 5, Section 63.

10   Human Rights Watch, "No Escape, Male On Male Prison Rape," online at www.hrw.org/legacy/reports/2001/prison/report.html.

11   *R. v. Brown* (1993), 97 Cr. App. R. 44, 1993 WL 963434 (HL), (1993) 157 JP 337, [1994] 1 AC 212, [1993] 2 All ER 75 (UK House of Lords).

12   The accused were charged under the Offences Against the Person Act 1861, Chapter 100, Acts Causing or Tending to Cause Danger to Life or Bodily Harm, ss. 20 and 47. Some theorists have speculated that the police felt compelled to lay charges to justify the exorbitant costs of their investigation. See Bill Thompson, *Sadomasochism: Painful Perversion or Pleasurable Play?* (London: Cassell, 1994), p. 2.

13   *Little Sisters Book and Art Emporium v. Canada (Minister of Justice)* 2000 SCC 69, [2000] 2 SCR 1120.

14   *Little Sisters Book and Art Emporium v. Canada (Minister of Justice)* (1996) 131 DLR (4th) 486, 18 BCLR (3d) 241 (BCSC) [*Little Sisters* trial decision].

CHAPTER 19

RUMINATIONS OF A DOMINATRIX

An Interview with Mz. Berlin

The final piece in our anthology is an interview in which Dave Monroe interrogates the Fabulous Mz. Berlin about the ins and outs of the porn business. Mz. B is a widely known BDSM dominatrix, actress, model, producer, and director who has appeared on many such (in)famous websites. She also works in "mainstream" porn, and thus has insight into several faces of the porn industry. Note that the purpose of this interview is to allow Berlin to put forward her thoughts for consideration by you, the reader. Dave makes little, if any, attempt to *argue* with her in Socratic fashion; it is an interview rather than a dialogue. Nevertheless, Berlin offers interesting insights on the nature and limits of harm, torture, the role of mental maturity in coping with the porn industry, and other titillating topics. Enjoy (and if you don't, prepare for a spanking)!

DM: Tell our readers about you and your educational background.

I am from Louisiana, where I attended Louisiana State University. I majored in Psychology and Communications, and was active as a member of the Student Activities Council. Although my formal education is simple and basic, I've spent most of the time since graduating from high school doing two things, learning about sex and people!

I'm 30 now, and was dancing when I was 18. By dancing, I mean stripping. After that, I got into fetish and bondage modeling, and for the last year and a half I've been working in adult films. One thing that attracts me to the adult entertainment industry is that I learn a lot about people and their behavior.

So you were dancing while you were in school?

Yes! [Laughs] Dancing is what helped pay for college! I'm that girl!

How does your education affect your experiences in porn? Do you see a resulting difference between your relationship to the industry compared to your fellows?

I think my education affects the way I treat other people more than it affects the way I think about myself. I'm better at evaluating people; especially as a dominatrix, which is what I am primarily. I think it helps me read and understand the body language of others, and communicate with the people with whom I work. For example, I am able to understand or discover the interests of guys I shoot with and ask them intimate questions without being insulting. Studying psychology also helps with humiliation – you learn what humiliates people, and that's part of the role of being a dominatrix. The communications part also helps in terms of public speaking.

However, there isn't for me a kind of "psychological separation," where I "blank out" while I'm shooting and am mentally disengaged. I really want to be there. I don't think that has anything to do with my education, but more with who I am. Being present, in the moment, no matter what the circumstances, is my main goal as a person.

Dancing aside, how and why were you drawn into the porn world in general, and into BDSM specifically?

I became obsessed with the fetish pictures of John Willie. I was attracted to the corsets, handcuffs, chains, and to the femininity of those images. I really liked the aesthetic, and I realized that I wanted to be in such pictures. So I met with photographers in California, Ken Marcus, Ian Rath of FetishNation.com, and said, "I want to look like a John Willie girl." We did shoots where I tried to emulate that vision of femininity. After a while, I began to see a progression in those pictures, an attention to detail, because I was becoming a different person and a better model. I was "becoming" Berlin. As far as film goes, the fetish producers realized that I like to talk and get into character while shooting – which most porn girls don't beyond the "oh yeahs" and "give it to mes" – so I started shooting short fetish film clips. But now I do everything: boy-girl, fetish, BDSM, mainstream porn, and so on. I'm also a "rigger," which means I tie people up, director and producer of Fetish/Bondage films, for my own company, and others. Oddly, I didn't get into the adult film side of things until I was 28 years old, so I entered the industry ten years too late! I'm too young to be a MILF, and too old to be a "barely legal." I have my own company called Em Kay Ultra Productions, and my own website (www.mzberlin. net), and I'm more proud of that than anything in the world.

Given that you wear several "hats," as it were, in the porn business, has your being a producer and director affected the way you view the industry, or the way you understand yourself in it?

Yes; it's given me more confidence as an actress. I feel comfortable asserting myself about being paid proper rates for scenes, and so on. In short, it's given me a lot more control. Being a director and producer has also given me a new perspective – you can't let the industry come in and use you. In porn, one works in a very physical environment; you're being touched intimately and so forth. A lot of girls in porn still connect physical engagement with emotional engagement, and this industry can tear them down. But taking the part of directing and producing has put me in a position where I can use the industry and it doesn't use me. I get what I want out of it, not the other way around.

It's also a bit like becoming a manager at any other job – you realize you're not just there to screw around. You're there to film porn. When I'm acting, I recognize that I am a commodity, there to be objectified by someone else and to perform. As a producer, I'm interested in the financial side of things, while if I'm directing for someone else, it's more about the shooting. If I'm producing, and it's my money being spent on making a film, you'd better believe that everyone is doing what they're supposed to and where they need to be!

You mentioned that some girls working in porn connect emotions with the intimate physical nature of the business, and that this can "tear them down." Will you say more about that?

I don't want to down the industry, but we do allow some things to happen that I don't think are emotionally correct. Some girls don't really understand what they're getting into. This happens most frequently with 18-year-old girls who show up LA with a suitcase wanting to be a "porn star" because they saw it on TV. The porn lifespan of such girls is likely to be short, because they don't understand how to set boundaries. I personally think that one shouldn't be allowed to do porn until 21. I believe this because generally these young girls don't recognize some of the long-term ramifications of what they're doing – there are videos of them having sex that are publicly available and around forever. Many young girls also simply can't cope with the "emotional drop" that comes with shooting porn. While making a film, there's a lot of adrenaline and a "rush" in the experience, like the experience of acting on stage. Afterward, there can be a bit of a letdown, and many young girls have trouble dealing with that. They simply haven't figured out how to reconcile their professional life as a commodity and their emotional states. The emotional effects also depend on the support system you have.

With my company, and the companies for which I work, especially in BDSM, we make a point of trying to inform actors and actresses about these pitfalls. Both TwistedFactory.com (a company I directed extensively for) and Kink.com are very scrupulous in this regard. We tell them exactly what we are trying to do, make it known exactly what to expect, and inform them about the possible consequences of their actions. In mainstream porn, AIM works to enlighten porn newcomers with a "Porn 101" DVD, but I think there should be more internal regulation.

We seem to be pushing in the direction of discussing some of the classic moral objections to pornography, so let's go there now. You've mentioned that you see yourself as a commodity and that the industry can "use" people and objectify them. It seems, then, that porn is, or can be, harmful to the women or men who make it. It seems exploitative, for one thing. What would you say concerning this objection?

With respect to objectification, I see how it can happen, but from my experience it generally doesn't, at least on a personal level. When I go on set, I make a point of making a personal connection with everyone with whom I'm working, so I don't see them as merely "things" rather than people. Producers and directors of porn may sometimes act this way, but that happens in any business. That our bodies are our commodity doesn't make it different. If we don't think in terms of religious morality, my body is mine to use in any way I see fit.

There are ways that porn seems to present women as objects, but it's not a problem unique to women. Porn also seems to objectify, in some sense, men, different races, ages, sexual preferences, and relationships, like the one between a "stepdad" and his stepdaughter. That's particularly true in marketing; the fantasies are objectified and push the envelope. They are selling an image – sexual excitement and "dirtiness." But this also isn't a problem unique to porn, and these things occur in any other industry. Advertising for Coke works the same way. Drinking Coke makes you young and happy? No, but the advertising and marketing are designed to get you to think that. If I am on a DVD cover, I don't feel objectified. If other people *see* me as an object, that's up to them. I can't control whether others see my work and objectify me, but am I objectified by merely being on the cover? I don't think so.

Sometimes my fetish work may involve me acting like an object, such as a chair, but that's the nature of those scenes. But my pretending to be objectified doesn't amount to my being objectified. I make a conscious, deliberate choice to take that role, and my choosing it makes it permissible. I am not being exploited, only seeming to be.

What about the objection that porn reinforces harmful attitudes toward women, such as perpetuating the "rape myth," and that it contributes to violence, rape particularly, towards women on the part of men?

I say fuck that – and I say that with conviction. I don't believe that pornography perpetuates harmful values and attitudes. If someone can prove to me, with hard evidence, that porn perpetuates these harmful attitudes, then we need to reevaluate not only porn, but entertainment in general. I don't have a television, but when I visit friends and we watch TV, I see nothing but murder, assault, and so on. There's a lot of violence in our entertainment. If entertainment is a value-teaching tool, then the whole system needs to be looked at. I don't think the evidence is there, though. For example, as the rate of porn consumption has increased, the rape statistics have declined. That suggests there isn't a connection.

Women don't like to be raped. Porn that shows what we in the industry call "forced fantasy" is made with women who consent to making it and aren't people who want to be raped. It's about playing with the fantasy. If some guy watching it gets the wrong message and doesn't understand the difference between fantasy and reality – he's just dumb, out of touch, and probably would commit a violent act with or without the extra input. Furthermore, when someone goes to rent or buy porn, they already know what they want to see. Porn is all about niches – bondage, anal, and so forth. The desire and attitudes toward a specific kind of porn are already there. No one is going to stumble across hardcore bondage or fetish movies and then come to the conclusion that that's how women in general want to be treated.

Do you think that porn damages interpersonal relationships, particularly romantic ones like marriage? Does it place unrealistic expectations and pressures on lovers?

I don't think it's necessarily destructive to these relationships. I think it's people's perspectives that are destructive to marriage, for example. Some people don't need to watch pornography. Some people may find it offensive, it may not be what they're into, they may rather read a novel. If porn is damaging to the relationship, it is more likely due to communication problems than anything inherently wrong with porn. If porn is hurting your marriage, that's indicative of a deeper issue. In our personal relationships, it's our job to communicate well and come to understandings about expectations.

Okay. What about BDSM and the fetish stuff you do? It seems that there may be special objections to that kind of porn, even if porn in general is free from the objections above. For example, BDSM is manifestly violent, kinky, and "perverse" in a way that "normal" porn isn't. It seems as if BDSM mixes torture and infliction of sometimes serious harms with sexuality and perpetrates these things on those involved in its production. If this isn't immoral, why not?

This is where we get into a discussion of informed consent. Anyone taking part in a BDSM film has given informed consent to what they're doing. I hate to hear the word "torture" used to describe a BDSM film. I've been tortured in real life, in a real-time situation in a real foreign country. I have also been involved in some of the most intense BDSM scenes ever created. I've done things that no other girl has ever done, as far as pushing myself physically.

Really tortured? Do you mind saying something about that? How did that happen?

I went to work at a strip club in a foreign country as a kind of "working vacation," and was stopped at the airport, basically because I have red hair and big boobs. I got mouthy, and was detained by security officers. I was tackled by a huge Samoan. I was made to strip down and was sexually humiliated by a group of female officers, threatened with tasers by male guards, and beaten to the point that one of my breasts and legs were bruised and swollen. So I have been really tortured. That's why I get upset when I hear that I make "torture porn." When you are really tortured, there's no consent. When I make films, it's always with informed consent and that makes all the difference. Real torture goes well beyond what we want and decide. The two contexts are not comparable. I went as far as being waterboarded under controlled conditions, because I wanted to confirm my belief that in the context of consent, even that does not count as "torture." Is waterboarding a horrible experience? Of course. But is it torture since I went through it voluntarily? No. Informed consent changes the context, and transforms what would otherwise be torture into something else. Consent is the entire heart of the argument – I wish I could go before Congress and tell them that.

So if I were walking down the street and saw you walking, and decided, without obtaining your permission, to tackle you, that would be wrong. But if I politely asked you if you wanted to be tackled and you said "yes," that would be okay?

Yes. But it's not *just* consent. It has to be *informed* consent. It must involve being informed about what's going on, understanding what's happening to you, and being okay with it.

Do you think that there are limits to the power of consent? Are there some kinds of choices that are inherently harmful enough that we might be willing to say "Nope. Even if you consent to this, we aren't going to allow it"? For example, let's suppose you and I were planning to make a film in which you kill me (for real) and mutilate my corpse. It seems that few people would allow my giving informed consent to trump the value of my life. If you think there is a limit to the power of informed consent, where would you draw that line?

Yes, I think if you have people agreeing to things that they don't understand, the shoot should be called off. For example, there are girls who sign up to appear on *The Training of O*, a heavy BDSM website. I know that several girls have had their shoots cut short because it was too emotionally/mentally taxing. I think that's wonderful. Producers have the power to say "when" when the actress involved is too stressed to continue. That's responsible filmmaking. Part of appearing on the site involves five days of intense "training," and there are some girls who get to day two and are broken. They didn't realize it's not like other porn shoots where it lasts a few hours and is over. So there are times on set when people become distressed, and that signals the end of filming the scene. Just another day, just another dollar; not a big deal.

So what you're saying is that in these cases there isn't informed consent, because they don't understand what they're getting into. That kind of consent, you might say, isn't genuine. But what about cases where a person really does understand yet still consents to something apparently immoral, such as your killing me on screen?

Again, setting aside the Bible and religious teachings, I think that one's body is one's own commodity, and that you can do whatever you like with it. I'm for selling kidneys; if you want to, then you should be able to. I believe you should be allowed to kill yourself, and I believe in physician assisted suicide. I heard of a case in Canada involving a husband and wife; the husband is terminally ill, and the wife, who is healthy, can't imagine life without her husband and wants to opt out. If she's giving informed consent, then why shouldn't she be able? However, I do think that people should undergo a process of psychological evaluation before being allowed to go through with those decisions. But if they make it through that, then who are we to decide what they should or shouldn't do with themselves? My body is my own commodity, and that need not end even at death. For example, I want to be put on display in something like the Body Worlds Exhibit – it's my wish, rather than to be buried in some mausoleum in New Orleans. Is it a popular decision? No, but it's mine. Can some of these decisions be creepy? Absolutely – but the fact that something is creepy doesn't make it immoral. After all, Catholics talk about eating the body and drinking the blood of Christ – isn't that creepy? So, I don't think that there are limits on the power of informed consent, but I also think there are people who aren't capable of giving informed consent. We should not let just anyone make these decisions – only those who are truly informed and okay with, or can handle, what they intend to do.

Again, it's worth stressing that informed consent is part of the activity of BDSM filming, both professionally, on the part of companies informing performers, and individually. Each participant gives informed consent.

A classic objection to violent porn, as we discussed above, is that it shows women in submissive roles in terms of their relationships with men. They are victims of forcefully asserted male power. However, your specialization in BDSM is being domineering – you're a dominatrix. Many of your films feature men in roles of powerlessness, being humiliated by women, being penetrated by women, and so forth. Do you think that the increased popularity of these films says anything at all about gender roles, or work to subvert traditional male hegemony, ideals of power and male dominance?

We've flipped the coin, haven't we? What I do, primarily, at this stage of my career is fuck guys in the ass and beat them up. I'm a dominatrix. I've been getting more and more calls to work on films like this because I know how to dominate a guy, and to make him feel dominated. It is sometimes funny to be working with a big guy, like 6 feet 5 and 300 pounds, and be dominating him. I can't help but think, "This dude could squash me." But it's really a mental thing.

You see sites like captivemale.com and meninpain.com out there now, and I think that this is more than creating a new market, but rather reflects an old market. I think many guys are tired of being the strong, tough guy and some just want to give up control. And it seems guys just like stuff in their butt – or the idea of it. Many guys who watch this would probably never do it, but seeing the porn gives them an outlet for those fantasies. Many men also fantasize about the woman in power – the idea or archetype of the big, strong woman who's in control. This kind of porn is an extension of that fantasy, just as fetish porn involving stockings, shoes, or what have you, is an extension of idealizations or fantasies men have based on ideas of women.

My personal "slave," or video slave, is your standard "tough" guy – he hunts and keeps a duck blind in his truck and feeds his family with what he kills. But I think in the moments when we shoot, he gets to say and mean and believe that he belongs to me. He fantasizes about giving up control to the strong female archetype, and realizes that fantasy in our scenes.

Our gender roles are becoming more fluid. San Francisco twenty or thirty years ago was pretty "gay." San Francisco today is "queer." We see a rainbow of sexualities based on a mix of gender roles – exploring roles and sexualities traditionally associated with masculinity and femininity that may differ from our biological sex. I'm not into some of that, I've always seen myself as a woman without having to make myself more masculine or ladylike. There are people out there, though, that don't have access to that sort of easy definition of themselves, so they're making their own definition of their sexuality. I think we'll see a wider variety of sexualities, and sexual practices in the future. I think as our gender roles blur, so will the practices.

If Catharine MacKinnon or Andrea Dworkin were to confront me about what I do for a living, I would invite them to sit down and watch my porn with me. I would ask them to consider the satisfaction that I get out of making femdom porn, the satisfaction that my partner gets, the satisfaction of the viewer, and the satisfaction of those who learn about new pleasures from watching. I'm sure that all that satisfaction would outweigh the discomfort of the few people who see my porn and freak out. Or I'd say "fuck you." I have no problem calling people out – I'm a loud voice in the industry.

Since we've been talking about the idea of shifting gender roles, it seems that we could address another kind of "shift." I'd like to ask you about the intersection of porn and pop culture. Watching porn is clearly more socially acceptable and widespread than it was even ten years ago, including "boundary" porn, like BDSM. Some porn stars are now celebrities, too, and we see celebrities acting like porn stars. For example, Jenna Jameson, Ron Jeremy, and the Girls Next Door are porn people who are pop culture icons. Need we even list the celebrities who gained fame as a result of sex tapes going public? As a result, one might observe that the "perverse" shifts over time. What are your thoughts on this? Is this normalization of porn a good thing or a bad thing?

When we consider this question, we have to look at the explosion of technology. Porn has become more accessible, and it's easier to make your own porn. We're lazy, and we don't want to be the person in the trench coat sneaking off to the video store. The effects of technological innovations have polarized the porn industry. One is either working toward making feature films for DVD, or Internet content. There really is no in between. One result, too, with the expansion into the Internet is that it has made the industry more responsive to the consumer's voice. It has also weakened the production pool, since porn now isn't just produced in Porn Valley. There are companies in south Florida, New York, and so on. So the industry has expanded, but the bubble is likely to burst and things may recede some. But things will never be the "same" as in the old raincoater days.

As we continue to grow in terms of "digital intimacy," porn will really bleed through into our everyday lives. I think that ultimately sexuality will just become a non-issue; we won't judge people in regards to their sexual preferences. I think we're on the verge of an American Renaissance, when we become a more cultured society – sort of like France, without the attitude! I'd like to see us come to a point where quality of life is more important than the quality of one's bank account. I think porn is contributing to this by presenting sex in a positive way, acknowledging that there are different sexualities, challenging gender roles and switching things up, and recognizing that there are shades of gray. Porn can play a beneficial social role.

How far are we willing to push the envelope? Are there some aspects of sexuality that we shouldn't normalize and accept? Where would you draw that boundary?

Well, I don't think that much of what's now heavy BDSM will ever be "normal" in the sense that most people will engage in it, unlike something like anal and oral sex with heterosexual couples. But things like using toys in sex won't be scary to men in ten years and that's not a bad thing. There are things, though, that I think will never be "okay" or "normal" sexual behavior, such as sex with children, animals, or the dead. In fact, I have a problem with any depiction, including comics and digital porn, of a grown man engaging in sex with anyone who's under the age of 18, or presented as being underage. I have a serious problem with "underage" themed videos. I think most reasonable people would agree that those are pretty hard limits with respect to normal sexual behavior, and being turned on by that is wrong. That stuff freaks me out, and if it freaks me out, one should be concerned.

Well, it looks like we're out of time. Thanks again for taking the time to share your thoughts with me and our readers.

You're welcome. I love to discuss the porn industry. I hope everyone profits from sharing my thoughts and experiences.

NOTES ON CONTRIBUTORS

ANDREW ABERDEIN, PhD, is Associate Professor of Logic and Humanities at Florida Institute of Technology. Much of his research is concerned with the interplay of formal and informal accounts of human reason. As a precocious but unworldly youth, his earliest exposure to pornography may have been reading philosophical arguments against it. He was later disappointed to discover that it wasn't half as exciting as those arguments had led him to believe.

THEODORE BACH is a PhD candidate in philosophy at the University of Connecticut and currently teaches philosophy at Southern Connecticut State University. He also enjoys simulating life in the possible world where philosophy professionals are paid porn-mogul salaries and porn moguls wait tables to make rent.

CHRISTOPHER BARTEL, PhD, is an assistant professor of philosophy at Appalachian State University. His research interests include philosophy of music, definitions of art, and theories of perception. In his spare time he enjoys playing bass, tattoo collecting, losing at poker, and trying to explain to his wife where all the money goes.

MZ. BERLIN is a dominatrix and bondage/fetish model, pornographic actress, producer, and director. Originally hailing from Louisiana, Mz. Berlin attended Louisiana State University where she pursued degrees in psychology and communications. She specializes in femdom porn, in which she dominates men and displays the archetype of the powerful female.

MATTHEW BROPHY, PhD, teaches ethics as a visiting professor at Minnesota State University, Mankato. He resides with his beautiful wife and above-average child in Minneapolis. Matthew, who received his PhD in philosophy from the University of Minnesota, strives to avoid the cyber-crack that is *Second Life* and virtual-reality based video-games. As you can imagine, his wife helps.

DARCI DOLL is a PhD candidate at Michigan State University. In addition, she is an adjunct instructor for Delta College and Central Michigan University. Her philosophical interests center around contemporary ethics and Ancient Greek philosophy. Her dissertation will be on autonomy and the correlating ethical obligations.

ANNE K. GORDON, PhD, is the worst kind of academic. She studies things such as human mating, with which she has had no direct, personal experience. She has never been kissed, never been on a date, and most certainly has never watched pornography. Everything she knows about human mating comes from reading psychology journals, watching Montel, and listening to hardcore rap lyrics. Anne is an Associate Professor of Psychology at Bowling Green State University. Her research areas include lying and deception, judgment and decision making, and human mating. Her main hobby is playing with her 14 cats, and her life's goal is to own an ant farm.

JACOB M. HELD, PhD, is assistant professor in the department of philosophy and religion at the University of Central Arkansas. He is co-editor of *James Bond and Philosophy: Questions are Forever*, as well as several essays on philosophy and popular culture. His academic interests include the philosophy of law, nineteenth-century German philosophy, and applied ethics, and his work can be found in such journals as *Idealistic Studies*, *Vera Lex*, and *Public Affairs Quarterly*. He is thankful Dave has offered him the opportunity to legitimate his inordinate porn consumption as research. Now he is not a pervert, but a dedicated scholar. Whew.

LAWRENCE HOWE, PhD, is Associate Professor of Philosophy at the University of West Florida. His special philosophical interests include environmental ethics, climate and philosophy, and the philosophy of Henri Bergson. He is co-founder and president of Citizens Against the Abuse of Air Conditioning (CAAAC). Among his personal interests are running, fishing, and sailing. He happily resides in Pensacola, Fla. *sans* air conditioner.

UMMNI KHAN, PhD, followed the path of many idealists: she went to law school at Osgoode Hall, focusing her studies on human rights. After dabbling in the real world of legal practice, she scuttled back to university to earn a Master's of Law from the University of Michigan and then completed a doctorate of law from the University of Toronto, writing her dissertation on the interpenetration of legal and cultural notions of SM. Her dissertation topic was a terrific conversation starter at law school schmooze functions. That is, when it wasn't totally awkward. She is now an Assistant Professor at Carleton University. When she is not challenging sexual totalitarianism, Ummni can be found snuggling with her sweetheart Brian or brainstorming costume ideas for the next Halloween.

SHANE W. KRAUS is currently a clinical-community doctoral student in the psychology department at Bowling Green State University. He has published two peer reviewed journal articles on pornography, one on pornography and adolescent sexuality and another on pornography use and adult sexual dysfunction. His current research focuses on understanding the influence of various legal elements and extralegal factors on jury decision making, and the treatment of addictive and compulsive behaviors (e.g., drugs and alcohol, pornography). He received his MA in forensic psychology from Castleton State College in 2007. In his spare time, which appears to be in short supply these days, he enjoys activities such as hunting, hiking, swimming, and spending time with his incredible wife.

CASEY MCKITTRICK received his PhD in English from the University of Texas at Austin in 2005. He has taught at the University of Texas, Rice University, and the University of Miami. Since 2005 he has held a tenure-track position in the department of English at Western Michigan University, where he teaches film, American literature, and studies in gender and sexuality. He is currently completing a book-length study called *Juvenile Desires: Visual Pleasure and the Mise-en-Scène of American Childhood*. He has published essays and reviews in the film journal *The Velvet Light Trap*, the anthology *Writing as Revision*, the *African American National Biography*, and *The Ethnic and Third World Review of Books*. He is thrilled to be contributing to this volume because the subject matter is close to his heart, and because he can finally surf porn websites without feeling professionally compromised.

MIMI MARINUCCI, PhD, has published on various topics at the intersection of philosophy, feminism, and popular culture. As Associate Professor of both Philosophy and Women's & Gender Studies at Eastern Washington University, Marinucci seduces students to participate in a perverse lifestyle choice of constant question, particularly with regard to established assumptions about sex, gender, and sexuality.

JONATHAN MILES, PhD, is an instructor of applied ethics at Bowling Green State University, a confirmed role-playing and comic book geek, husband and father, and passionate free speech advocate, even going so far as to co-host and produce his own political talk show called *Political Animals*. He has also contributed to *Heroes and Philosophy*, another anthology in the Pop Culture and Philosophy series by Wiley-Blackwell. When he is not teaching or rough housing with his toddler, he can be found yelling at less intelligent political talk shows or playing various role-playing games.

DAVE MONROE is an instructor of applied ethics at St. Petersburg College and adjunct instructor of philosophy at the University of Tampa. He is also the co-founder and current president of the Lighthearted Philosophers' Society, a group of philosophers meeting annually to seriously discuss humor and laugh at the seriousness of philosophy. *Porn – Philosophy for Everyone* is the second Philosophy for Everyone volume he's edited; the first is *Food and Philosophy* (Wiley-Blackwell, 2008, with Fritz Allhoff). In his spare time, Dave loves spending time with (and creating culinary experiments for) his inspiring and beautiful wife, Rhonda, obsessing over the Detroit Red Wings and Tigers, laughing, and watching naked people do naughty things.

CHAD PARKHILL sometimes envies real philosophers who work on real problems, until he realizes that being a real philosopher involves writing detailed papers on problems of reference and possible world theory. Not being a real philosopher, Chad gets to write papers on things like Daft Punk's existentialism, "girl–girl" pornography, Stephen King's homophobia, and the perverse history of heterosexuality. He is working on a PhD at the University of Queensland; when he graduates and finds himself jobless he may well revise his position on the kinds of papers he ought to be writing.

ROGER T. PIPE is an adult movie critic and journalist. He has spent the last sixteen years reviewing over six thousand adult movies and websites for his website www.RogReviews.com and was inducted into the X-Rated Critics Organization's Hall of Fame in 2009. When he is not steering readers away from bad porn, Roger enjoys reading anything by Stephen King, caring way too much about his devolved Boston Celtics, and spending time with his incredibly understanding wife and their two sons.

GRAM PONANTE (an anagram of "Porn Magnate") is an editor at Hollywood-based Mavervorl Media. He self-applied the honorific "America's Beloved Porn Journalist" in 2005 and, for lack of any competing interest, it became true. His trenchant, grave, and often flawed observations about the fascinating business of American and international pornography are consumed by thousands of readers daily on his virtual home base at GramPonante.com. Ponante lives in Los Angeles with his wife and two children and, like Wittgenstein, keeps in mind that "even if in such cases I can't be mistaken, isn't it possible that I am drugged?"

DAVID ROSE, PhD, knows too much about French cinema, given his adolescent years and having to watch the BBC 2 film club for any hint of eroticism. Now, he need only turn on the TV after 10 p.m., but is busy working out the parental controls because his kids are getting too big. He also thinks that Google Chrome's Incognita mode is advertised falsely and dreads the day his children work that one out. He is employed by philosophical studies at Newcastle University and every so often he writes articles on Hegel, Vico, and moral stuff.

DYLAN RYDER is a native Californian and an adult film actress who has appeared on most of the popular mainstream porn websites, including brazzers.com and bangbros.com, and has appeared in DVDs from companies such as Devil's Films, Third Degree, and Hustler. Dylan has also worked for a non-profit organization offering substance abuse counseling to inmates in California prisons. She remains close with her family, who support her with her various endeavors, including porn.

TAIT SZABO, PhD, is an Assistant Professor of Philosophy at the University of Wisconsin College, Washington County. In his spare time he consumes far less pornography than his involvement in this anthology may seem to indicate, preferring instead a wide variety of cinema, television shows, magazines, and other entertainment.

FIONA WOOLLARD, PhD, spends most of her time thinking about sex and death or, as she puts it on her academic homepage, has research interests in philosophy of sex and normative ethics, particularly issues surrounding killing and letting die. This makes her a hit at dinner parties. She is a lecturer in philosophy at the University of Sheffield. When not in Sheffield, she lives with her fiancé Ryan in a small village in Oxfordshire and enjoys running by the Thames.